HIGH-PERFORMANCE Dodge Neon

Builder's Handbook

MIKE ANCAS

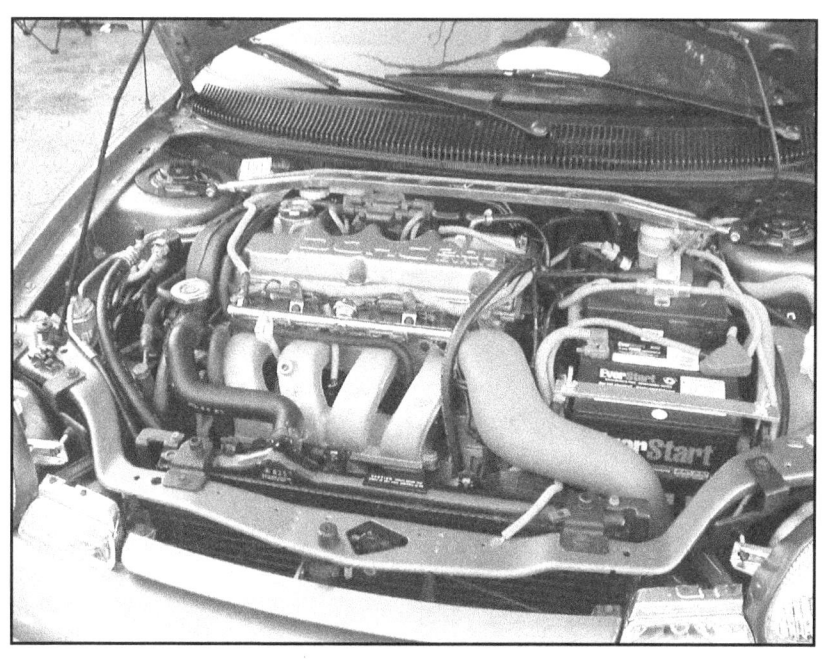

CarTech®

Copyright © 2005 by Mike Ancas

All rights reserved. All text and photographs in this publication are the property of the author, unless otherwise noted or credited. It is unlawful to reproduce – or copy in any way – resell, or redistribute this information without the express written permission of the publisher.

All text, photographs, drawings, and other artwork (hereafter referred to as information) contained in this publication is sold without any warranty as to its usability or performance. In all cases, original manufacturer's recommendations, procedures, and instructions supersede and take precedence over descriptions herein. Specific component design and mechanical procedures – and the qualifications of individual readers – are beyond the control of the publisher, therefore the publisher disclaims all liability, either expressed or implied, for use of the information in this publication. All risk for its use is entirely assumed by the purchaser/user. In no event will CarTech®, Inc., or the author, be liable for any indirect, special, or consequential damages, including but not limited to personal injury or any other damages, arising out of the use or misuse of any information in this publication.

This book is an independent publication, and the author(s) and/or publisher thereof are not in any way associated with, and are not authorized to act on behalf of, any of the manufacturers included in this book. All registered trademarks are the property of their owners. The publisher reserves the right to revise this publication or change its content from time to time without obligation to notify any persons of such revisions or changes.

Edited by Travis Thompson
Designed by Christopher Fayers

ISBN 978-1-61325-006-8

CarTech®
39966 Grand Avenue
North Branch, MN 55056
Telephone (651) 277-1200 • (800) 551-4754 • Fax: (651) 277-1203
www.cartechbooks.com

OVERSEAS DISTRIBUTION BY:

Brooklands Books Ltd.
P.O. Box 146, Cobham, Surrey, KT11 1LG, England
Telephone 01932 865051 • Fax 01932 868803
www.brooklands-books.com

Brooklands Books Aus.
3/37-39 Green Street, Banksmeadow, NSW 2019, Australia
Telephone 2 9695 7055 • Fax 2 9695 7355

Front Cover: A stock SRT-4 is even better equipped to take to the track than a stock Neon. But suspension changes are also recommended for the SRT-4 as long as class rules allow. No upgrades are needed for street driving, as the stock suspension is excellent. We are well aware of the fact that spirited street driving is common, but without race tires and a great track to run on, the limited thrill of street racing is not worth the risks.

Inset Left: You can have the power of an SRT-4 in your older Neon chassis. One way is to swap the whole engine, but another is to find an SRT-4 head/manifolds/turbo and swap it all onto your 2.0.

Inset Center: Neons typically will lift a rear tire during both autocross and road racing. The author clips a cone on his way to an eventual second place overall (out of 114) at a Steel Cities SCCA Solo II. Without that pylon, 2004 Steel Cities autocross champ, Miata driver Nick Flynn, would have been taken down as well. (Photo courtesy Jim Weslager)

Inset Right: If you're serious about handling, you might want to step up to a set of coil-overs. They also allow you to adjust the ride height of your Neon. (Photo courtesy Chris Malluege)

Back Cover Bottom Right: Intakes come in all shapes and sizes. One of the benefits of the Neon powerplant vs. the traditional Honda OHC engine is that the intake faces forward. Open a hole in the hood, and you'll have direct access. (Photo courtesy Gil Diaz)

Back Cover Top Right: Probably the hardest part of swapping throttle bodies is swapping over your sensors. You will need a set of torx bits or wrenches, and be warned – the factory wasn't afraid to use a little thread lock on the bolts! Be sure to use the correct sensors for your particular Neon. (Photo courtesy Michael Carpenter)

Back Cover Bottom Left: Local drag racing events are easy to get addicted to. Going to sport compact days, test and tune days, or just bracket racing events is a great way to get to know your car and have fun. Don't worry, even if your car is stock, there'll definitely be somebody slower (cough*Honda*cough). (Photo courtesy Chris Malluege)

Title Page: Installing an aftermarket intake system is probably the best bang for the buck for a Neon 2.0-liter powerplant. The potential for gain is even higher for a 2001-'04 R/T and a 2001-'02 ACR. This is an Iceman intake on a first-generation Neon. (Photo courtesy Patrick O'Hara)

	Introduction 4	Chapter 9:	Body and Interior Modifications 75
Chapter 1:	Neon History 13		Gauges 75
	First-Generation Cars: 1995-'99 14		Cockpit Comforts 77
	Second-Generation Cars: 2000-'05 15		Weight Reduction 78
	Neon Racing Legacy 16		Steering Wheels 80
	The SRT-4 18		Exterior Modifications 81
	The Future of the Neon 20		Body Kits 82
Chapter 2:	Suspension and Handling 21		Functional Body Modifications 83
	Bigger Bars and Heavier Springs 22	Chapter 10:	Turbocharging, Supercharging, and Nitrous 85
	Sway Bars 23		Turbocharging 85
	Struts 24		Superchargers 89
	Strut Tower Bars 24		Nitrous Oxide 89
	Final Suspension Tweaking 25		The SRT-4 90
	Corner Weighting 25		
	Alignment 30	Chapter 11:	Transaxle Tech 93
Chapter 3:	Wheels and Tires 32		Neon Transmissions 93
	Street Wheels 32		Aftermarket Clutches 95
	Tires for the Street 34		Lightened Flywheels 96
	Autocrossing 35		Limited-Slip Differentials 96
	Racing Slicks 39		Gear Oil 98
	Road Racing 40	Chapter 12:	Engines 99
	Drag Racing 40		First-Generation Powerplants: 1995-1999 99
	Tire Pressures 42		Second-Generation Powerplants: 2000-2005 100
Chapter 4:	Braking 44		Blocks 102
	Road Racing 46		PCM Tech 102
	Autocrossing 47		First-Generation Swaps 103
	Cars With Boost 47		Second-Generation Swaps 104
	Engine Transplants and NWHSS 47		SRT-4 Swaps Into non-SRT-4 Neons ..105
	Aftermarket Brake Pads and Rotors ...48		Underdrive Pulleys 105
	Brake Fluids 49		Motor Mounts 105
Chapter 5:	Intake System 51		Engine Care and Lubrication 107
	Throttle Bodies 55	Chapter 13:	Modifications on a Budget 109
	Porting, Polishing, Extrude Honing 57		Dual Duty 111
Chapter 6:	Exhaust System 59		Full Race 116
	Headers 61		Where Do We Go From Here? 118
Chapter 7:	Ignition and Fuel 64	Chapter 14:	Don't Just Sit There – Go Racing! 119
	Ignition Systems 64		Solo II Autocross 119
	Wires and Plugs 66		Solo I Hillclimbing, Track Events, and Driver's Schools 123
	It's a Matter of Time – Understanding Advance and Retard 67		Road Racing – Improved Touring 124
	Electronic Fuel Injection Tips 69		SCCA National Road Racing 125
Chapter 8:	Camshafts and Heads 71		Driver's Schools 125
	SOHC Neons 72		Drag Racing 125
	DOHC Neons 73		
	SRT-4 73		Source Guide 127
	Cam Timing 73		
	Cylinder Heads 74		

INTRODUCTION

A Book About Neon Performance – It's About Time!

The first time I approached a publisher about writing this book in 1999, the response was: "Sorry, but there is not enough interest among the target market." Forget the fact that SCCA Neon racing was the hottest thing going, not to mention the Chrysler contingency money that was being paid to competitors (largest cash payoffs for any car in SCCA history). I felt that the Neon had made a serious impact on the sport compact market the day it was first introduced five years earlier. But still, no publisher was willing to take on the project. However, when CarTech® got wind of the project – they jumped on it. So you can thank them for funding this project, and for having a finger on the pulse of the current performance market. I'd also like to thank Michael Charpenter for his help throughout the project.

In the Beginning

One of the first people to recognize that the Neon would make an impact on the performance market was John Fernandez at Chrysler. Even before Chrysler started cranking out thousands of these puppies every month, Fernandez's motorsports program saw to it that a significant number of these first production Neons were ACR (American Club Racing) versions. At that time, the general public had a hard time visualizing that these "grocery getters" would someday be hitting the amateur racing circuit. If you recall, Chrysler was pro-

The author and founder of Speednation got his hands on one of the first Neon ACRs to roll off of the assembly line. In conjunction with Grassroots Motorsports magazine, the car was gradually developed over several years until it found its way back to Chrysler to be crushed. The author continues to actively race and crash Neons in SCCA hill-climbs (pictured), road races, and autocross. This Neon was totaled 30 seconds after this photo was taken. (Photo courtesy Keith Bower)

moting the Neon as a cute little economy car (Hi!), but many SCCA racers were thinking to themselves: "2,300 pounds with 132 horsepower – sounds like a winner to us!" It wouldn't take long for the import racing movement to take notice, either.

At that time, Honda was dominating the movement with its quick little Civics, and it seemed like everyone was walking around wearing t-shirts covered with Japanese writing and characters. I always wondered what the Japanese letters I had on my racing Civic actually said. In my own defense, however, I was racing Civics back in 1986 before the import performance movement started. But I wasn't too blind to notice the introduction of the Neon and the potential impact that this car would someday have on that culture.

In early 1994, Gary Johnson, part of the Fernandez motorsports program, approached *Grassroots Motorsports* magazine about developing a project racing Neon. Publisher Tim Suddard had the insight to take him up on the offer. After a year of SSC racing in the Southern Florida SCCA region, I was given a chance to further develop this cool project car.

For those who aren't familiar with it, the Showroom Stock class (SSC) of the SCCA is exactly as it sounds to be – racecars that are still in stock trim, nearly identical to the way they came off the showroom floor. Just add a roll cage, fire extinguisher, and window net, and go racing. *Grassroots Motorsports* was graced with an early ACR. The car was also what the industry refers to as a "white body" car, destined to end its short life in the crusher once its purpose has been fulfilled. I was determined to see that its life would have meaning. By the way, one of the guys who started it all, John Fernandez, is still racing Neons in the SCCA SSC road racing class, finishing second in 2003 and just missing the podium in 2004.

One of the First Modified Neons

In 1994, the staff at *Grassroots Motorsports* magazine and I were given the task of taking a successful, well set-up, virtually stock SCCA racing Neon and further modifying it so that it would go faster and handle better. But first, I had to get to know the car, so it was off to the 50th Annual (and final) Chimney Rock Hillclimb in Asheville, North Carolina. The only modification we had time to do before this event was to replace the stock 14-inch alloys with larger, custom-made 15- x 7-inch wheels. Racing against seasoned veterans, the car managed to take home a trophy in the large C Street Prepared class. Then it was off to the 89th running of the Giants Despair Hillclimb in Wilkes-Barre, Pennsylvania, followed by the Weatherly Hillclimb in Pennsylvania (it has a cool jump near the end), and some serious testing at Road Atlanta.

This whole time, we were in search of aftermarket parts to help improve both handling and power. We added adjustable Tokico inserts, a Supertrapp exhaust, an air velocity intake system, etc. Back then, of course, no one was yet manufacturing any of these parts, so we had to improvise. Attempts to secure a limited-slip differential from Chrysler proved futile, as these were still in the development phase until 1996. A header also eluded us during the first year of modification. Trying different injector sizes along with modified throttle bodies just seemed to piss off the onboard computer and make the car slower. Over the next year, after a lot of testing and tuning on the SCCA autocross circuit, we were faced with a sad truth: our Neon handled worse and was no faster than when we started. After winning a regional autocross championship despite our mistakes, I reluctantly waved goodbye to the Neon as it headed back to Detroit.

In 1996, the car was painted nitro yellow green, and it continued its development under the direction of J.G. Pasterjack and Tim Suddard of *Grassroots Motorsports* magazine. It received a DOHC transplant, an Electromotive EFI system, and a better suspension. Still, very few aftermarket products were

When first introduced to the public, Chrysler wanted to promote a fun, clean, happy image. Remember the "Hi!" horn-beeping commercials? Thanks to thousands of sport compact enthusiasts, that image has changed.

The sport compact enthusiast movement started in the UK when the Austin Mini was introduced. Bobby Eakin is shown here autocrossing his Cooper S. The Japanese followed suit with offerings such as the popular Civic, seen here (piloted by the author) at the Weatherly Hillclimb in SCCA GT-5 trim.

Introduction

The Grassroots Motorsports (GRM) Neon ACR was developed and raced by the author, but back in 1994-'95, there were few performance parts available. Autocrossing was used as a tool to help sort out the handling. This first step is recommended before attempting high-speed competition.

available, so after sitting in J.G.'s backyard for a year, it finally met its fate in 1997. I still really miss that car.

Of course, now there are hundreds of aftermarket drivetrain parts available for the Neon. Most work, but most also fail to deliver on their promised horsepower gains. Many suspension improvements work, but some do not. The problem still encountered is that "out of the box" aftermarket suspensions fail to meet the specific needs of the owner who is looking for both a competent street car and a weekend racer. We hope to shed more light on both areas in the pages that follow.

Building a Better Wheel

The biggest problem we faced in 1994 was trying to sort out which products actually worked, and which ones didn't. We had little to work with, and results were usually disappointing. Then, all of a sudden, aftermarket performance companies started coming out of the woodwork. We were excited, and testing continued, with mixed results. Nowadays, it seems there are new companies springing up daily. The big question we still have is: "Who are these guys?" Many sell exactly the same product as everyone else but simply re-label it and market it as their own. Even Mopar is guilty of this practice, though the products that bear their name are of good quality. But in the high-performance aftermarket overall, it seems that the "what works" to "what doesn't work" ratio is getting worse, not better. So how do you know if the product you are about to spend your hard-earned money on really will improve your Neon's performance? Test it on the dyno.

The Importance of Dyno Testing

Did you hear the one about the two guys who brought their cars to a chassis dyno? They had identical DOHC first-generation Neons, except that one was stock, while the other had a few of today's popular modifications.

The guy with the stock Neon (we'll call him Kyle) was first to get strapped on to Speednation's Mustang Chassis Dynamometer. The results showed a healthy 124 horsepower at the wheels. This figure is very consistent with other stock Neons that have been tested given the parasitic loss that all cars experience (more on that later).

Next, Kyle decided to do some quarter-mile runs. Yes, a Mustang dyno can do that, too. Kyle sat in the driver's seat, and when given the word by the dyno operator, he dumped the clutch and went through the gears just like he would if he were at a drag strip. Of course, he didn't have to worry about reaction time or drifting into the other competitor's lane. As long as you don't accidentally step onto the dual rollers, drag racing on a chassis dyno is a very safe activity. However, if you do happen to step on the rollers at 100 mph, you'll get sucked down into the dyno's interior like Wile E. Coyote into a giant Acme vacuum cleaner.

Anyway, Kyle's Neon again performed predictably, ripping off a few runs ranging between 15.9 and 15.7 at 87 mph. Again, what we have here is a healthy, but bone stock, DOHC Neon. This was the end of Kyle's session, so he made way for his friend (let's call him Eric) to take a turn. As the straps were being loosened on Kyle's car, he exclaimed: "Wait until you see the power of Eric's car. He really pulls away from me on the highway."

As we were strapping Eric's modified Neon onto the dyno, he also indicated that he felt that the modifications he had performed on his Neon would register much higher numbers than Kyle's car. Over the past few months, he had installed an aftermarket exhaust, header, cold-air intake, underdrive pulley, performance chip, and adjustable cam gears.

A few minutes later, after running a routine parasitic test to determine the amount of torque lost between the crankshaft and wheels, both Kyle and Eric were highly anticipating the first power run. However, a minute later, when the run was completed, both were completely speechless. The dyno screen was flashing "122." And no, that wasn't the temperature that day. A second run was made just to be sure, and again, their eyes were fixated on the "122" that appeared on the screen. "Okay, what's the deal here?" exclaimed Eric. "How could my car have less horsepower than Kyle's?"

Was it possible that a modified Neon would have less power than a stock Neon? In this case, obviously, it was. The dyno doesn't lie – it always tells the cold, hard truth. We can't tell you how many disappointed car owners we've seen over the years at the Speednation shop. They expected to gain 15 horsepower from their exhaust system, 12 from their intake, 15 from their header, and 25 from their chip. That adds up to 67 horsepower! Of course, their 4-cylinder engine ended up with only 6 horsepower total from the mods they performed. How can that be? The manufacturers of those products make claim to these high numbers, and often the magazines substantiate these claims.

A Few Words About the Truth

We need to take some time here to clear up a few misconceptions. The truth is that nearly all the major automotive magazines cater to their advertisers. They don't make money from selling magazines; they make money from selling advertising. The more subscribers they have, the more they can charge for their ads. Did you ever wonder how they can afford to charge so little for their subscriptions? Most magazines would lose money if all they had to count on was revenue from magazine sales.

So that brings us to the truth. Do you think the magazines want to upset one of their advertisers? Of course not. That's why you rarely see a manufacturer's product depicted in anything but positive terms. Why do you think that most magazine product tests end up concluding: "all of the products performed well." Their project cars get sponsorship from the manufacturers, which is why you see every system being replaced with an aftermarket performance part.

The truth is that many of these products are hype. You won't get 15 horsepower by adding an exhaust. Of course, under certain circumstances, in a sterile engine dyno lab, using 115 octane fuel, and artificially creating a situation where an engine is choking on its own exhaust gasses, you could get 15 hp by adding an exhaust system. You are replacing a component that was designed to be the weakest link. For most Neon owners, we will be lucky to get 5 hp from an exhaust, if anything, and low-end torque may likely be sacrificed. Ignition components will typically

*After you get your Neon's handling sorted out, it will be ready for more spirited competition. The **GRM** Neon is seen here attacking the Giant's Despair Hillclimb, which is the oldest motorsports event in the USA.*

add zero horsepower, except under certain conditions or in very high-performance applications.

We experienced this phenomenon first hand. One of our earlier project cars was given head work, bigger injectors, a header, exhaust, an air intake, and throttle body. So we were getting much more air through the system, and then we added more fuel to the equation. The result was disappointing. We had expected more horsepower with all of the work we had done. But then we added hotter camshafts. The dyno results could have made the car a poster child for the company that made the camshafts. The car just seemed to wake up, and all of a sudden we had gobs more power. But looking at what we had done, it was obvious the camshafts were simply taking advantage of all the other components we had added previously. All they did was to balance out the system. We had unknowingly created a situation in which the stock cams were the weak link in the powerplant. When we gave the engine what it was craving for, voilá – power. But for most stock Neons, adding hotter cams will likely do very little without also adding a performance PCM (powertrain control module) to help advance ignition timing, plus some extra air and fuel.

So a very important thing to remember when buying aftermarket parts for your Neon is that you can't add up the horsepower numbers claimed by the individual manufacturers. The truth is you will be lucky to get a fourth of what is claimed by adding multiple components. Adding just one component will probably only net you half of what is claimed. Of course, this is dependent on what else you have done to your car. You could get more, but you may also get zero. Now don't get us wrong. You can get some good information from a magazine, but you need to be cautious of the claims that are made. Books, however, contain no advertising, so we authors are free to tell it like it is.

However, at the same time, we owe a debt of gratitude to the manufacturers for creating the products that do work. Without them, there would not have been a performance movement in the 1990s. But the truth is that most brands of headers, air intakes, and exhaust systems are almost the same when it comes to adding power. The difference between a $400 intake and a $100 intake is simply $300 and a cool "name." Whether you use the cheap part or the brand-name part, you'll likely get the same minor power increase.

Anyway, back to Eric's dilemma. He lost power despite making the most

Introduction

All of the tips and suggestions found in this book are based on reality – not hype – courtesy of Speednation's Mustang Chassis Dyno. We've done extensive testing to help Neon fans get the most for their money when buying performance parts. Speednation's Michael Carpenter is shown here helping to fine tune the ex-Daddio Turbo Neon.

popular street/racing mods, but he and Kyle were convinced that the modified car was faster than the stock car. It was true that Eric's car was louder, and at 6,500 rpm when Kyle's power was starting to drop off, Eric's power was increasing. This would account for the "numerous tests" they performed on the highway at 70 mph where Eric was able to pull away from Kyle.

The most common mistake that car owners make when adding modifications to their cars is that they trust their "butt dyno." The car feels faster when doing a "seat-of-your-pants" run on the highway. Actually, what frequently happens is that the car sounds louder, or your wallet tells you that the car surely must be faster given the amount of money you just spent, and that influences your experience on the highway. This phenomenon is called cognitive dissonance. It's what keeps wackos camped on the top of a mountain week after week waiting for aliens to land and greet them. They are convinced, based on their cosmic calculations, that this is the weekend that the aliens will land. Their entire club is convinced of this, and they have constructed a lifestyle around this philosophical truth. So even though the aliens disappoint them one week after another, they simply decide that their calculations for this week's landing were incorrect, and that actually it is next weekend when the landing will take place. So they go home anticipating that the magical event will take place next week.

Of course, it is their entire philosophical belief system that's flawed, not their calculations. To accept the first premise is to accept that all you have been working towards is without merit.

Back again to our Neon boys. Before he came to the dyno, Eric was unwilling to accept that the money he had spent would not result in more power, so all of the "seat-of-the-pants" testing he did was influenced by this fact. Needless to say, he was shocked when he saw the truth on the dyno.

We seldom encounter a situation that can't be helped by some dyno-directed tuning. With Eric's Neon, we were able to play with cam timing (on most other cars, ignition timing can usually be adjusted) to net some free gains. Using the dyno as a guide, we were able to get more power. In fact, after a few dyno tuning runs, it became apparent that the cam gears were installed incorrectly. Both cams were one tooth off. By correcting that problem, and letting the dyno guide us as to how much advance or retard to dial in, Eric left our shop in a much better mood. I'm sure he is really leaving Kyle in the dust now, as he gained 16 hp on the day. Of course, that's only 14 hp more than Kyle, and most of that was still in the higher RPM range.

Since every engine is slightly different, and the possible combination of modifications that an individual car can have is astronomical, what works for one car may not work for yours. There is only one way you can know for sure whether what you have planned for your car will really work: get your car to a chassis dyno.

What You Should Do With an Hour of Dyno Time

First, Get a Baseline Reading

Before you do anything to your car, you should find out how much torque and horsepower your engine is currently producing. That way you can compare anything you do in the future to your baseline reading. Even if your project car is well on its way, the next 20 horsepower is often harder to get than the first 20. Make log entries each time you add performance parts to your car, and also each time you go to the dyno.

Adjust Ignition Timing

Unfortunately, this isn't going to be an option for Neons, as they have distributorless ignitions. But if you have added a stand-alone, programmable ignition system, you can retard or advance timing to help fine tune your torque curve, adding either more high-end or low-end torque.

Adjust Your Cam Timing

If you have installed adjustable cam timing gear(s), a dyno is the best way to determine the proper setting for both your cam gears and ignition timing. Although this is often a trial-and-error process, more horsepower can usually be found by making simple adjustments to your cam gears while it's still on the dyno.

Experiment With Air/Fuel Mixture

If you have an aftermarket fuel-injection system, a fuel pressure regulator, or aftermarket computer, then a dyno will accurately measure the horsepower changes you will get following each fuel adjustment.

Compare Your Car's Horsepower to Other Cars Just Like Yours

Most dynos usually have graphs stored for each car that has been tested. Your car's graph can often be compared to other cars similar to yours. You can see what gains have been achieved by adding various performance parts, and that can help you determine what parts you should (or shouldn't) buy for your car. Also, by viewing the curves of other cars, you can often learn their secrets to gaining more power.

Quarter-Mile and 0-60 Times

Not all dynos are created equally. Our Mustang dyno's computer takes into account your car's weight and the dual rollers and eddy-current magnets that can put load on the rollers to simulate inertia. The computer incorporates data published by the EPA that corresponds to the horsepower required to keep your car traveling 50 mph on a flat road. When you start out, you must overcome the initial inertia similar to the friction you encounter by the pavement on a road. Also, in real life, the faster you go, the more drag you encounter as your car attempts to push itself through the air. Mustang dynos automatically compensate for this by increasing the load on the rollers as you accelerate. The result: extremely accurate quarter-mile and 0-60 times.

Determine the Best Shift Points

What makes you think that the RPM shift points you have chosen are optimal for your car? Was it based on your car's torque curve? Is your car continuing to generate horsepower over 7,000 rpm, or should you short-shift at 6,000 rpm? The only way to know for sure is to do a shift-point analysis on a dyno that can give you quarter-mile times.

For almost as long as there have been cars, guys have been tuning their cars based on quarter-mile runs. You make an adjustment in the pits, and then see if what you just changed will translate into a faster quarter-mile time. It can make for a long day, and often, you'll have to come back another day. The problem is, temperature and humidity conditions will likely be different when you return, so your quarter-mile times will vary.

Then you have the human factor. Did you do everything the same on your last run as you did this run? If you've ever been to a drag strip and taken three runs in the same day, it's unlikely that you had three identical times. If you did, then put down this book right now and get to the local strip as fast as you can. You could make some serious money in bracket racing. Since most of us are unable to perform identically from run to run, trying to find out if your car gained power by retarding or advancing cam timing by 1 to 2 degrees based on quarter-mile times is an exercise in futility. The bottom line is that when you're looking at very small horsepower gains, there will be no way you can accurately measure the effectiveness of your tuning at a drag strip.

It seems that there is more misinformation out there than there is information. Hopefully, after you finish reading this book, you will be armed with enough information that you will be able to prevent some of the same mistakes made by our buddy, Eric. Here are a few important pointers you should always keep in the back of your mind when planning your Neon project.

Five Important Rules to Follow When Modifying Your Neon

Lesson 1: Buy Someone Else's Neon that has Already Been Built

There are few things in life as rewarding as turning the key and driving down the road in your newly completed Neon project car. After all, it was your sweat, blood, time, and money. The only thing we have found to be more rewarding is to buy someone else's completed project!

No, you didn't build it yourself. Yes, it's probably not in perfect shape and may need some minor work, but you couldn't build one for less money. So what about that wonderful feeling of accomplishment you won't get to experience by having done it yourself? We don't know about you, but we've been able to get over that. Add a few customizing touches, and you will soon forget that someone else did all of the work (and spent all the money). After you own the car for a few years, it'll feel like part of the family. The best part is that if you get sick of it in the future, you can always sell it without taking a big loss.

At the time of this writing, I found a 1995 Neon ACR ready to go racing for $1,500! Granted, that's a "friend" price, this SSC-legal Neon included a full cage, racing seat, exhaust, quick-release steering wheel, fresh clutch, logbook, and had never been crashed. I couldn't get the cash out of my wallet fast enough. I also found several other racing Neons prepared just as well, ready for Spec Neon or SCCA IT (regional) racing for well under $3,500. Keep your eyes open, as the Neons competing in SSC become ineligible for further competition due to SCCA's 10-year rule. Some Neon racers will be dumping them for pocket change.

Lesson 2: Be Prepared to Spend Money on Your Project That You Will Never Get Back

If you insist on hopping-up the car you already have, then you must be willing to accept this fact. Now don't get us wrong – the process of building up your car may be worth the price you pay. It can form a bond between the car and owner that non-enthusiasts won't understand – it also forms a bond between you and your Visa card. For many people, researching the parts to get, and then installing them, is just as fun as having a hopped-up ride. So if you choose to take this path, hold onto this book, and we can help you get the most for the money you spend on performance improvements.

When it comes to performance, despite all of the tuning you do to your Neon and all of the parts you install, the truth is in the racing. It isn't that hard to get involved in local events. Even if your car is stock, you can still go out and have a blast.

Introduction

When shopping around for a good project Neon, it makes the most sense to buy one that's already finished. This will save you lots of time and money. I purchased this 1995 SSC Neon ACR for $1,500 (plus another $200 for 4 sets of wheels and tires) from all-around nice guy, Gordon Wise (pictured racing the car before it was sold). The same day I bought this car, I drove it to a new SSC lap record at Summit Point racetrack (Jefferson circuit).

Lesson 3: Establish a Budget for Your Money and Time

When you set out to build the project Neon of your dreams, you should set a budget. Even if money is no object, a budget can be extremely helpful. Setting limits will help you to prioritize how your money is being spent based on what aspects of the project are most important to you. That's why even large, multi-billion-dollar corporations have budgets. Those budgets serve to help keep the companies focused on their goals. For the rest of us without unlimited funds, we'll be operating under a budget whether we like it or not. A mandatory budget will help you prioritize what parts to buy, based on your end goals.

Many auto enthusiasts make the mistake of buying a Neon, then immediately purchasing a cool set of rims, a slick-looking rear wing, or installing a killer stereo. Then a few months later, when their project car starts to come together and they decide to do some racing, they could regret some of their earlier choices. That cool wing may then become a wasted expense, as it provides no performance improvement and will likely cause you to be excluded from the stock or entry-level classes. Then there are those wheels, which could also take you out of certain classes, plus pose some additional problems. For instance, did those aftermarket wheels change your final drive ratio so that you are not as quick off the line as your competitors? Do the best racing tires come in sizes that will fit on your new wheels?

How often do you see nearly brand new parts being sacrificed by people who didn't take the time to plan out their project? The parts that they initially purchased no longer meet their needs because their goals have changed, so the parts are sold for a fraction of the original purchase price. If you plan your project well, you can pick up some of these parts, and their loss can be your gain. Avoid buying parts that don't fit your goals, and you won't end up selling them at a loss down the road. Remember, even the top racing teams have budgets. It's important to have the overall picture in place before you go out and buy film.

In addition to the financial aspect, you also need to budget your time. In a perfect world, you could wake up in the morning, go out to the garage, and work on your car all day. But unfortunately, most people have to go to work. Then there are friend and family responsibilities, and all of the other time constraints that come with life in the 21st Century.

Don't underestimate the importance of setting a time budget. Relationships are often put into some degree of jeopardy when you get really involved in your automotive project. Often, your spouse (or friends) may feel that spending time with your car is more important to you than spending time with them. But there are ways to avoid these potential problems.

First, limit the time you work on your car when your spouse is home. If you have children, try to involve them in your project so that there is a family element to what you are doing. And most important, empower your significant other. Give them the power to decide, for instance, how long you will work on your car for a given day. All this holds true for your friends, too. Invite them over to help on a project; sometimes two or three heads (or sets of hands) are better than one.

Time management is also important when it comes to deciding on the amount of time that you want to spend on specific phases of your project. Sometimes paying someone to do something for you is much easier than doing it yourself. Spending five hours in the dirt wrestling with your exhaust system, for example, may not be worth the $100 you could spend to have it installed at a muffler shop in 45 minutes. Your budget, mechanical abilities, and shop facilities will help you make these decisions.

A close friend of mine has several projects he is trying to get off the ground, all at the same time. For the three years I've known him, he hasn't completed a single one, but keeps adding more. For the most part, the only cars he has been able to consistently race during that time have been the ones he bought from me (complete, ready to race) and the one we bought together (also a turnkey racecar). So be realistic and honest with yourself. If you have the time, then go for it. But if you don't, then please refer back to lesson one so you can start having fun this weekend.

Lesson 4: Read the Whole Book

Although the performance parts and modifications outlined in this book have been proven to work, your results may vary. Your particular car, depending on its age, engine type and efficiency, gearbox, etc., may respond differently to performance modifications. Often, the addition of a single performance component may not yield the targeted performance improvement. There can be many reasons for this, but often it's that all the components in a system (intake, exhaust, combustion) need to be properly matched. Horsepower gains often only take place when the individual performance parts in a system complement each other, so read the whole book, and keep a grand view of the whole project car in mind.

Since Neons are such great cars to start with, sometimes you can do more harm than good. We know that from personal experience. Please, we hope you learn from our mistakes. Chrysler engineers have already designed the engine components to be both efficient and powerful. You would think that by adding hot cams you could really increase performance. But the gains would likely fall below your expectations, especially if adding the cams is the first thing you do. This is also true when making modifications to the intake and exhaust system. It's a sound decision to add an air velocity intake system, header, and a cat back exhaust, and expect improved performance. However, if you then spent money on a monster throttle body without considering how to balance your system with more fuel, then you may again be disappointed in the result. Your PCM, injectors, intake, and exhaust must work in harmony with the changes you make. The first few horsepower may be easy and inexpensive to get, but as you get closer to your goal, the "power/dollar spent" ratio will start to increase.

One final thought. If a particular type of performance part is not mentioned in this book, it's probably because it doesn't work. Don't listen to the claims made by some companies that boast of horsepower increases that seem too good to be true – they probably are. Even "dyno tested" claims can't always be tested. Using an engine dyno under the right conditions, someone could probably show that adding dirt to your engine will increase power. The real test involves putting the engine in the car and driving it over a period of time. Then a chassis dyno plus some serious track time will tell you if a product passes muster. So the best advice we can offer is to read this entire book before you get on the phone to start ordering parts. You could save yourself a lot of time and money.

The Speednation turbo Neon was purchased from legendary SCCA autocrosser Mark Daddio for $6,000. Daddio drove this car to an SCCA National Championship in D Street Prepared, but was no longer nationally competitive in Street Modified. After a few tweaks to remove some of the toe out and negative camber, the car found new life in high-speed events, and broke two Solo I records before crashing. Don't worry; the SRT-4/Razor turbo powerplant survived.

Lesson 5: Keep Up With Current Information

This book is not designed to be a step-by-step repair manual. You can purchase a factory service manual for that information. Also, there are many resources where you can find information on how to install some of the performance parts we will be reviewing. We recommend that you visit both www.Neons.org and www.allpar.com to see the unbelievable amount of information there specifically organized to help you select and install parts. Websites and message boards can change and grow on an hourly basis, so they're a great way to

Pictured at the 2001 Mopar Nationals are a who's who of Neon performance. Shown left to right are Len Ayala, Gary Howell of Howell Automotive, Dick McMullen, and Craig Martinelli. (Photo courtesy Howell Automotive)

Introduction

Creating a Budget/Project Plan

Budgets can be a very personalized thing, but all budgets should take into consideration the basic components of your car. To get started you should first take a look at the chapters in this book and decide on your car needs. All this, of course, should be based on what exactly it is you want to do with your Neon. Suspension, engine, intake, exhaust, ignition, and appearance should all be listed as categories. Even if you are not anal retentive, making a list can be very helpful, especially if you have a computer. Start by listing these categories, and then add sub categories based on the sections in each chapter. For example, under suspension, you should have springs, shocks, sway bars, wheels, tires, etc. Even if you already have a nice set of wheels, put a "$0" on the line next to "wheels." Under "shocks and struts," however, you may want to upgrade to an adjustable Tokico or Koni system, therefore you'll need to research how much they cost, possibly including installation, and keep track of that in the budget.

This itemization will also serve another purpose. If you are using a computer program that can calculate your expenditures, you will have a running total of what you've spent on your car. This will help keep your head out of the clouds and your feet on the ground, protecting you from spending more money on the car than it's worth. It will also help you to keep track of exactly what you have done, essentially giving you a readout of your car's modifications.

Finally, the budget could help with an insurance claim in the event that your car is stolen. Receipts for both aftermarket parts and labor should be kept in a folder accompanying the hard copy of your budget. You may as well put a "before" photo of your car in the folder, as well as any other photos you take during the build up. Those who take the time to compile this information will be glad they did when their project is completed, as it will serve as a tribute to the time, effort, and money that went into their Neon. And if the day ever comes that you decide to sell your baby, prospective buyers will recognize that you are a detail-oriented person who likely took good care of your car. It will prove, for example, that there actually is a limited slip installed in the transaxle, or that the engine really was completely rebuilt a year ago, or that the timing belt was just replaced at 60,000 miles.

Wheels and tires will eat up a good chunk of your budget if you're not careful. Whether for show or for go, as in Mike Crawford's SRT-4 drag car, you need to factor these costs into your budget. This factory backed car runs in the eight-second bracket. (Photo courtesy Howell Automotive)

You can also learn a lot by going to Neon gatherings, or by joining a sport compact or racing club. Make sure that you have an open mind when someone is telling you about their mistakes and successes. (Photo courtesy Howell Automotive)

stay up to date on current parts and procedures. Websites can be very helpful and informative, especially when it comes to specifics that we have no room to address in this book. Magazines also contain a lot of new and useful information, but read them with a skeptical eye. Remember, the magazines will rarely tell you when a part that they have tested doesn't work.

Your best source may very well be the Internet and the tuners who successfully race their Neons. Thousands of Neon performance pages exist, and there are hundreds of forums and posts. Also, skepticism is the right approach when reading about someone else's project Neon. They may be trying to sell their car. But more likely, they have spent money on their car that will make it difficult for them to admit that their modifications don't live up to the manufacturer's claims. Remember the story of Kyle and Eric?

The Importance of Balance

Keep in mind that some modifications work well alone (i.e., addition of an air intake system), but most others require a fine balance of components in order to achieve desired results. The key to building a successful Neon project car is to keep balance in mind, from the first time you pick up a wrench. Audiophiles know this concept well. A great stereo won't sound very good if you listen to it through a cheap pair of speakers. Try to keep this in mind when reading the rest of this book, as it will serve you well in the end.

CHAPTER 1

NEON HISTORY

The import/tuner movement emerged in the mid 1980s, and it continues to grow today. Back then, it was the Hondas and VWs that were dominating the new front-wheel-drive tuner market. This eventually gave birth to the hugely popular sport compact phenomenon. Sport compact enthusiasts look for style, power, and handling in a car they can drive on the street and also take to the track on weekends. When Chrysler cranked out the first Neon in 1994, they found a car that had instant appeal to this demographic, but were they too late?

The Neon wasn't the first sport compact Chrysler produced. In fact, the first true front-wheel-drive subcompact car ever to be built in the US was the Dodge Omni/Plymouth Horizon. They were both peppy and economical cars, and sold nearly 200,000 units in 1978, their first year of production. They were also a dominant force in the subcompact market through 1990, when production finally came to an end.

The 1983 VW Rabbit GTi had a big influence on the sport-compact market, as did the Honda Civic. In 1984, the same year that Honda unveiled the new 1.5-liter Civic and CRX, Chrysler introduced the Omni GLH. Whereas the Mazda GLC stood for "Great Little Car," Dodge's GLH referred to "Goes Like Hell." Appropriately, the man who inspired this creation was none other than the legendary Carroll Shelby. That first year, the GLH sported a 110-hp naturally aspirated 4-cylinder powerplant. A performance camshaft was one of the reasons for the increase in power

Even in non-turbo trim, the Dodge Omni and Charger were popular as racecars. SCCA Solo I hillclimber, Joe Foering, is seen here at the starting line for the Weatherly hillclimb. He is always in contention for the PHA Solo I ITB championship.

over the stock Omni – this sounds like a sporty tuner car to me.

The following year, a 146-hp turbocharged 2.2-liter engine was offered as an option. As you can imagine, a turbocharged GLH could blow the doors off Honda's new Civic and CRX Si. The GLH's power, handling, cool alloy wheels, and ground effects set this Mopar performer apart from the rest of the pack. In 1986, a few hundred GLH-S models even came with Koni adjustable shocks and struts, 15-inch alloy wheels with performance Goodyear tires, and a further modified 175-hp engine.

Chrysler really seemed to be on the right track with the Omni GLH. No other sport compact was a match for that kind of power-to-weight ratio. The GLH had never received the respect it deserved, but it still has a cult following among Mopar fans. If, however, it had been produced in Japan, things would probably have been different. For some reason, in the late 1980s, if it wasn't from Japan, then it wasn't cool. That attitude changed in 1994, when Chrysler introduced a car that would capture the hearts of both Mopar and sport compact fans around the world. The first Dodge Neon made its way to showrooms in January 1994 as

Chapter 1

Shelby versions of Omni and Charger were big hits with the Mopar community. With 175 hp on tap, they were quick cars. (Photo courtesy Michael Carpenter)

Below: One of the larger Neon gatherings used to take place every year at the Belvedere assembly plant in Illinois. This little car has sparked an enthusiastic following, and this book is dedicated to all who love the Neon and SRT-4. (Photo courtesy Patrick O'Hara)

an early 1995 model. They were affordable, quick, nimble, cool – and they were the answer for enthusiasts who wanted a legitimate sport compact but didn't want to buy an import.

First Generation Cars: 1995–1999

For the first-generation cars, two chassis were available: the coupe and the sedan. There were SOHC (single overhead cam) and DOHC (dual overhead cam) 2.0-liter engines available. The SOHC made 132 hp and 129 ft-lbs of torque, while the DOHC made 150 hp and 133 ft-lbs of torque. There were only a few different handling and optional equipment packages that could be ordered during the first generation of production.

It all began in January of 1994 when the first Neon 4-door sedans rolled off the assembly line. Even the SOHC was a highlight in an otherwise torque-challenged sport compact market. At that time, Honda was only offering its 125-hp, 106-ft-lb motor in its 1992-95 Civic Si. When the Si failed to return to the market the following year, some of the Honda loyals defected. I was one of them. After racing Hondas for five years, I found the Neon to be a breath of fresh air. Although slightly heavier than the Civics, the Neons could out pull them on the racetrack as well as on the street.

These new Neons started to appear on TV sets across the nation on a regular basis. From the catchy commercials, to the SCCA Challenge and Celebrity road races, the Neon received a lot of attention from the media.

The first year of production was highly successful, and not much changed in 1995. However, there were a few changes for the 1996 model year. Base cars now came equipped with 14-inch wheels, and the gray bumpers were replaced with a body-colored piece. This was also the first time that antilock brakes were offered as an option on all cars.

In 1998, the base model was eliminated and replaced by the Highline, which became the new entry-level Neon. If you are building a racecar from scratch, the earlier base model or Highline makes a good donor car. They are the cheapest to buy anyway, and since you'll probably be replacing the struts, springs, wheels, etc. anyway, you may as well not butcher up an ACR. Save those cars for the guys who need to race in a stock class in which major modifications are not permitted.

Expresso/Sport (1997–1999)

The Sport and Expresso models varied from year to year. Expresso started life as the "white wheel" package for both Plymouth and Dodge; early Expressos had either white wheel covers, or alloy wheels, along with special white badging. Later Expresso became the Plymouth counterpart to Dodge Sports. Early Sport sedans, and all later Sports (both coupe and sedan) were basically a fog light and spoiler package for a Highline, as they did not get a special suspension. Some later cars did get the DOHC as part of the package, making them attractive to an enthusiast who would redo the suspension anyway.

The Sport Coupe (1995) and R/T (1998–1999)

The 1995 Sport Coupe was essentially an ACR, but with all of the available options. They shared suspension with the ACR, except for the special struts. All of the options were available, so the weight varies widely.

The R/T was introduced in 1998. It essentially brought back the original

Sport Coupe, but with racy new graphics. It was available as either a coupe or sedan. The R/T is the car to have if you don't want to do too many modifications and also don't want to do any serious racing. It has a great mix of driver comforts along with a good suspension, DOHC motor, and the performance gear and final drive ratios in the transmission. If you aren't necessarily looking for super high-end racing equipment, the R/T's stock parts will work great, keeping the cost of your project down. Keep in mind that because of its more extensive list of options, an R/T won't be as light as an Expresso or ACR.

The ACR

The American Club Racing (ACR) versions of the Neon are easy to spot. They came from the factory with fog light holes in the front fascia, but no fog lights. The other big difference is under the hood. All sedans had the SOHC motor, and all coupes had the DOHC. Both came with adjustable Koni struts, and were no-option cars, which made them the lightest Neons available. ACRs could still be optioned with A/C and the basic stereo.

The fastest of the bunch are the 1995 SOHC ACRs (due to weight and cam profile) and the 1996–99 DOHC ACRs. All are faster than any other Neon produced from 1995–2005, except for the SRT-4, of course.

Second-Generation Cars: 2000–2005

In early 1999, the next and final generation of Neons hit the showroom floor. This was a great time to pick up a good R/T or ACR, since there were tons of the previous generation cars left at the dealerships. The big change was that the DOHC engine was gone, and so was the coupe – all 2000+ Neons are 4-door sedans with SOHC engines. Several versions were available, including the ES, R/T, and ACR.

The main difference between the R/T and the ACR was that the ACR remained a stripped-down version designed to appeal to hard-core racers, while the R/T

Although it was planned as a grocery-getter, the Neon was also marketed to the racing community. Chrysler provided lots of contingency money for successful SCCA racers who chose to race a Neon. No other car in recent history made as great an impact on road racing and autocrossing. The Mazda Miata is a close second.

Of course, Neons owe their racing heritage to the muscle cars that came before them. The t-shirt in this photo reads: "My Neon's Daddy is a Hemi Road Runner." Poking fun at the imports, it also says: "Your Honda's Daddy is a Trail 90." (Photo courtesy Howell Automotive)

was more of a high-performance street version. Depending on the options you ordered for your R/T, the ACR remained 50 to 100 pounds lighter. But even with better torque and improved technology, these cars were no faster than the first-generation DOHC Neons (they're about 100 to 200 pounds heavier).

For race fans stuck in stock classes (in which an addition of a rear sway bar is forbidden), the chassis you want is the 2000 version that came with both front

Chapter 1

The Neon ACR (American Club Racing) was designed to live its life as a racecar. No radio, air conditioning, floor mats, fog lights – nothing to make it heavier than it needed to be. The earlier ACRs also came with a "trunk kit," which refers to some SCCA legal bolt-ons that literally came in the trunk: Koni shocks, stiffer springs, and a rear sway bar. Since these parts officially came as part of the car, they were legal for SCCA stock class competition.

The R/T Neon was basically an ACR with a few street comforts. The sport suspension made it an excellent-handling street car, plus it had a radio and air conditioning. (Photo courtesy Patrick O'Hara)

and rear sway bars. If a front bar comes on a car from the factory (a standard feature – not an option), then you can retain it. The 2001–2005 cars only had a front bar, so fine tuning your stock racer is more of a challenge. The problem is, there was no ACR or R/T version available in 2000, so although the chassis is desirable, the powerplant is not.

The other option that stock racers should look for is the SOHC high-output Magnum engine that was available from 2001 to 2004. This engine differs from all other second-generation SOHCs in that the Magnums produced 150 hp and 135 ft-lbs of torque. The 2001 Magnum is the specific one to look for as it had a hotter cam. In 2002+, that cam was re-profiled for less strain on the valvetrain.

Neon Racing Legacy

Interestingly enough, most of the initial TV ads for the Neon were designed to appeal to the average female buyer, which was the largest part of the targeted demographic. Those "Hi" commercials were certainly cute. Many buyers put a "Hi" on the front of their cars. It was inviting and friendly. The Neon was a friendly car.

But behind the scenes, Chrysler had launched one of the best promotions to ever appeal to racecar drivers. Chrysler's Motorsports program began planning for the Neon's unveiling back in 1991. The end result was a program devised by Chrysler's Motorsports Team to encourage men and women racers alike to dump their current racecars and hop into a Neon. The reason was simple: cash! Chrysler wanted you to know that if you won a race in their cute little Neon, they would give you a cute little bag 'o cash.

Chrysler was even offering a special Neon ACR (American Club Racing) version for $10,500 – as long as you produced an SCCA card at the dealership. Put in a roll cage, and you were ready to go that weekend. But some dealers didn't get it and sold a few ACRs to unsuspecting buyers! The ACR was one of the first American cars of recent times to offer what serious racers really wanted: a lightweight factory car with none of the frills that added weight to the chassis, plus an engine with great torque.

The difference between an ACR and a regular no-option Neon is that it weighed approximately 50 lbs less. That doesn't seem like much, but for a 2,500-lb car, 50 pounds feels like having 5 extra horsepower. If you add any options to the regular Neon, it could end up weighing 200 lbs more than an ACR.

The ACR also came with a better suspension than the regular base Neon. By 1998, all the ACR's suspension but the shocks turned up in the Neon Sport and later R/T. Other notable extras for the ACR included better gearing, 4-wheel disc brakes, quicker steering, and a different computer program that allowed a higher top speed. I can't remember a better deal in recent racing history.

But the racing public was a little slow at first to get on the SCCA Neon

Above: Neons were born to compete in racing venues. The second-generation cars are not the best choice for autocross since they are heavier than the earlier cars, but they're still competitive. Keith Lucas switched from a Mustang to a Neon and is successful in the G Stock SCCA Solo II class. (Photo courtesy Bob Killmer) Below: Neons are also right at home on the track. Lapping days, high-performance driving events (HPDs), and formal SCCA and NASA racing venues are littered with Neons. If you're on the East Coast, you might run into Howell Automotive testing one of their cars. (Photo courtesy Howell Automotive)

bandwagon. Only 200 units of the special ACR sedan sold in 1994. Chrysler was hopeful that the program would grow when the 2-door DOHC Neon was introduced just before the 1995 season. And they were right. That following year, they sold 10 times as many SCCA ACRs. The reason for the success of the Chrysler racing program was obvious. They were offering a complete package: a turnkey racecar that could be serviced at your local dealership, lots of contingency money, plus a full factory warranty. Nowadays, if an auto manufacturer finds out that you're racing your car, they may void your warranty. There are even rumors that one company is monitoring autocross results looking for violations, and then sending out letters to buyers informing them that their warranty has been voided. Give me a break! Autocross? You could autocross most new cars until you corded the tires without doing any damage to the vehicle. At most, you only get 5 to 10 minutes of

Chapter 1

Need a more upscale look for your Neon? Howell Automotive manufactures this fiberglass nose for 2000-newer Neons. The styling is reminiscent of the Hemi-powered sports cars built by Briggs Cunningham in the '50s. This one is fitted with a Chrysler grille, but for serious airflow, some users leave the grille out entirely. (Photo courtesy Howell Automotive)

track time per weekend at a Solo II event. Times have certainly changed. But back then, Chrysler was proud of its Neon, and encouraged buyers to go racing. Thankfully, this practice is still alive. Subaru gives new WRX buyers a free membership to the SCCA, which is paramount to a license to race. But with the $10,000 that SRT-4 owners are saving over a WRX STi, they can afford to buy their own SCCA membership.

The success of the SCCA Club Racing and Solo program are excellent examples of how marketing and racing can get together to boost sales, and the Neon program was one of the most successful programs of its kind. In the first two seasons of eligibility, Neons took home National Championships in both Showroom Stock C (SSC) and Showroom Stock B (SSB), as well as in two different Solo II classes, and Neon sales to the general public soared.

Mopar Performance (Chrysler's high-performance parts branch) initially didn't offer many hop-up parts for the Neon. There was no real urgency for Mopar to offer options for Neons as long as they were running in SSC and SSB, where few mods are allowed. But that changed in anticipation of the Neon moving into IT (improved touring) classes, which was initially expected to take place in 2000. However, it was delayed until 2005 partially due to the unbelievable popularity of the Neon in Showroom Stock racing. Mopar now has a great line of performance parts for both the street and the track.

The next big transition for Chrysler that caused the sport compact community to take notice was the introduction of the Dodge Razor at the 2002 Detroit auto show. This rear-wheel-drive concept car boasted a 0–60 mph time under six seconds, and a top speed of 140 miles per hour. Under the hood was a 2.4-liter turbocharged engine that made 250 horsepower and 230 ft-lbs of torque. Although it didn't look like the Razor would ever make it into production, you could tell that Chrysler was up to something.

The SRT-4

What has a faster 0–60 time than the Porsche Boxster S, Beetle Turbo S, and the Nissan 350Z? What car did *Sport Compact Car* magazine name its "Sport Compact Car of the Year" the first year of production? What did Speednation name as the "best bang for the buck" of any street car or racecar on the planet? Okay, we made the last one up. Anyway, the answer is obvious, mainly because we told you at the top of this paragraph – it's the SRT-4.

This great sport compact first started taking shape in 2000 when an SRT-4 concept car was introduced. Whether or not it would ever go into production was anyone's guess. But as more and more radical cars were paraded in front of our curious eyes, we were hopeful that something would come of it. Chrysler was up to something, and it was good.

The Street and Racing Technology (SRT) department inside Dodge is responsible for the new line of performance-tuned Dodges. The number "4" obviously refers to four cylinder, just as the Viper SRT-10 indicates that the Viper has 10 cylinders, and the SRT-8 has 8 cylinders.

It's hard to come up with things to say about the SRT-4 that haven't already been said, but I do have a few more observations to share. I believe the reason why every car enthusiast doesn't have an SRT-4 in their garage is because of clever marketing by the competition. If you simply look at the SRT-4 on paper compared to every other sport compact car on the planet, it's obvious which car stands out. With 0–60 times under 5 seconds, quarter-mile times dipping below 14 seconds, and a top speed of nearly 150 mph, the 2,900-pound SRT-4 has few rivals. Then factor in the excellent handling and price tag of just over $20,000, and the choice is clear. Now that a few are showing up on the used market, the deal is even sweeter.

However, I think that the low price may be an obstacle in elevating the car to a more legendary status. If the price was closer to $30,000, the car would no longer be considered "cheap." Let's face it, one of the stigmas the Neon has endured through most of its production life is the fact that people view it as a cheap car, or a rental car. It doesn't have the fit and finish of a BMW, but if you blindfolded a racecar driver and put them on the track in a BMW and then into a Neon . . . they would probably be killed. Bad analogy. But the point I am trying to make is that when it comes to choosing between form or function, the Neon is equal to many high-end sports cars in the function category, but loses out when it comes to form.

That stigma causes many people to view the SRT-4 as simply a Neon on steroids. Although it is a fair analogy on one level, it is likely the reason the SRT-4 isn't more popular with the Honda and Subaru crowd. Speaking of Subaru, they managed to shake off the cheap stigma in the late 1990s. I remember just how unreliable, unexciting, and poorly made the early Subarus were. Remember: "Inexpensive, and built to stay that way"? Now, thanks to some great marketing and cool cars like the STi, Subaru is viewed with much higher esteem. Of course, the "inexpensive" part of their early slogan did not "stay that way" after Y2K.

But the SRT-4 has a destiny all its own. If you can get past the fact that it is not an import and doesn't carry a high price tag, you will find yourself driving a car that will blow the doors off of most of the popular sport compact cars. It is also clearly the best bang for the buck in this market.

The reason for its success is simple – the 2003 version came standard with a turbocharged 2.4-liter powerplant that cranks out 205 horsepower and 220 ft-lbs of torque. It's built at the same assembly plant where all Neons are made. Only about 3,000 units were originally projected for construction that first year, but due to the popularity of the SRT-4, four times that number rolled off the assembly line in Belvedere, Illinois, in 2004.

With the addition of a limited-slip differential (LSD) in 2004, the SRT-4 started tearing up the autocross track. The LSD helps get all that power to the ground and makes the car a real blast to race. Neon-legend Mark Daddio switched to an SRT-4 in 2004 and was very successful (what else is new?). Pictured is a novice getting some instruction at a local SCCA Solo II. (Photo courtesy Jim Weslager)

The SRT-4 comes in a very nice package, which can be easily upgraded thanks to Mopar Performance. You can add a Stage 1, 2, or 3 kit specifically engineered to bolt right onto your SRT-4. No guessing, no trying to match components – just pick up the phone and get a proven horsepower package to meet your need for even more speed.

Chapter 1

The actual computer and head from the Razor concept car ended up on the Speednation turbo car, shown here right before it set a few new SCCA Solo I records. Unfortunately, it took out seven guard rail posts at the Pagoda Hillclimb.

The list of impressive features seems to be endless considering the low price tag. You get an efficient Mitsubishi TD04 Turbocharger with a cast-aluminum intercooler that will move the boost gauge as high as 14 psi. The 2.4-liter engine was upgraded to produce 230 horsepower at 5,300 rpm and 250 ft-lbs of torque. A high-performance 5-speed manual transaxle, 17-inch alloys, equal-length halfshafts, and a performance clutch help take full advantage of all that power. A muffler-less, dual-outlet exhaust system with 2.5-inch polished stainless tips, a larger-diameter throttle body, and a high-flow intake manifold add to the efficiency of the powerplant. An ABS system and four-wheel 11-inch disc brakes with larger-diameter calipers and rotors can stop the SRT 60–0 mph in less than 120 feet. This level of performance exceeds that of the concept car that inspired the SRT-4.

For 2004, there were more improvements made to the platform designed to elevate both power and handling to a level that caused tuners and racers to take notice. A limited-slip differential, designed to get the power to the pavement more efficiently, was now standard.

The Future of the Neon

With the production of the Neon expected to end in 2005, the future of the SRT-4 is also in question. Originally, only 3,000 units were planned, but so far over 20,000 have been sold. These numbers caused some corporate heads at Chrysler to take notice. The SRT-4 may help keep the Neon around a few more years, but both may fall by the wayside for Chrysler's new PM platform. This new platform, which should include a hatchback version similar to the Ford Focus, will be a mix of technology and design from Mitsubishi, Chrysler, and Hyundai. Neon and SRT-4 fans hope the PM will be a fitting replacement. I fear it may not be, however. When I asked an unnamed Chrysler engineer what "PM" stood for, he replied with an answer that I can't repeat here. Let's just say he isn't thrilled with the project. Neither were the Honda CRX guys when it was canceled and replaced by the Del Sol, but that turned out okay. Sorry, poor example. In the rough draft of my first book, the *Honda Performance Handbook*, I was planning on referring to the Del Sol as a boat anchor, but I changed my mind so as not to get the Del Slow owners angry. Let's hope that the Neon doesn't evolve into a heavy, underpowered boat anchor.

So what about the Razor? What became of it and are there production plans? Rumor has it that the computer and SRT-4 prototype cylinder head ended up in Mark Daddio's Turbo Neon, which is now in the hands of my company, www.speed-nation.com. The problem is, I totaled the car after setting a new class record at the 2004 Pagoda Hillclimb. However, the powerplant survived, and will soon race again. As for the Razor project and the future of Chrysler, there are mixed messages coming from the company regarding the feasibility of the project. But remember, this is the same company that produced the Prowler, so I wouldn't be surprised if we see some incarnation of a Razor in the near future. Until then, we have the Viper, and for those of us with smaller wallets and a strong desire to race, we have lots of Neons and several thousand SRT-4s out there to play with.

If you already own a $2,000 Neon, this book can help you build up your Neon to match the performance of a $20,000 SRT for half the price. For SRT-4 owners, there are many upgrades revealed in this book that can help take your car to an even higher level of performance.

Chapter 2

Suspension and Handling

Neon owners will tell you that one of the best things about their car is its great handling. The unibody construction, high structural rigidity, and fully independent suspension provide the driver with excellent feedback as to the road conditions. But as good as they are from the factory, most tend to understeer, also referred to as "push" or "plow." Chrysler engineers probably feel that for the average Neon owner, understeer is easier to control than having the tail hang out around every turn (oversteer). However, the best-handling Neons have been modified to decrease understeer and induce oversteer when driven with a degree of skill.

This chapter can help you transform your daily driver into a weekend racer, as well as give you better control on the street. Of course, we do not endorse fast street driving. Racing should be reserved for the track – not the street. But a better-balanced vehicle will offer better control, and could help you avoid obstacles in the road, allowing you to drive away from dangerous situations.

Although Neons are one of the best-handling cars you can buy right out of the box, there are many changes that can be made to improve on the factory performance. One way to increase understeer is to equip the front end with stiffer springs than the rear, which is how the Neon comes from the factory. The front springs are 150 lbs, and the rears are 120 lbs. However, the best handling setup for a front-wheel-drive car is the opposite – the springs in the rear should be stiffer than in the front. Since this is contrary to what the manufacturers recommend, you may find that many aftermarket parts distributors will try to talk you out of making the rear stiffer. This may be because they are following your car's

Neons have great torque right out of the box, so the first thing you should do before you go racing is upgrade the suspension. A good-handling Neon, such as Michael Carpenter's car, can really bring in some low lap times.

High-Performance Dodge Neon Builder's Handbook

A set of lowering springs is one of the first steps many enthusiasts take with their Neon. Some of the most affordable lowering springs are available from Mopar Performance Parts. (Photo courtesy Mopar Performance Parts)

original suspension design. The springs they may send you will probably make your car lower, but not correct the understeer condition. A good parts distributor should be able to quote you the spring rates of the suspension package you want to order. If they don't know the spring rates, then they are probably poorer-quality springs and will not give you the handling you desire.

A second word of caution: a competition spring setup is not for everyone. It takes a good driver to take full advantage of a properly balanced suspension. The best way to sort out which suspension setup may be right for you is to take your car out to a local autocross. If the understeer you experience causes you to yearn for a more balanced car in the turns, then you may be ready to change your stock spring setup. But by no means should you drive fast on the street with this setup, as it may end up biting you in the end.

Bigger Bars and Heavier Springs

The rear suspension is where you'll find the biggest controversy in the book. Let me summarize the two schools at work. The first theory is that Neons handle much differently than other FWD cars, such as Hondas, so what works for them won't work for a Neon. According to this theory, the proper way to set up a Neon for racing, and I stress racing here, is to get the front suspension just right, and then move on to the rear. This philosophy involves buying the proper front sway bar, and front springs and struts, and then worrying about the rear later. If you do it like this, the front spring rates will be much stiffer than the rear.

Here's some compelling evidence to support this theory. Mark Daddio won D/Street Prepared (a class in which lots of suspension mods are permitted) in the Neon that we at Speednation now own. He set the car up by modifying the front first, and then in order to get the rear end to rotate, he simply inflated the rear tire pressures to 70 psi. We're not talking about a street tire here – these were very sticky, shaved race tires. Several other drivers have cited this setup as the way to go, and Neons have done extremely well nationally in both Street Touring and Street Modified using this philosophy.

So here is my counterpoint, or the second school of thought for modifying Neon suspension. Mark Daddio is an exceptional driver, and a better driver than I am. He could beat most racers driving a Neon even without the tire pressures he likes. He has National trophies in driving everything from muscle cars to formula cars. But if you were at the track when Mark crossed the finish line in his Neon, and put a pyrometer on the rear tires, what do you think you

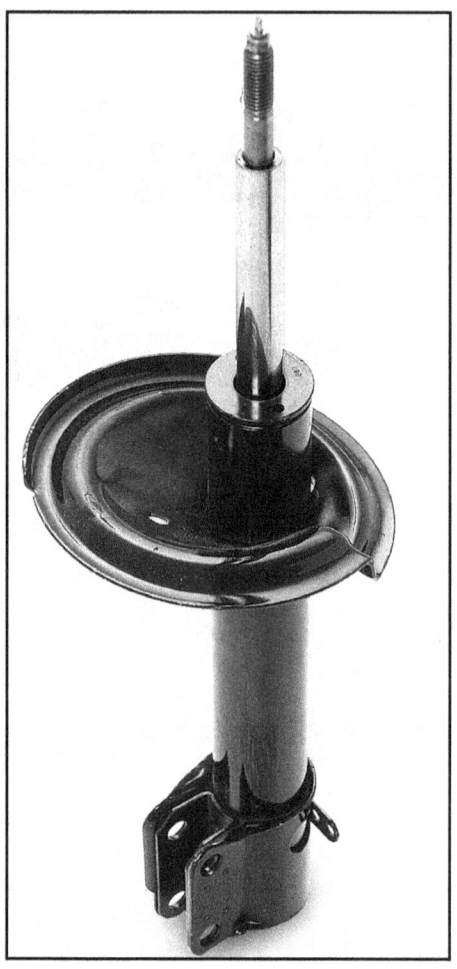

When you add a set of lowering springs, it's a good idea to add some performance struts to help control the compression and rebound. If you want to upgrade your Neon to ACR specs, these Mopar Performance ACR struts are available for first- and second-gen Neons. (Photo courtesy Mopar Performance Parts)

would find? The rears would be very hot in the center of the tread, and cooler near the outside of the tire. This is not an optimal use of a race tire. The ideal setup is to have even temperatures across the entire width of the tire. Mark, and others, were able to win because: 1) Neons are very forgiving cars, and 2) these guys are exceptional drivers.

Ideally, the rear pressures should remain between 25 to 35 psi in order to keep an even temperature across the tire. That way you'll have the biggest, stickiest tire patch you can get touching the pavement. This will give you the best traction and handling. If Mark was driving a car that had a stiffer rear end, he

Suspension and Handling

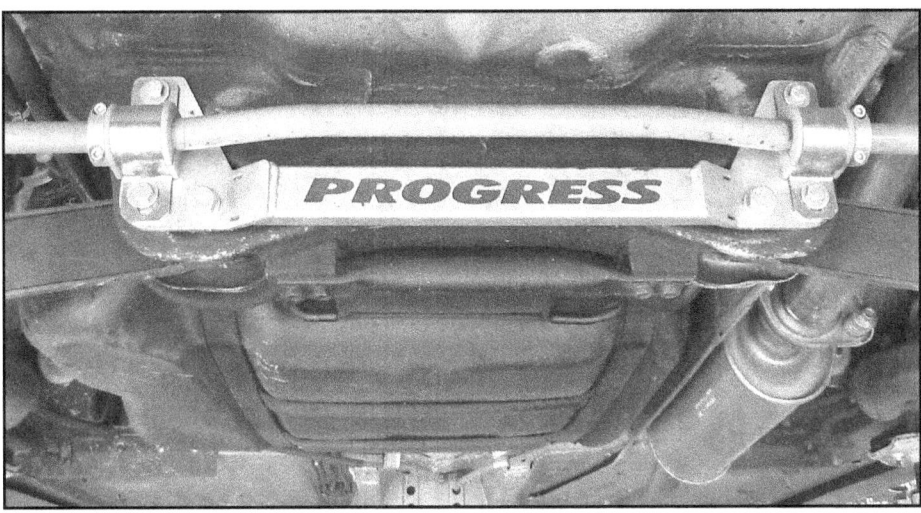

Progress is well known for making suspension components for Hondas, but they also make sway bars and suspension components for Neons.

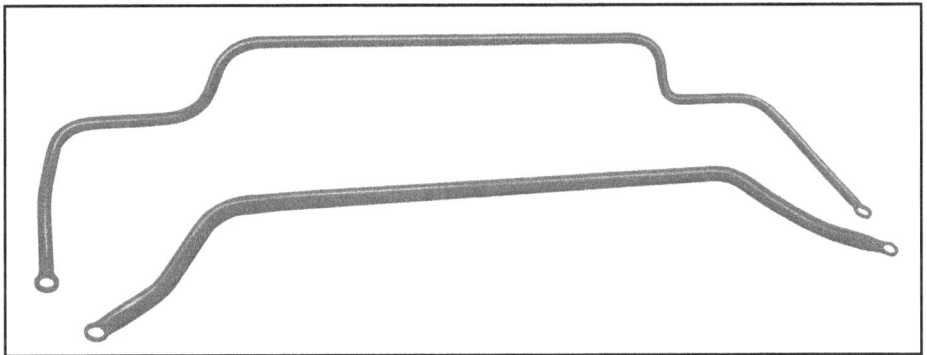

Mopar Performance Parts offers upgraded sway bars for most Neons. You can upgrade your Neon to ACR specs, or get even larger bars. (Photo courtesy Mopar Performance Parts)

spring rate of 300 to 500+ lbs. But remember, if a manufacturer can't tell you the spring rate of their springs, it's likely no better than what you already have on your car. We experimented with our factory ACR Neon back in 1994 and found that many springs we tried were no better than the well-designed ACR springs. Of course, things have changed since then and many reputable companies have designed systems that work well on both Neons and SRT-4s.

Sway Bars

The main function of a sway bar is to reduce body roll, but just because a car has body roll doesn't mean it won't handle well, and vice versa. Adding a larger sway bar to the front or rear will make that end of your car stiffer. Remember, if you buy aftermarket bars, be sure to get polyurethane bushings. Sway bars are an inexpensive way to reduce understeer, but unless your Neon came with a Touring (front: 20 mm, rear: none) or Sport (front: 22 mm, rear: 18 mm) suspension, you have none. Even if you have an RT, ACR, or SRT-4, a sway bar upgrade is a very worthwhile option to pursue. A stiffer front bar will induce understeer (plowing), but the tradeoff is helping to keep the front end square when turning. This cuts down a little on inside tire slippage under hard cornering. Adding or replacing a smaller rear bar with a thicker one tends to induce oversteer. Aftermarket sway bars are available from companies such as Suspension Techniques or Modern Performance.

For serious racers, an adjustable rear bar is recommended so that you can dial it in based on what type of racing you want to do. Wait until your entire suspension package is in place, however, before you decide how stiff to make the rear bar. The best way to proceed with sway bar adjustment is by starting with the loose setting (the outermost holes on the bar), and working your way in to fine tune the overall rear stiffness. This is best accomplished at a local autocross test and tune. Once you get the proper setting, be prepared to back off one or two holes if you decide on entering a high-speed event. Autocrossers like to

wouldn't need so much tire pressure in the rear, and he could have a larger contact patch. However, if you are racing a Neon in a class that doesn't allow bigger rear bars or stiffer springs, then the only thing you can do is to go with stiffer struts and play with your tire pressures. That is precisely the situation with SCCA Showroom Stock racing, where my Neon handles best with 32 psi in the front tires, 38 psi in the rear, and Koni struts all around.

This discussion could go on forever, but there is one thing that most Neon racers will agree on, and that is that Neons are better racecars when you can get the rear end to rotate. The biggest problem with stock Neons is understeer. In other words, when you enter a turn carrying too much speed, there is little chance of being able to negotiate that turn. The front tires screech, lose traction, and tend to keep on going straight. This could put you into the weeds – or worse, the wall – because you can't steer the car.

If, on the other hand, traction is lost with the rear tires, steering is still possible. That's why a little oversteer (in capable hands) will enable you to go around turns carrying more speed, with more g-force, and under better control. And the best way to reduce understeer (or induce oversteer) is to start with the rear suspension. In fact, if you're on a budget, you can save money by leaving the front suspension alone and just making the rear a little stiffer.

Some aftermarket "competition" springs are available for less than $150/pair, but most of these only lower the car about an inch and do not correct the understeer problem because their spring rates aren't much stiffer than stock. For racing, I recommend a rear

If you can afford it and your class rules allow it, you should buy an adjustable sway bar. It can help fine-tune your Neon's handling on the track, but there's no need for one on the street. This sway bar has multiple attachment points to adjust the feel.

Neon ACRs came from the factory with adjustable struts. Twisting this knob adjusts the strut from pretty stiff to really stiff. (Photo courtesy Chris Malluege)

be on the edge of hanging out the rear end, but at 100+ mph, you want that rear end to stay put.

You may also want to consider loosening the front sway bar to further reduce understeer, but this should only be done for pure racing vehicles. This is a nice trick if you have installed a limited-slip differential (LSD). An LSD will typically increase understeer, so you end up plowing into a turn. Never install an LSD unless you also upgrade the rear sway bar, because the first time you try to turn the car at high speeds you'll end up going straight. A stiff front bar will make this situation even worse. A loose bar won't engage completely when you initially start turning, but once you are in the turn, as your car starts to experience some body roll, the sway bar will grab and help keep your car flat through the apex and track out portion of the sweeper.

Struts

Moving on to the struts, external adjustability is what to look for if you want to do a little amateur racing. Even if you just want to upgrade your handling for the street, depending on the terrain where you live, adjustability will give you options so that you can dial in the best performance for your car and how you drive it. Koni is really the only choice right now for serious racers, but KYB also offers a less expensive solution for street driving. You do, however, get what you pay for.

If you are planning to install aftermarket struts yourself, make sure you use the proper manufacturer's torque settings when securing the fragile tops of the new struts. We watched in horror when a local muffler shop used too much force when installing a new strut on one of our racecars (we were trying to save time). You should see all the cool stuff that squirts out of a compressed strut when the top breaks off. We stopped laughing when we found out that the shop had no spare, and we remembered we had to leave for a race the next morning. We were surprised, however, how well the car still handled with one Koni and one stock strut up front.

Strut Tower Bars

Adjustable strut tower bars are a good choice for most Neon street and dual-duty cars, and they are available for both front and rear. They are not intended to take the place of sway bars, but they will add stiffness. They can either be homemade, or purchased for approximately $50 each. If you have a full cage in your racecar, however, you won't need to spend the money on this bolt-on.

One final word about the stiffer rear-end controversy. I have raced both Neons and Hondas, and they are not much different. The fastest Honda guys will tell you that the key to exceptional handling is to make the rear stiffer than the front. Most of the really great Neon autocrossers have not tried the stiff-rear setup, and few have had a great deal of experience at 100+ mph racing. A much more precise car is required at those speeds, and you need full traction from all four tires to keep yourself from getting seriously injured or killed. So my advice is to do what works for you with what you have to work with. Most aftermarket handling packages do not come with stiffer rear springs, therefore you may have to inflate the rear pressures (as Mark did) to get your Neon or SRT-4 to rotate. But if you can find a stiffer rear set-up, you'll be able to optimize the efficiency of your tires and generate more g-force in the long run, which will net faster lap times.

Suspension and Handling

The coil over spring in the left picture is a two-stage spring set-up on our turbo Neon. In the center picture, you can see the small spring at the very top of the assembly. It's designed to compress easier to help smooth the ride slightly. We removed these springs since we would no longer be driving on the street and didn't want any delay in compression when entering a turn. On the right, we're replacing the old spring with a single, heavyweight spring for more predictable handling.

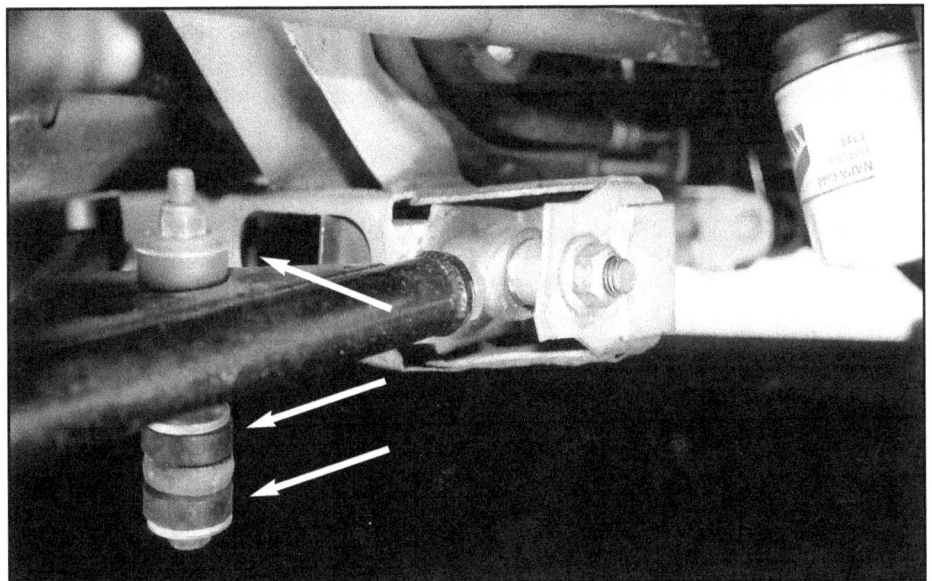 

Polyurethane is a wonderful compound. The racing world would not be the same without it. This high-strength material is used in the sway bar bushings seen on the Speednation turbo Neon (left), and Booger shifter bushings for the SRT-4 (right). Both serve to replace standard rubber bushings, making for a stiffer feel.

Final Suspension Tweaking

Once you've installed all your suspension parts, set your struts halfway between stiff and soft, and then get yourself to an autocross. You should only make adjustments to the struts, sway bars, and tire pressures when you can see the result of your changes in the way your Neon feels and handles. It'll probably take a few events to sort everything out, so be patient. Don't make more than one change at a time, or you'll never know what was responsible for changes in your handling. Even if your handling gets worse, that's a good thing because it'll tell you what didn't work. In the long run, if you've taken good notes along the way, both the good changes and bad changes will show you the way to an excellent-handling Neon.

Corner Weighting

A poorly balanced car could give you a lot of unwanted thrills if you are racing when competing in high-speed

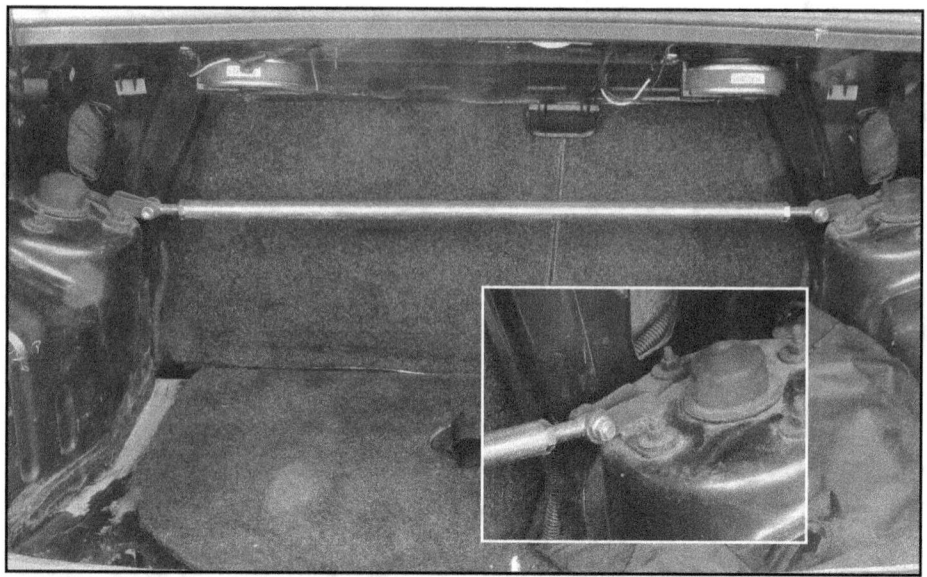

One affordable upgrade that's easy to install is a pair of strut-tower braces. The one shown here is in the rear of a first-gen Neon, and was purchased on eBay for about $40. It really helped stiffen up the rear end and keep it flatter in the corners. (Photo courtesy Travis Thompson)

If you're really serious about handling, then you should cornerweight your Neon. This is really only possible if you have adjustable spring perches making it possible to raise and lower each corner of the car. Do this before you get your Neon aligned, as changing ride height will effect both toe and camber.

events such as Drag Racing, Solo I, or Road Racing. Downshifting and hard braking at 100+ mph will exaggerate any weight imbalance your car may have, even though you may not have noticed it at slower speeds. In fact, you may not notice any real balance issues unless you are driving your Neon at its limit. Trail braking and heel/toe downshifting can help smooth over an unstable chassis, but a properly balanced car will react in a much more predictable fashion, allowing the driver to push the limits of tire adhesion without excessive twitch and roll.

So, what does it take to engineer a well-balanced machine? For many vehicles, all it takes is access to accurate scales, help from a friend, and about an hour of your time. You need to have the ability to raise and lower each corner of the car, however, to make this work. That will require a fully adjustable aftermarket suspension. Actually, any Neon that you intend to race seriously should have coil-over springs, which allow you to adjust your ride height, if competition rules permit.

Grab a buddy, get a note pad and pen to record changes from inside the cockpit while your friend reads the weights, and push your Neon onto a set of electronic scales. Make sure that you have the car in racing trim. I recently helped my friend, Glenn, corner weight his 1985 ITA MR2. After going through a few cycles of raising and lowering the corners, Glenn realized that he had his 40-pound Easy-Up pit tent in the trunk of his car. It was funny for a few second, but then we realized that we had to start all over.

To help you avoid a similar incident, we'll walk through a sample corner weighting session. These are the actual results of the first time we put the Speednation 1996 Turbo Neon on the scales. By the way, even though this car was a National Championship Solo II car in the competent hands of Mark Daddio, there was no way in the world I was going to drive it at 120+ mph up a 1½-lane-wide mountain road until it was as balanced as possible. Good balance equals predictability.

A few notes about the Speednation Turbo Neon. It has two lightweight racing seats, a complete interior in the forward cockpit, but is completely gutted behind the driver's and front passenger seat (SCCA Street Modified rules). A full, SCCA-legal roll cage (the same one that Daddio originally used in SSB) was reinstalled for this Neon's second life as an autocrosser.

Before pushing the car onto the scales, make sure that they have been leveled. Once the car is on the scales, rock it a little to settle the suspension. The first thing to write down is the dry, or curb weight, of the car. These numbers won't be of much use unless you're planning to pilot it by remote control. The heaviest weight you will ever add to your car is you, so you should be in the driver's seat when the car is on the scales. So, therefore, the next step is to get into the car. Refer to the chart below to see the dry weight compared to the weight of the Turbo Neon with me in it. Look carefully. Where did the majority of the weight go? Surprise – nearly 60 percent of the weight ended up in the left (driver's) rear corner! The LF (left front) gained 62 pounds, 56 pounds went to the RF (right front), 106 pounds went to the LR (left rear), and only 5 lbs went to the RR (right rear). Worse yet, the LF/RR diagonal gained only 67 lbs, while the RF/LR diagonal gained a whopping 162 lbs. You want the diagonals to be even so you have the same amount of understeer or oversteer in right and left turns.

Dry Weight

LF: 772   RF: 760
LR: 418   RR: 454

LF + RR = 1226
RF + LR = 1178

W/ Driver

LF: 834   RF: 816
LR: 524   RR: 459

LF + RR = 1293
RF + LR = 1340

Regular street driving will not work your suspension like racing will. At 100+ mph, every little imperfection in the pavement will make itself known to the driver. Your car must be predictable for you to trust it. Often, you'll even get some air at high speeds, depending on bumps and dips in the track. (Photo courtesy Keith Bower)

Okay, so I weigh 229 lbs. I was eating to compensate for the stress I felt trying to get this book finished on time. Anyway, to try to balance out the weight, the first change we made was to lower the RR and raise the LR. Two principles are at work here. The first is that vehicle weight is not balanced from one side to another, but on a diagonal. For instance, if your Neon is relatively well balanced, except for the LR, which is too light, you can't just add some weight to that corner and expect to solve your problem. If you do, prepare for a shock. Sure, some of the weight will go to the LR, but the RF will also increase substantially.

The second principle is that raising a corner will make it heavier. That doesn't seem to make sense to a lot of people. If you think about it in terms of what is happening to the wheel, you will understand more clearly. You're not so much raising a corner of the car as you are pushing the wheel down towards the ground. We found a very easy way to remember this very important principle: Lower equals Lighter.

After you set up your Neon, take it to an autocross to see how it behaves before you go high-speed racing. Even at the track, we took it easy the first day just so that we could be sure how the car would handle. After dialing out some of the camber and toe out that Mark Daddio was using for Solo II competition, the car was still unstable at 120+ mph in a straight line. We eventually put the front toe setting to 0, and that cured the wandering, though turn-in suffered slightly.

1st Change

LF: 860   RF: 793
LR: 500   RR: 480

LF + RR = 1340
RF + LR = 1293

So, back to the scales. After this initial adjustment, we gained 26 lbs in the LF and 21 lbs in the RR, so that diagonal gained 47 lbs. The other diagonal lost 24 lbs in the LR, which is where all the weight of my butt went, and 23 lbs in the RF – a total of 47 lbs lost. So far, so good – or so we thought. Losing the 24 lbs in the LR was great, but the weight lost in the RF shifted the RF+LR/LF+RR diagonal from 1340/1293 to 1293/1340. The rear of the car was very close to balanced,

Chapter 2

The Speednation Neon's suspension is far from stock. We don't recommend this for the street simply because custom end-link joints like these will wear out and fail with repetitive movement. Most racecars will only log 100 to 500 miles per year.

We wish we had invented coil overs with these adjustable spring perches. They're one of our favorite mods because you can use them to adjust ride height for maximum balance and handling, plus they can provide precise tire clearance in lowered cars.

with only a 20-lb difference, but the front was still way off. The diagonal didn't change at all – it just reversed itself. We hadn't solved anything.

2nd Change

LF: 845 RF: 805
LR: 514 RR: 469

LF + RR = 1314
RF + LR = 1319

After my friend/helper quit and went home frustrated, I was still at it two hours

These complete coil-overs are available from Mopar Performance Parts for your SRT-4. They give you the ability to adjust your ride height, which will help you corner weight your car. (Photo courtesy Mopar Performance Parts)

later. Every time I tried to get the car a little more balanced, it seemed to just get worse. And I am no novice at this, having corner weighted over 100 cars. After a lot of trial and error, the weights ended up being 845 LF and 805 RF (very close for most cars), and the rear was 514 LR and 469 RR (also very close). But the best part was that the diagonal was 1319/1314. To be honest, it was mostly luck, with a little skill and perseverance.

We recommend that you don't drive yourself too crazy trying to reach a "zero" differential (perfect balance), since a change at any corner will affect the other three as well. As you can see, weight can be added (or removed) to make subtle changes in your car's balance, but you should never add any weight in front of the front axle or behind the rear axle. Also, remember to move the car off the scales each time you make a change and rock the car again before you push it back on to settle the suspension.

Relocating or changing the size of the battery is a common trick that we practice in all of our racecars, class rules permitting. With your car on the scales, experiment with placing the battery in different locations before bolting it down. Hint: the best place isn't always in the RR. We find that it is often better to get it as close to the passenger seat as possible, depending on your weight and how your car is configured.

Corner weighting can be a relatively simple procedure if you have an easily adjustable suspension. But if you can't take advantage of the aftermarket suspension systems and/or are not permitted to alter ride height, don't be too discouraged. There are still some options available. For example, experimenting with different spring rates can also change the balance of a vehicle. This would involve much more time, since the springs would have to be removed and replaced, then the car reweighed with each combination you attempt. You can see how long it took us to get our Neon right, and that was with a simple adjustable spring perch system. But, in principle, the stiffer the spring, the less the spring will be able to compress, resulting in more weight transferred to that corner.

But is it a good idea to have different spring rates on each corner of the car?

Sure it is – circle track and road race drivers have been doing this for years. Even in stock classes, some car builders shop for natural variations that can occur in stock spring rates, and bias the car based on these variations. That is way too extreme, however, unless you are extremely competitive. Another trick is to use older, worn "stock" springs in some corners, and fresh new

Suspension and Handling

Relocating the battery is a common mod for racecars. Before you decide where you want to put your battery, get to a set of racing scales to determine the best location. However, since the development of new smaller, lightweight batteries, relocation is not as popular.

Camber and caster are easily adjusted with adjustable camber plates. In a stock Neon, it's possible to get one degree or more of negative camber, but you can get three or more with camber plates.

springs in others to create the desired effect. There are also variations in the thickness of "stock" strut tower bushings, which can alter ride height.

Finally, there is a theory that you can gain about 10 to 15 lbs in spring rate by pre-loading the bushing at the bottom of the spring. If you loosen the assembly (as if you were planning to remove it), you can twist the bushing so that it's in the wrong position, then tighten everything back up. When the car is back on the ground, there will be added tension on the bushing, essentially causing it to have its own spring rate. This is a trick only used by those racers competing in stock classes. As far as we're concerned, it is still just a theory – we haven't had nearly enough patience to try it.

So will all this actually make your car handle better? If the car is poorly balanced (like our racecar was), the answer is yes. But if the weight is already within 2 percent from the left to right side (that's about 50 lbs in a 2,400-lb Neon or 60 lbs in a 2,900-lb SRT-4), then be prepared to accept a tradeoff if changes are made. Remember the cardinal rule of fine-tuning: changing one thing usually affects something else. So if your car understeers when turning right (a common FWD problem), you can improve this situation if you're willing to sacrifice some of the good handling you're experiencing when turning left. Here are a few lessons to keep in mind when approaching this project: 1) Have a definite plan in mind before you begin, 2) Don't make too many changes at one time, and 3) Don't get greedy.

A strut bar or brace will improve front-end rigidity, which will help overcome the tendency of your SRT-4 or Neon to understeer. (Photo courtesy Howell Automotive)

A good alignment is essential for a good-handling Neon. We don't recommend straying from the factory settings for a street project, but a racecar will live or die based on the alignment.

Alignment

An alignment is the last thing you should do before you hit the track. Any further lowering of the car or shifting of weight anywhere in the car will require another alignment. Even adding racing seats, a carbon hood, or getting lighter rims will change your alignment settings.

Don't ever take a good alignment for granted, as it is extremely important to a good-handling car. There isn't too much you can do to a stock Neon or SRT-4, and competition rules forbid making changes to the factory setup in many stock racing classes. If you only intend to use your car on the street, then you should skip this section, as most changes will drastically reduce the life of your tires, and could make your car unstable when driving on a crowned surface (such as the street) at high speed.

Camber is the angle between the vertical axis of your wheel and the perpendicular centerline of your car (if you have negative camber, the bottom of your tires stick out farther than the tops). The Neon chassis is camber challenged from the factory, but you can get a small amount of negative camber by loosening the bolts on the top of the strut mount and pushing the strut in towards the engine compartment as far as it will go. Pre-1998 ACRs and many other models have slotted mounting holes, allowing camber adjustment with the stock bolts. You have to do this with the front end of the car in the air. Some racers will actually elongate the holes for the upper strut mount to squeak out up to one degree of negative camber. With factory "crash" undersized bolts and slotted struts, 2.5 degrees of negative camber is possible. Speednation's Michael Carpenter has had a lot of autocross success running his Neon (named *Tess*) with 1.5 degrees of negative camber with this set-up.

The only way to get any sort of real control over your Neon's camber setting is by using aftermarket camber plates. We recommend only making changes to your camber plates when your car is on an alignment machine. That way you can really see what is happening to both camber and toe.

Speaking of living and dying, the Speed-nation Turbo Neon met its end at 110+ mph at the 2004 Pagoda Hillclimb. This legendary hillclimb is run only once per year, and has been a staple in the PHA series for the past several decades. After setting a new class record by over two seconds on the one-minute hill during Saturday's competition, the author got greedy and took out seven guardrail posts on Sunday.

In layman's terms, toe in is when your tires look pigeon toed. Toe out is when the fronts of the tires are spread apart (it looks like your car is trying to turn in both directions). Dialing in 1.5 to 3 degrees of negative camber in the front is a good starting point, along with ⅛ to ¼ inch total toe-out, which will help the car turn in quicker. Any additional toe-out will cause major tire instability when going fast in a straight line. We had to change the alignment characteristics of Daddio's autocross Neon before we took it high-speed racing. The car was wandering back and forth at 80+ mph, and when the turbo kicked in, it was very difficult to control. That all changed when we took the toe-out setting back to zero. The car didn't turn in as well when autocrossing, but at higher speeds, it was much easier to trust. Remember that Neons have a tendency to go slightly toe-out under acceleration, and toe-in under deceleration.

Make sure that you sit in the car during the alignment process to insure true settings. If you didn't believe us when we stated earlier that any weight changes made to your car will affect alignment, try this experiment. While sitting in your car on the alignment rack, shift your weight from side to side and watch the alignment computer. If you can't see the alignment screen, you will surely be able to hear the alignment guy yelling at you to "sit still!" Your own weight is even a factor in toe and camber setting. But again, for pure street driving, you don't need to sit in the car during the alignment since you won't be pushing your car to the limits on the street. If you do drive at 100 percent on the street, then camber settings are the least of your problems – you may need to get your brain aligned instead.

So what about the rear end? Negative camber in the rear will resist spinning out, but could increase plowing (understeer). The same goes for toe adjustments. Toe-out in the front helps your car turn in better, but toe-out in the rear does the opposite. It really gets confusing. We recommend starting with the front alignment and leaving the rear neutral until you get a chance to test your car. Then continue to make adjustments to the front until you get the best possible handling. Only then should you move on to the rear to see if you can improve on what you've already accomplished. If you know of a driver who successfully races a Neon similar to yours, ask them what settings they use. That could also be a great starting point for your car, assuming the person giving you advice is actually winning races.

Summary

When I took out seven guardrail posts at 110 mph at the Pagoda Hillclimb with the Speednation 1996 Turbo Neon, it was a case of simply overdriving the car. The corner weights were set, the alignment was perfect, the tire pressures were right on, but you can't make a car defy the laws of physics. Still, if I had one more foot of roadway before the rear end touched that first wooden post, I probably would have been able to drive the car out of that drift. Even a perfect-handling car will bite you if you don't have respect for the road. It may be the first Neon I wrecked, but it won't be the last. When you're trying to break records that have been on the books for nearly 100 years, you need every last tenth of a second – if you have the guts.

There are so many choices for tweaking your suspension. The trick is to develop a balance. The system you select for the front must be compatible with your rear setup. There is no perfect formula that will work for every Neon and SRT-4. Driving styles differ, and unless your weight (both the weight of your car and your body) is exactly the same, handling will always differ slightly from car to car. That's why we recommend buying an adjustable system. Spring perches are a great start as they can accept springs of varying rates and can also be raised or lowered. Add adjustable sway bars and you'll be able to infinitely tweak your suspension as you move from the street to the track, or from one racing venue to another. In the future, you may decide to remove weight from your Neon or get a heavier audio system. You may change the size of your wheel/tire combination or relocate your battery. No matter what you do, with an adjustable system you can make adjustments in your suspension so that balance is maintained. Also, as you do more testing, you'll be able to fine-tune the car's handling characteristics to complement your particular driving style.

Just because your Neon is lowered and has stiffer springs doesn't mean that you've improved its handling. On the contrary, we learned that lesson the hard way back in 1995 when we were developing the GRM Neon. After re-sleeving the shocks, getting stiffer springs, adjustable spring perches, and 15 x 7-inch wheels, what we ended up with was a car that didn't handle as well as what we had to start with. Sure it was stiffer and lower, but in autocross competition, we still were getting beat by D Stock Neons. (Photo courtesy Howell Automotive)

CHAPTER 3

WHEELS AND TIRES

Neons don't come from the factory with the best setup for performance driving, so often the best thing you can do to improve the handling is to upgrade your wheel/tire combination. But before making a decision about what wheels and tires are right for you, it's important to decide what you primarily want to do with your car. For a cool street look, there are many options out there. Most street drivers simply choose a wheel with good looks to complement their car's personality, but if racing is your priority, the selection of available wheels is more limited. Wheels for racing have an emphasis on function, and are generally not as attractive as those designed for street looks. You may end up choosing a wheel based on weight, specific diameter, width, backspace, and price, with little regard for looks. If winning is at the top of your list, then looks should not factor into your choice, but the type of racing you do should.

One of the best things you can do for your racing Neon is to invest in a set of race tires. There are many different compounds to choose from, so read this chapter carefully before you spend your money. These are shaved and heat cycled 225/50/14 Kumho Ecsta V700 tires from The Tire Rack.

Street Wheels

Never in automotive history has there been a larger selection of aftermarket wheels from which to choose. Prices range from $50 apiece to upward of $2,500 per set. But how do you decide which wheel-and-tire combination is best for your car? There are several factors that can help you make this often difficult, but mostly fun, decision.

If you're not concerned with a budget for your project, then looks should be the priority. The particular design of the wheel selected should be one that enhances the overall look that you have planned for your vehicle. Shop around, as prices can vary as much as $100 per set for the more expensive brands.

If you've taken the advice in the Introduction and have created a budget, then your budget will help you decide what wheels will best meet your needs. After buying the stereo, spoiler kit, intake, exhaust, and header, you may find that you won't have enough money left over to get some super expensive wheels. Then again, wheels may be more important than that stereo. A budget is all about compromise, and it will help you to make sound decisions guided by your head, and not so much by your heart (or the limit on your Visa card). Remember, you need to have enough money (or credit) to go have fun with your car after the project is finished.

One of the big decisions you'll have to make in choosing a wheel/tire combo is the diameter. Keep in mind that the larger the diameter, the lower the final drive ratio. In other words, a larger combo makes fewer revolutions than a smaller diameter for a given distance. The results of this change are far reaching,

Wheels and Tires

Choosing the right wheels for the street is more a matter of form than function. Pick the wheel that best fits the personality you want your Neon to present. But keep in mind that the bigger the wheel, the more expensive the tire. (Photo courtesy Howell Automotive)

impacting many of your vehicle's operating systems.

Stock Neon wheels are 14 x 5.5-inch wheels, with the 5 x 100-mm bolt pattern, and 40-mm offset. ACR and R/T wheels are 14 x 6-inches. The most popular sizes for performance (not looks) are 14 x 7 and 15 x 7 inches.

Since larger-diameter wheels go around fewer times for a given distance, your tires will last longer (unless you're doing burnouts). However, tires come in different compounds; this point is only valid when comparing tires of similar composition. Stickier tires will generally wear out sooner. Your car's speedometer will also be affected by a wheel/tire combination that is larger than the stock diameter. The common result of this phenomenon is a speeding ticket. The speedometer is tricked into thinking that your car is going slower than it actually is because there are less tire revolutions per mile.

A positive effect of changing to a larger diameter setup is that your wheel bearings may last longer, but you'll be putting more stress on your transmission. It's much easier to turn a small wheel than it is to turn a larger wheel. That also explains why you'll feel a reduction in torque when you use a larger wheel/tire combination. The good news is that although you may not be quicker off the line, you will be able to hold first and second gear longer before having to shift. This effect, however, is undesirable if you want a lot of low-end torque, as most autocrossers do. A smaller combo will help keep the RPMs up slightly when you are trying to exit a turn. At any given point, acceleration with a smaller wheel will likely be livelier than with the bigger tire/wheel.

Then there is the cost of the tires. For a given brand and model of tire, the 14-inch size will be cheaper than the 17-inch version every time. Of course, some high-performance street tires don't come in 13- or 14-inch sizes, but there are always alternatives. Just because a specific tire brand is "cool," doesn't mean that you won't be able to find your size in a different brand that will match or outperform your friend's "cool" tire. A 15 x 7–inch wheel is probably just the right size for most Neon applications because there are more performance tires available in that size. Of course, 15-inch

The tires you choose for the street should be researched before you buy a set of wheels. You may discover that the tire brand and compound you want isn't made in a size that will fit on the wheel you just bought.

Chapter 3

There are a lot of great tires out there that outperform your stock tires, but still have great tread life. This is a Falken Azenis Sport. (Photo courtesy Chris Malluege)

wheels and tires are more expensive than 14s.

An important advantage of larger wheels and tires is that you can fill up your fender wells without having to lower your car to the point where you won't be able to straddle road kill. You car will look lower than it actually is. Dropping a car too far also adversely affects your suspension. So, a larger wheel will help you achieve that "racing" look without giving up your car's streetability.

Tires for the Street

There is less of a selection of quality street tires than of cool wheels. The question asked most often is: What tires are best? There really isn't a single answer to this question. The tire you select should be based on what type of driving you want to do. Usually, you get what you pay for. But if you buy expensive tires expecting that they will be good for both the street and occasional track use, you will be disappointed. Tires come in different compounds. In general, a softer compound will offer better handling, but will wear out sooner than a harder tire. A racing tire may handle well on dry pavement, but not in the rain, and vice versa.

So how do you decide? Forget the hype about one tire being so much better than another. We have been participants and judges in many tire tests, and when comparing tires with similar design and compound, there's usually no significant difference between the major brands. That's not to say that purpose-built tires are all the same. For instance, snow tires will provide better traction in the snow than regular tires. So comparing a Bridgestone Blizzak with a Pirelli P6 is not a fair comparison. The P6 will outperform the Blizzak every time on dry pavement, but won't get you stopped as quickly on an icy road. Off-brand tires, however, usually do not perform as well as the major brands.

There is a big difference between the different models offered by a given company. Tire manufacturers offer many different designs and compounds, in the same way that GM builds Corvettes and Cavaliers. Take a BFG ZR and a BFG Touring TA, for example. The top-of-the-line BFG ZR tire is a much better performer than the bottom-of-the-line "touring" design. However, the top-of-the-line performance tires offered by BFG, Kumho, Yokohama, Michelin, Falken, and Nitto all compare favorably. Once you narrow down all the brands that make a tire for the particular use you have in mind, you can go pick the tire that's on sale, or that has a cool name. It's very similar to choosing which sneaker you want.

The first thing that you need to do before you choose a street tire is to decide what type of driving you want to do. If you don't plan on doing any racing, then a harder compound will do nicely. Traction in the rain and snow will not be compromised as long as you stick with good name brands. If you care more about handling than tire wear, select a softer compound performance tire. But be careful when using these softer compound tires on your daily driver. Dry performance will be superior (if not exhilarating), but under any other conditions, you could be putting yourself at risk. In other words, if you live in Arizona, go for it – but for Seattle, a more conservative compound would be a better choice.

The only problem is that it isn't always easy to compare compounds from one brand to another. The government created its UTQGS (Uniform Tire Quality Grading System), but each manufacturer has a slightly different system of grading treadwear. A 250 wear rating on a Goodyear tire may not compare to a 250 on a BFG. But within the same brands, the rating is more of a constant. For example, a BFG tire rated at 250 is softer than a BFG rated at 300, and will usually provide better traction.

Tire sizes can also be very confusing. For example, both a 225/50/15 and a 205/50/15 will fit on your 15 x 7-inch wheel. Your first impression may be to go for the 50-series tire, since you think it has a smaller overall diameter. That, however, would be an incorrect assumption. Actually, these sizes have the same overall diameter. The first number in the tire size is the width in millimeters. The second number, "50," is a percentage of width vs. the height of the sidewall (distance the tire extends above the rim). In other words, a given "series" indicator (which is a percentage) is not constant. In this case, the height of our 225/50/15 is the first number (225 mm wide) multiplied by the series number (50%), equals 112.5 mm in height. For our narrower tire, the 205/50/15, the height is 205 mm x 50% = 102.5 mm tall. Therefore, the 225/50/15 has a sidewall that is 10 mm taller than the 205/50/15.

In order to calculate the overall diameter of your wheel and tire combination, you need to convert inches (wheel size) to millimeters. One inch equals 25.4 millimeters, but don't get out the calculator yet. Let's say you and your friend have identical Neons. He has 15-inch wheels mounted with a set of 205/50/15 tires. But you want to go one step more radical than your friend, and you want to go with a 17-inch rim. Let's do the math. The distance from the center of a 15-inch wheel to the outer edge of the rim (radius) is only 7.5 inches, while the radius of a 17-inch rim is 8.5 inches. The wheels you want to buy

Choosing the right wheel and tire size to best fit your street car's needs takes some degree of planning. How wide can you go without rubbing the suspension or the body? Buy your wheels to fit your car; don't modify your car to fit your wheels. (Photo courtesy Howell Automotive)

are two inches larger than his, but only one inch will stick up into your fenderwell (8.5 vs. 7.5 inches above the center of the wheel). The other inch will be lifting your car off the ground (8.5 vs. 7.5 inches below the center of the wheel).

In order to retain the same look, you need a 17-inch tire with the same overall diameter, so what tire size do you need? There's no reason to do more work than you have to – Tirerack.com has the dimensions of all of the tires that will fit under a Neon. Or you can always check manufacturers' websites to find the overall diameter of their tires. For our example, the average 205/50/15 has an overall diameter of 23.2 inches, while a 205/50/17 is nearly the same diameter, at 23.5 inches. Some tires, however, seat lower in wheels than other tires (like the Michelin Pilot). Also remember, if you buy a wider wheel, the tire will usually seat lower than with a narrower rim. Tires wider than 225 mm won't usually fit on a Neon without modification to the fenderwells.

Since there are several factors that come into play, the first decision to make is what suspension setup will be best for how you want to use your car. Then measure the opening you have to work with, do some of the math above, and call a reputable dealer and ask questions. Feel free to shop around, but don't always go with the best price. Good customer service is also important. If the company with the cheapest prices can't answer your detailed questions, but a place like The Tire Rack takes the time to work with you, don't turn around and buy the stuff from the other guy just to save a few bucks. Chances are, the other guy won't be able to help if you run into problems.

Autocrossing

Generally, if you want to compete in a stock class, you will be restricted to retaining your stock rim size. The newer Street Touring and Street Modified classes allow for wider wheels. Currently, the Street Touring has rules regarding tire compound and won't allow super sticky tires that are rated less than 140. Falken Azenis tires are very popular for the treadwear-restricted classes. Most nationally competitive Solo II drivers use this tire. It is about as sticky as you can go and still be within the rules. Check with the SCCA first before buying tires if you plan on competing in these classes.

Since alloy wheels are lighter than steel wheels, they are a better choice. Many racing wheels weigh only 9 to 12 lbs! That can help you save 5 to 10

If you live in an area that has poorly maintained roads, stay away from 18-inch or larger wheels, unless you know someone who repairs bent wheels for a reasonable price. The smaller the sidewall, the closer the ground is to your wheel, and the better chance you'll damage your rims.

Choose a wheel with a finish and shape that complements your car. The owner of this red SRT-4 went with a gun-metal gray wheel to give it a more sinister look. (Photo courtesy Chris Malluege)

pounds per corner, which adds up to 20 to 50 lbs overall. That's a huge weight savings – not to mention that reducing rotating mass will increase your Neon's ability to accelerate off the line and out of a turn. It's much easier for your Neon to get the lighter wheels moving.

The Chrysler factory alloys are good choices for autocrossing in stock classes. You would think that the more expensive aftermarket wheels would be lighter, but that isn't always the case. Stick with the stock wheels, and spend your money on good DOT (Department of Transportation) racing tires.

Some clubs even offer "street tire" classes, so you can use the same rubber on the track that you use on the road, saving you from changing wheels and tires when you get to the track.

If you want to be more competitive, here's the short list of tires with the highest percentage of stock class wins for the past 10 years: BF Goodrich G Force, Hoosier Radial A3S04 and A3S04, and Kumho VictoRacer, Ecsta V700, and the new V710. The Nitto 555RII also shows some promise, but Nitto is still behind BFG and Hoosier in soft-compound race-tire development. During the late 1990s, Goodyear stopped making a competitive, soft-compound autocross DOT radial, and Yokohama made little changes in their first-generation A008R over the years. Their new effort, named the A032R, doesn't seem to be the choice of the champions. Since the race-tire market changes from year to year, you may want to check with your local autocross club to see what the current hot tires are, or you can go online with one of the autocross discussion forums like www.team.net or log on to Tirerack.com. The Tire Rack is a major sponsor of SCCA events, and most racers buy their race rubber there.

One of the advantages of buying your race rubber at places like The Tire Rack is that you can get them heat cycled. Unless your race tires are properly heat cycled, they will tend to harden more quickly between races and will not wear as intended. Plan on using your race tires no more than one season. Many of our racer friends boast about how good their particular choice of tire was, stating: "I have been racing on them for three years now and there's still tread left." My response is usually something like: "Do you ever wonder why you never win races?"

If your race rubber is lasting three years, it's no longer race rubber. It has probably lost too much stick and is now no better than your average 350-wear street tire. There is a way to check if your tires are beyond their shelf life. Tire durometers will tell you how soft your tires are. Once your tires get too hard, there is little you can do. We have successfully used Formula V Traction Treatment on our slicks, especially when it's late in the year and we don't want to buy new rubber just for the last few races. If you follow the instructions on the bottle, after you paint the kerosene-like substance on your tires, they get stickier. Expect them to wear out quickly once they've been treated. Formula V sells for about $40 for a gallon jug, which will last most racers two seasons or more. Most of the time, however, the only way to truly restore stick is to buy fresh rubber.

Another reason to get your tires heat cycled is to keep them from developing the dreaded "groove of doom." Heat cycling cures the compound. Otherwise, varying temps across the tire can cause it to separate near the center tread line under hard cornering, exposing the steel cord below. The rest of the tire could be fine with lots of rubber remaining, but once your tires show cord (anywhere), you will not be allowed to compete until the tire is replaced.

There are several differences between the top three brands – BFG, Hoosier, and Kumho. Kumhos wear better, and will last longer, and despite initial trouble with the design, their new V710 compares well with the stickier Hoosiers and BFGs. We do use Kumho VictoRacers on our turbocharged Speednation Neon since we wanted to add some track events to our autocross schedule. The autocross compound Hoosiers and BFGs tend to be too sticky for driving schools and track-time events, but there are harder road-race compounds available.

Road-racing compounds are designed to be harder so that they don't overheat as much on the track, but we don't recommend them for serious autocrossers. Autocrossers on a budget could benefit from going to the racetrack from time to time to look for good used tires (sometimes for free). Some of the very serious road racers use a sticky autocross tire for qualifying, and then switch to a harder compound tire for the actual multi-lap race. They often just throw out their qualifying tires after they mount up their race rubber. Ask the tire suppliers at the tracks; you may just get lucky.

Depending on the type of racing you want to do, choosing a wheel-and-tire combination is as simple as researching what combination the class leaders are using. Of course, you'll have to remember your budget. A Hoosier radial will tend to be more expensive than a Kumho, and both cost more than a Toyo or Falken. These inexpensive, lightweight spun-steel Diamond Racing Wheels can be ordered to meet any application.

For autocross, especially on asphalt, we like the Hoosier radial or BFG radial because they stick nicely even while cold. Neons have very little weight bearing down on the rear tires, which can keep them from reaching proper operating temperatures on an autocross course. Kumhos are also great tires, especially if you only want to buy one set of autocross tires per season.

Racing on concrete is a different story. The super-sticky bias-ply Hoosier Autocrossers or qualifying Hoosier slicks (25 compound) don't work as well on concrete, which has a more abrasive surface than asphalt. These bias-ply tires tend to overheat and get greasy. For that reason, most racers run the radial Hoosier, or a Kumho or BFG. For Race Prepared classes, a slightly harder Hoosier slick (35 compound) or Goodyear slick will generally be a little harder and won't overheat as easily. Since the tire companies are constantly changing compounds, it's impossible to make an absolute recommendation here. By the time you read this, the recommended compound may no longer be available, or a new compound may have

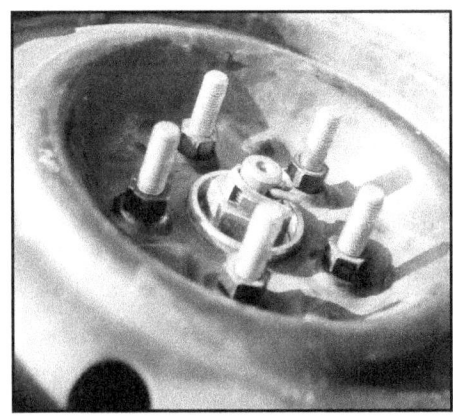

You may need to replace your stock wheel studs with longer ones if you're planning to use a wheel spacer. If you can avoid using a spacer, you'll be better off. Simply decide how wide you want your Neon's stance, and buy wheels with the proper backspace to make that happen.

been developed that is better for one application or another. The best thing to do is to ask successful Neon racers what they use, or just call The Tire Rack and they will tell you what the proper tire is for your racing venue.

If you choose to leave the stock class and move up to Street Prepared or Street

Chapter 3

Choose your autocross tires based on your budget and the class in which you wish to compete. The cheaper Falken Azenis, seen here on one of Michael Carpenter's Neons, are probably the best bang for the buck you can get for the SCCA Street Touring classes, which won't allow a tire stickier than a 140 compound. (Photo courtesy Bob Killmer)

For the SCCA Stock classes, the Falken Azenis is a cost-savings alternative ($60/tire). However, you won't be competitive unless you shell out $140/tire for the Kumho V700 or Kumho V710 (V700 shown on Rich Shank's G-Stock Neon) or spend $180/tire for the Hoosier A3S03. (Photo courtesy Bob Killmer)

Modified, then there are no restrictions on wheel size. SCCA Street Prepared history has proven that for Neons, the best choice in wheel size is 14 inch. This is because the smaller-diameter wheel will provide better low-end torque, a very valuable commodity in autocrossing.

Specifically, consider using a 14 x 7, 14 x 8, or larger wheel and 225/50/14 tires. We use Diamond Racing wheels, which are made of lightweight spun steel and hold up well under severe racing conditions. They can be custom ordered with any diameter, width, and backspace for less than $350/set. Expensive aftermarket alloys can be pricey ($200+ each) but you will save 5 lbs per corner. On the other hand, you may be able to find a good used set of 14 x 8 or 15 x 8 lightweight alloys, but expect to spend over $600. Don't go smaller than 8 inches wide, unless there is a wheel restriction in your class.

So why a 14 x 8-inch wheel? We actually tested 7-, 8-, and 9-inch-wide wheels mounted with the same size and brand of tire. On a 60-second autocross course, we found that there can be as much as a two-second difference in times between the wheel sizes, depending on driving style.

Forget about the FWD myth that the rear wheels and tires don't do as much work as the front, therefore, their tire patch is less important. In fact, one of the largest gains we saw was when we replaced the rear 14 x 7s with wider 14 x 8s. Big 14 x 9s seem to be overkill, and can cost a lot more than the smaller sizes, but they look really cool, especially before they have tires mounted on them.

Why not 16- or 17-inch wheels? Simple – the smaller-diameter wheel will give you a better final drive ratio. For autocrossing, this will give you more torque coming out of a turn and in accelerating. If you don't believe this, go to a drag strip (like we did) with 14- and 17-inch wheels on hand. The 14-inch wheels will always give you faster quarter-mile times.

There are some applications where a larger-diameter wheel (15 inches and above) would be preferable. Some high-speed courses may require an extra shift before a particular turn, often requiring an immediate downshift before exiting the turn. That can waste precious time, but sometimes there isn't much choice. You can't afford to ride along on the rev limiter for more than a second, or you'll waste more time. In this case, a larger-diameter wheel could be used to slightly change your final drive in the other direction, helping you to avoid that extra shift. The only problem with putting this sound theory into practice is that you have to bring along an extra set of wheels and tires to events.

Even if you're competing in a modified class, a 14-inch wheel is still the best option; 15 x 8 and 15 x 9-inch wheels might also be good choices. Even with tons of horsepower, like the 300+ hp we have in our Speednation Neon, 14-inch wheels are still the best.

One of the problems that must be anticipated when you add larger/wider wheels with sticky tires is that your stock wheel bearings and hubs may not be able to stand up to the increased g-forces. Road racers need to change their hubs every 12 hours of track time, whereas autocrossers may get a few years of events on one set of hubs. If you do have to replace them, you should consider upgrading to ACR hubs, which are 10 mm thick, as opposed to the 8-mm hub that came on pre-2000 cars. Even the R/T, which came with a heavier-duty suspension, did not have the thicker ACR hubs.

Racing Slicks

At events or in classes where DOT-approved tires are not required, racing slicks are an even better choice. They can also be much cheaper, especially if you buy used. It's not often that one service stands out above all others, but when it comes to used slicks, we have to mention John Berget Tire (262) 740-0180, out of Wisconsin. The price of a new slick is usually around $130+ each, but you can get two for that price through Berget. John also has access to new slicks at discount prices. They are sent COD to your door in only a few days, and for good customers he will often throw in a free tire from time to time.

But are slicks that much better than the DOT-approved autocross tires mentioned above? Yes, and for one good reason. They have no tread. The tread on a tire will bend slightly when you throw your car into a hard turn, causing some slippage and loss of grip. Since slicks have no tread, they avoid this problem.

If you're new to the sport, we recommend that you don't go out and buy a new set of street tires to use for autocrossing. A full-treaded tire will slip and screech all over the track, and although this can be entertaining for the spectators, it does not translate into fast times. If you're on a very tight budget, then use the baldest used street tires you can find, as long as they don't show cord, which can cause a blowout. You won't be competitive, but you'll sure have fun.

The 14 x 7-inch alloy sold by Mopar Performance is the trick wheel for ITA competition. As far as we know, this wheel is no longer available new. A much cheaper alternative, although heavier by four or five pounds, is the spun-steel Diamond Racing wheel, which comes in any offset and size.

The Kumho V710 is a great tire, but its debut was far from successful. They were recalled just a few months after being released due to, well, just look at the photo. This was from a road-racing application where tires will get really hot and stay hot. We didn't hear of this happening when the tires were used for autocross, though. Kumho fixed this problem in mid 2004, and the V710 is now one of our favorite tires.

There are several good slicks on the market, and despite our love for Hoosier autocrossers, we have to give the nod to Goodyear when it comes to pure race tires. Over the years, the Goodyear slicks have demonstrated two big advantages over their competitors. First, they resist heat cycling. Hoosier slicks seem prone to harden once they've been heated and cooled several times over several races. The other problem with Hoosier slicks is that the sidewalls are so thin, they tend to leak air directly through the rubber – often as much as 5 lbs per hour. As far as rubber compounds go, both Hoosier and Goodyear offer some excellent choices. From super sticky (used for qualifying or autocrossing) to

Chapter 3

Race tires are great. They can do miraculous things for handling, but you can overdrive even the best race tire. Rusty Hopkins comes out of a turn at Summit Point a little too fast, and the SSC Neon (owned by Bill Silvers who is watching this sequence in terror) gradually loses traction and leaves the track, ripping the tire right off the rim.

endurance tires (harder, tend to last longer), there are several compounds from which to choose. Typically, the lower the compound number, the stickier the tire. Of course, the stickier the tire, the more quickly it wears out.

As far as size goes, there are no slicks available for 14-inch rims, so you'll need to step up to 15 x 6- or 15 x 7-inch wheels. You may need a little more backspacing to run 23 x 8.5- or 23 x 9.5-inch tires, since some of the extra rubber will stick out inside the wheelwell.

Road Racing

You shouldn't run the same tire for serious autocrossing as you would for road racing. After several hot laps, a sticky tire will often overheat and become "greasy" and lose traction. The softer-compound autocross tires also won't last for an entire road race. However, autocross compound tires are often used for qualifying. When you can start in front of the pack, there is less chance of getting taken out by one of the many passing mishaps common in road racing. Most race tire manufacturers we've already mentioned make tires for road racing. The only difference is usually compound. Road racers using slicks have additional choices in how soft they want their tires to be. Besides that super-sticky autocross compound, there's usually an intermediate soft and full hard tire.

Sometimes, Mother Nature likes to add her own challenges during a road race. For these times, there are rain tires. Made out of a super-sticky compound, rain tires have grooves (you could call them tread) designed to channel rain and optimize contact with the pavement. Despite these grooves, the rain tires are not DOT approved. Class permitting, autocrossers also use these rain tires when the going gets wet.

Drag Racing

When it comes to tires, drag racers have a decision to make just like the autocrossers. Do you go with a street/drag tire, or with a pure race tire? Or, do you just use what you have and head out to the strip? Entry-level drag racers can have tons of fun with little or no money in their wheel/tire budget. But in order to bring down those quarter-mile times, a good FWD drag tire is needed.

The most popular drag tire with the sport compact crowd is the 555R Nitto Drag Radial. This tire is constructed with "R" compound rubber, and is the stickiest DOT-approved tire that Nitto makes. The problem is that there are only a few sizes available. If you're sticking with the stock wheels, a pair of 205/55/14s will work well. In the tire testing that we conducted, the Nittos were no faster than the BFG G-Force or the Hoosier Radials, which come in a

Don Howard is known for winning burnout contests at the Mopar Nationals and was one of the first engine builders to explore the limits of the 2.0-liter Neon engine. He's shown here getting ready to do a quarter-mile run using very sticky drag tires. Drag tires hook best with about half as much air pressure as autocross or regular street tires.

larger variety of sizes. Rumor has it that the new G-Force may have an edge over all of these, but we haven't had the opportunity to test it yet.

If your goal is to reduce your quarter-mile times, and you want to use an "R" rated tire (which will wear out quickly on the street), then you should have an extra set of wheels so you can change over from your street tires to the racing rubber. This also makes it easier to run lower pressure in your race tires, without having to worry about airing them back up to drive home. Just start at the stock pressure, and then adjust down to find what works best. If you run with an extra set of wheels and tires for the track, you should try to fight the urge to use a 17-inch wheel, and stick with 15s or 14s in the front for the track. This will increase your low-end torque and give you faster quarter-mile times. The only problem with this setup is that it may require you to make an extra shift before the finish, which will cost some time.

If you haven't started drag racing seriously, then just bring your car to the track in street trim and check out the cars that are similar to yours. What size wheels and tires are they using? Are they

Gary Howell is the premier Neon engine and quarter-mile car builder. His Hoosier drag tires are very sticky and help him launch his car down the strip faster than most other Neons on the planet. (Photo courtesy Howell Automotive)

crossing the line at high or low RPM? If they made their final shift just before the finish line and ended up crossing at low-

er RPM, then a smaller diameter wheel may provide them with enough time to get the car's power band after that final

Chapter 3

The right tire pressure is critical for racing applications. Often, racers will have different pressures for each corner of the car (to coincide with different corner weights). An autocross test and tune is the best place to determine the correct pressures for your Neon. Adjust your pressures, record the pressures, take a run, and make notes on whether the car was under or over steering. Then try another set of pressures.

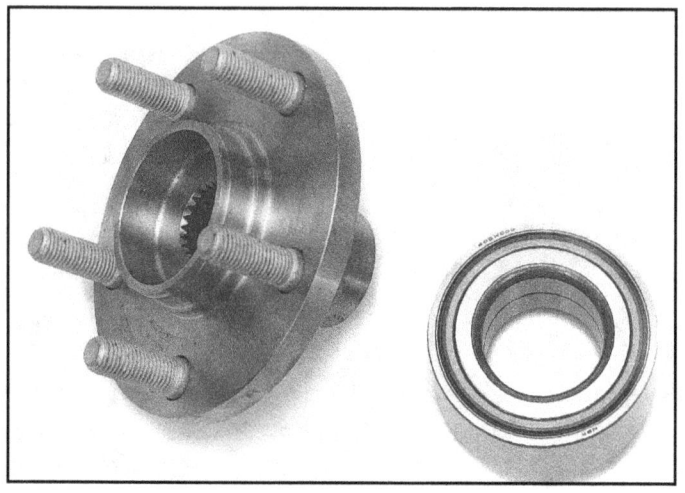

Mopar Performance Parts sells this ACR hub and bearing kit to upgrade your standard Neon, or service your ACR. The beefed-up hub is better able to withstand the rigors of racing. (Photo courtesy Mopar Performance Parts)

shift before crossing the line. It will also provide more torque at the starting line. On the other hand, if the cars you see are crossing the finish at high RPM (without bouncing off the rev limiter), they probably have just the right wheel/tire combination for their car.

For the most part, unless your quarter-mile times are under 13 seconds, stock wheels and tires are fine for the rear. But once you are breaking the 100-mph mark, then having grip in the rear is also important. Since most serious drivers set up their cars so that the front end is heavy (especially if there has been a more powerful and heavier engine transplanted), that leaves the rear end light. There may come a point where the rear becomes too light, which could be dangerous without sufficient rear-end stick.

When it comes to pure drag tires, there are only a few choices. Mickey Thompson has long been one of the most popular tires among drag racers. The 20 x 6 x 14-inch size works well for the stock wheels. These slicks require much less tire pressure than the street/race tires mentioned above, so discuss this with your tire dealer before you get started. You'll need more pressure the heavier your car is. In general, you can start at 20 lbs and work your way down.

Here is the real secret for choosing tires. First, choose the venue in which you want to compete. Then, find out what brand and compound the really fast, nationally competitive guys are using, and buy that exact brand, size, and compound.

Tire Pressures

A whole section related to tire pressures? You've got to be kidding! In the previous chapter, we covered many ways to improve your car's handling, all of which involve spending money. In this section, we'll discuss one of the most effective and cheapest ways to fine tune your handling. The last time we checked, air was still pretty cheap.

Many people both overlook and underestimate the effect that tire pressure can have on handling. But when it comes to changing handling characteristics, adjusting pressures is one of the best tools you can have at your disposal.

For racing suspensions, a good starting point for most Neons using DOT race tires is 30 to 35 psi in the front, and 28 to 32 psi in the rear. Our Turbo Neon, fitted with Kumho V700s, ran with 34 psi in front and 32 in the rears. If you have a heavier car, you should be in the higher end of this range. If you find your car pushing in the corners, you should raise your front pressure and/or lower your rear pressure. Start with higher pressure and work your way down. You can mark the edge of your tires with chalk or shoe polish to see how much of your tire is rolling over during cornering. If there is not enough rollover, then lower your pressure. If there is too much rollover, then increase the pressure in that tire. You usually want the tire to only roll over to the edge of the tread.

Mark Daddio, who drove our car to an SCCA Solo II National Championship in D Street Prepared, used 30 to 35 psi in the front and 65 to 70 psi in the rear. Now keep in mind, he is a phenomenal driver. Since he's able to do things with a car that most drivers can't, he's been nicknamed "the Alien." He drives like he is from another planet. We don't recommend these pressures for any other human. His driving style is so smooth, he rarely jerks the steering wheel. He needs the back end of the car to be loose, so that it rotates easily. By over inflating the rear tires, the back end gives up its stick and rotates very well. The same is true when you drastically under inflate a tire. But when you're working between 25 and 45 psi, the higher the pressure, the greater tendency the tire has to stick. The lower the pressure, the less traction you'll get. Remember, oversteer and understeer also have to do with what pressures you're running in your front tires. You just have to play with the pressures to get the best results for your Neon and the way you drive.

The more scientific way to adjust pressures is with a pyrometer. They are relatively inexpensive (under $100) and can tell you the surface temperatures across your tire patch. If the center section of your tire has higher temperature readings than the outer tread, then you may want to lower the pressure. If the outer portion is hotter, then you should increase pressure.

The best way to do it is by racing the car to see how it drives. If the car is loose as a goose (oversteer – rare with stock Neons), then lower the front pressures and add air to the rear. The theory for most motorsports that take place on asphalt or concrete is: increased pressures result in increased traction. Adding air to the front tires will cause them to stick better, and your car will pivot around that point and cause the tail to swing out (oversteer). Increasing pressure to the rear will cause the back end to stick better, and will induce some plowing (understeer).

Drag racers tend to run very little air in the front tires. This is contrary to the theory above. But drag tires need to flex so that initial grip can be maximized. Ask your drag tire dealer for the correct pressures for your car. Even when running street tires, we tend to drop our pressures to 15 to 20 psi at the strip. This works better if you have a taller sidewall. Shorter 35-series tires may not be able to handle low pressures like these without causing damage to your rims. If you don't have a pyrometer handy, do a nice burnout and observe the strip(s) of rubber left behind. Dark edges tell you your pressure is too low, whereas a dark center indicates that the pressure is too high. You want to strive for an even patch.

Michael Carpenter (NeonMike22 on Neons.org) decided that he wanted to take his 1995 2-door Neon drifting, and came up with this setup. He slapped a pair of MT Drag Slicks (22 x 8 x 15) on the front and pumped the pressure up to 50 psi. He left his rear tires alone (cheap 175/70/14 radials). With that combination, he was able to out-drift many of the rear-drive cars, proving that with the proper (or improper) tires and pressures, you can get your Neon to do just about anything.

For the most part, Neons come standard with understeer at no extra cost. But by following the guidelines outlined in this chapter, your car can be transformed into a well-balanced and more predictable creature.

The owner of this SRT-4 bought an extra pair of wheels and tires for the drag strip. With a smaller-diameter wheel, he can fit a bigger slick in the wheelwell. Look at the contact patch in the picture on the right – now that's a drag tire. (Photo courtesy Chris Malluege)

Chapter 4

Braking

When the first ACRs were introduced in 1994, their competent braking system was a pleasant surprise to the racers who bought them. At that time, I was racing two different Hondas, but my first few laps in the prototype ACR Chrysler had provided me with these two observations. The first was that this new SOHC 2-liter motor had great torque under 5,000 rpm. The second was how quickly I could bring this 2,300-lb car to a stop. I wasn't expecting great braking, since the Hondas I had been racing weighed less than 1,900 lbs. But I was so comfortable and impressed with the handling and braking of the ACR that I chose my first race in the car to be North Carolina's dangerous Chimney Rock Hillclimb. That level of confidence in a car and its braking system can really help you get the extra few tenths of a second required to put a driver on the podium. Since then, I have raced many other cars, a few with better brakes, but most with systems that required much tweaking in order to give you the level of confidence necessary to master threshold braking.

My favorite braking story takes me back to the 2000 Weatherly Hillclimb. I wasn't planning to go (too many broken racecars – too little time for repairs), but I received a call informing me that if I came, the promoter would have a car waiting for me. I gathered up my racing gear and was on the road less than 30 minutes after the call, thanks to a very tolerant wife. When I arrived, I found a Shelby Cobra in the pits waiting for me. For those who are not familiar with the venue, hillclimbs are high-speed SCCA Solo I events that require the same level of preparation as road racing, but the danger is inherently greater. On average, nearly 5 percent of the cars that enter on Saturday morning end up wrecked by Sunday afternoon.

Generating a high degree of friction between your pad and rotor will stop your car faster. The tire's contact patch must also generate friction with the asphalt. A racing pad may generate more friction between the pad and rotor than the tire can between the contact patch and the road, making your tires the weak link in your braking system. This could cause your brakes to lock up and your car to slide under braking, so choose the compound pad best suited for your tires and your racing venue. (Jim Weslager)

So there I was, sitting in the Cobra at the starting line staring at turn one, which is a blind 70+ mph sweeper. When the green light came on, I was on the throttle with a vengeance, spinning the rear wheels, and pitching the car sideways as I accelerated up the ⅛-mile straight. Did I mention that the asphalt was wet from a morning rain? Second gear produced even more torque than I anticipated, and the car again pitched to the side. I was told later that the owner of the car, having seen that, asked the promoter: "Are you sure Ancas knows what he is doing?" But as I got closer to turn one, knowing that I had to rely on 40-year-old braking technology (the car was running in a vintage class – no mods allowed), I thought to myself: "Let's

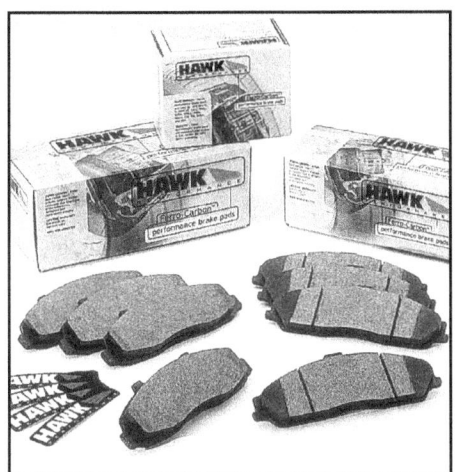

High-performance and racing brake pads, like these from Hawk, can be a good upgrade, depending on what type of racing you're doing. However, they'll probably generate more brake dust and wear out your stock rotors faster than stock replacement pads.

see, this car is worth $200,000, and right now I have $200 in my checking account, so I'd better get on the brakes early." It's a good thing I did, as I ended up having to use both feet to slow down the car just enough to slide it through the turn. By the end of the day, I had a better feel for the brakes, but still had to use both feet. My times were good enough to beat all of the vintage drivers that had raced on that hill for the past 30 years. But the next time I went to Weatherly with a high-horsepower car (turbocharged 1996 2-door Neon ACR), I was over seven seconds faster on this one-mile long, six-turn hill! The Speednation Neon didn't have more horsepower than the Cobra, but what it did have was great brakes, and that made all the difference.

Even when a Neon's horsepower is increased by 50 to 100 percent, the stock brakes still work great. I still use stock brake pads and rotors, despite the fact that brake manufacturers are always trying to send me free brake components. However, there are several situations that dictate when you should upgrade your brake system listed below. If you decide to do so, the aftermarket brake market is filled with great items that will not only look great on your car, but will stop it even faster. On the other hand, just because there are fancy brake parts available, it doesn't mean that you have to buy them.

If you have a budget for your project, then some of the modifications mentioned in this book other than braking should take precedence in terms of both your time and money. We're certainly not advocating that the brake system should be ignored; on the contrary. You should check your fluid level often, and your entire system should be flushed every two to three years to avoid moisture buildup. Moisture in your brake lines can increase your stopping distance and lead to corrosion on the inside of your brake components and lines. Calipers and pads need to be checked yearly, and rotors should be cut whenever new pads are installed or replaced if they are too worn or warped. But beyond this routine maintenance schedule, you should consider

Modern braking systems will consistently outperform the brakes on vintage cars. After racing Neons and Hondas, when I got behind the wheel of this SVRA Vintage legal Cobra and tried to stop, I almost pushed my foot through the firewall. For street applications, a Neon's modern braking system is more than adequate. No upgrades are necessary. (Photo courtesy Jim Mistick)

Chapter 4

The Neon's front disc brakes feature vented rotors, which help dissipate heat better than solid rotors. Aren't you glad you don't have to go out and buy rotors like this as an upgrade?

Turbo cars tend to carry a lot more speed into a turn as opposed to a normally aspirated Neon. An SRT-4's braking system has taken that into consideration, but if you add a turbo to a regular Neon, you may want to consider upgrading the brakes. (Photo courtesy Keith Bower)

sticking with the original braking system. As I mentioned above, there are at least two instances in which brake upgrades are recommended.

Road Racing

The first thing that most novice drivers realize after finishing their first event is just how brutal road racing can be on a car and its components. Any time you abuse your brakes, such as in road racing, track events, or driver's schools, an upgrade is required. The heat that can be generated from constant high-speed racing has been known to melt a wheel's center cap, warp a rotor, boil brake fluid, or even turn a brake pad into dust. As stated before, Neons have excellent stock braking systems, so all that may be needed is to change to a performance brake pad. I recommend Hawk blue pads in front, and Hawk street pads in the rear. You'll also need to completely replace your brake fluid after each event due to the heat build-up. We recommend using a fully synthetic brake fluid with as high a boiling point that you can find. Also, the harder the pad you choose, the more your rotors will be abused. Obviously, something has to give. If you use a stock pad, you probably won't wear out your rotors, but if you use a hard racing pad, you will cut a three-inch groove in your rotors.

Recently, I performed an impromptu pad and rotor test. I was on my way to Virginia International Raceway (VIR) to participate in a high-speed Solo I event. However, my friend Glenn and I never made it. We instead stopped at Summit Point Raceway and entered a driver's school. The cost for the VIR Solo I was $125 and that would net only about 30 minutes of track time, while the driver's school cost $350 and would provide over two hours of track time. The choice was obvious, but there was one problem. My Showroom Stock Neon was prepped for a Solo I, not a road race. The brake pads were brand new, but were stock. Could these pads withstand that much abuse? Since I didn't have any spare pads with me, I decided to take it a

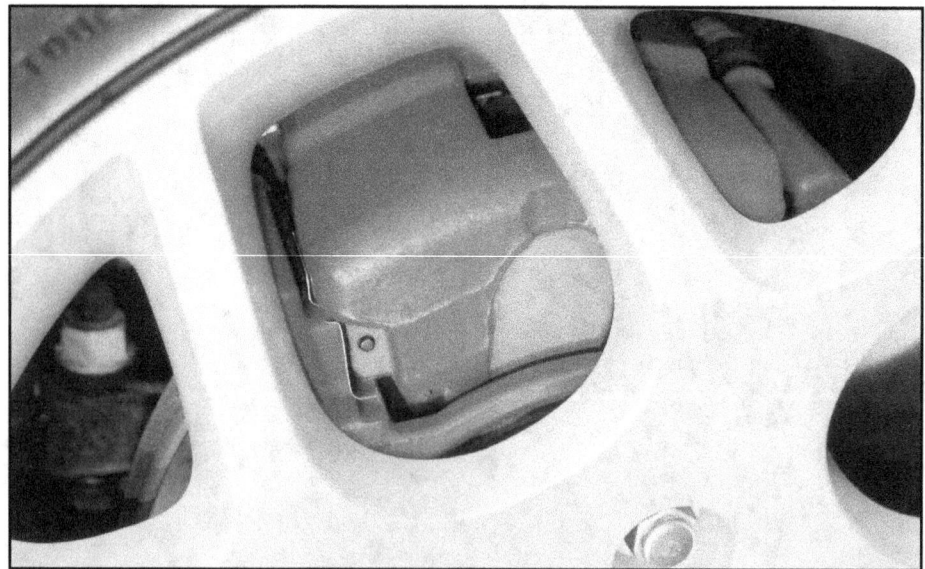

SRT-4s have better brakes than regular Neons straight from the factory. Check out this heavy-duty caliper making itself known behind the stock SRT-4 wheel. They're fine for the street, but for serious racing, an upgrade may be in order.

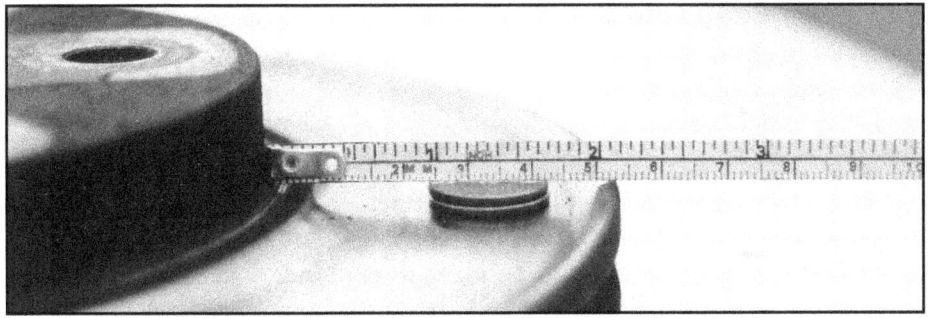

When you switch to a racing pad, your Neon will stop faster. But something has to give when you increase the friction against the rotor. With performance pads, the rotor can actually wear out before your pads. When we replaced the brakes on our Showroom Stock Neon after only two road races, look how much material was removed from the rotor!

little easy so that the pads and tires would last the weekend. That strategy only held up for as long as it took for the first Spec Miata to pass me on the inside of the braking zone in turn one. My assigned running group consisted of three SSC cars, two IT cars, and 23 Spec Miatas. The Miatas did have better brakes, but that was the last time I let a Miata pass me under braking. I did leave that weekend with two different shades of Miata paint on my Neon's butt, but I also left with fully functional brake pads. Granted, they were nearly worn out, but they lasted an entire weekend. My friend Dave, who races a modified GTi, had to change his expensive pads halfway through the event. Of course, expensive race pads will stop your racecar faster, but make sure you bring along an extra set – along with spare rotors and fluid.

Autocrossing

Autocrossers usually don't need to use a harder pad. The reason is that performance pads are designed to disperse heat better than stock pads (to stay cool), so they don't heat up as easily. In SCCA Solo II, you want pads that will heat up to their operating temperature quickly so that they'll stop you more efficiently. I discovered first hand that competition pads can be overkill. With stock pads, there is good balance between the pads and tires. Upgraded pads grip harder, and unless your tires can grip harder, they may just lock up and slide. The first time I autocrossed my SSC Neon with Hawk Blue pads, I locked up the wheels in the first hard-braking area. I realized that I was used to the pads being the limiting factor, or the weakest link in the system. But in this case, the tires were the weak link. After you flat spot a brand-new $160 race tire, you learn your lesson quickly.

Cars With Boost

For those who stray from the naturally aspirated crowd, you might want to think about upgrading your brakes. Given the fact that you will likely be going faster and carrying more momentum into a turn, it follows that you'll need to use your brakes more often than before. The first time I put the turbocharged Speednation Neon on the track, I attempted to use the same braking points I was familiar with when I was at the track a dozen times before. What I hadn't considered was that I would be going so much faster than in the past. Instead of 100 mph at the end of the straight, I was going over 130 mph. The result was not an off-track excursion, but there was some screaming (at least inside my head), a bit of drifting to scrub off speed, and another flat-spotted race tire! This was starting to get expensive. However, the problem was a result of physics coupled with a miscalculation on my part and not a fault of the braking system.

Engine Transplants and NWHSS

Looking to run 10-second quarter-mile times with an all-motor car? Then the 2.0-liter motor your Neon came with may not be big enough. A larger, heavier, 2.4-liter engine may be just the ticket. If your Neon has added weight from a motor swap, or if it's an NWHSS (Neon With a Huge Stereo System), you will be carrying more momentum into a turn than a stock, lighter-weight car. For that reason, you may want to consider a brake upgrade. Of course, the NWHSS cars usually have 17- or 18-inch wheels,

With a good braking system, you can get on your brakes later in the corner. The ability to carry more speed into and through corners will lead to faster lap times and higher finishes. (Photo courtesy Etechphoto.com)

Chapter 4

For autocross applications, a soft OEM pad is just fine. They will tend to heat up faster, giving you more bite when you enter the first couple of turns, as demonstrated by Rich Shank. A racing pad won't start outperforming an OEM pad until the last few turns when they get up to their operating temperature. (Photo courtesy Bob Killmer)

NWHSS (Neons With Huge Stereo Systems) carry a ton more weight than a stock Neon. Many are all show and no go, so it's harder to get them moving, and harder to bring them to a stop. Larger, heavier wheels also add to your stopping distance. If your Neon looks like this, you might want to consider a brake upgrade. Some big, slotted rotors would look better behind these wheels, too.

so they can't get going fast enough to need the better brakes.

Aftermarket Brake Pads and Rotors

What harm could possibly be done by investing in a set of trick brake pads? You would expect these expensive, high-quality pads to stop your car quicker, and with less brake fade. Often, this is the case, but there's a hidden price to pay.

Everyone knows that friction is required in order to make brakes operate properly. However, friction causes wear. As mentioned earlier, a stock Neon braking system is designed to wear the pads, but if you upgrade to performance pads, you'll be adding more wear to your rotors. The last time we looked, pads were cheaper and easier to replace than rotors.

Using competition brake pads on the street can also cause your rotors to warp. This also happens if you abuse your stock pads. One solution is to buy performance rotors, and then send them off for cryogenic treatment, which is proven to resist warping. A cheaper way to cut down on warping is to be conscious of any time you're using your brakes more than usual; for example, driving down a long hill that has a long red light at the bottom or making an unexpected panic stop. Your pads and rotors will be hot, and if you keep your foot on the brake pedal (for the duration of the red light, for example), the surface where the pads are contacting the rotors will stay very hot, while the rest of the rotor will start to cool. If possible, release the brake pedal from time to time (creep up to the light) so that the rotor cools evenly. Also, when pulling into the pits after your autocross or drag race run, don't engage your parking brake and let your car sit. If you are on a flat surface, just leave your car in gear without the parking brake. I never have that problem since both my 1996 Turbo Neon and SSC Neon have nonfunctional parking brakes. Mark Daddio, the former owner of the Turbo Neon, made sure that the parking brake would never offer any resistance during a Solo II run, where hundredths of a second often meant the difference between winning and losing. The former owner of the SSC Neon, Gordon Wise, used the same philosophy during road racing. Having no E-brake also keeps you from instinctively engaging it in the pits after completing a racing session. All these tricks will help keep your rotors from warping whether or not you're using performance pads.

If you do decide to upgrade your braking system, there are many different brake pads on the market, composed of everything from asbestos (old type) to Kevlar. As a general rule, the cheaper the cost of the pad, the more the pad tends to wear, and the longer they take to stop your car. Aftermarket rotors are also a

Braking

There are many different aftermarket pads and rotors on the market. Your first attempt at selecting a pad for your car may not be optimal. Try a few different pad compounds and manufacturers before you decide which you want to stick with for the long term.

If you use your brakes hard and often, slotted rotors will stay cooler and warp less than standard rotors. They also help dissipate heat from the pads, which will increase their lifespan, too.

stop the car better. That, however, is not always the case. A rotor with holes has less contact surface for the pads to grip. As long as your stock pad is not overheating and causing brake fade (vapor lock), stock rotors should stop better than drilled rotors. However, if heat is an issue, then cross-drilled or slotted rotors may be the way to go.

Another thing to be keep in mind is that it is possible to over-engineer your brake upgrade. There is a point where the weak link will become the friction your tires have with the road. Your new brakes may work so well to the point that your wheels lock up. You can't overcome the laws of physics. Don't assume that the $1,000 brake kit will stop your car faster than the $500 upgrade. If your wheels are locking up with the $500 brakes, then it will be physically impossible to stop any faster with the $1,000 setup.

Stainless steel braided brake lines are only recommended if you plan on beating the crap out of your braking system, such as in road racing. The stock rubber brake lines are just fine, but under very hard braking situations, the hydraulic pressure can slightly inflate the rubber lines. If the brake fluid starts to boil, the rubber lines could give way, especially if they are old and cracked. Stainless steel lines dissipate heat better and eliminate this ballooning effect, making for a firmer pedal feel.

One last thing – doing an expensive brake upgrade means you should also upgrade your tires. Wider rubber and/or a stickier compound tire will better help your new brakes do what you pay them to do.

Brake Fluids

There are definite advantages to replacing your stock fluid with synthetic or high-performance fluids. Brake fluids are graded based on their boiling point. Regular over-the-counter fluids are fine for regular driving, but when you add more weight or power to your car, there will likely be more demand placed on your brakes. Also, if you live in a part of the country that is particularly hilly, such as San Francisco, you

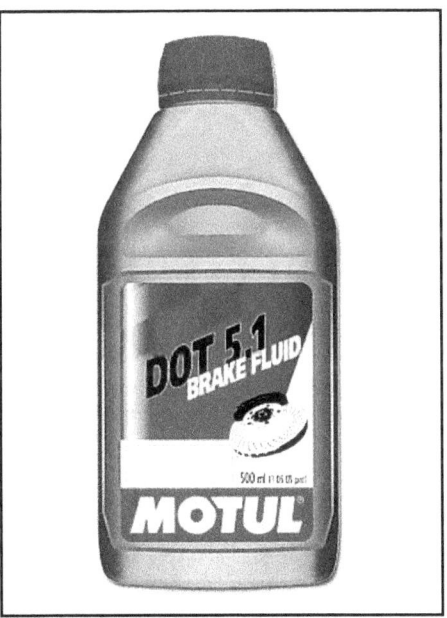

Virginia International Raceway has one of the longest straightaways you may ever encounter at a race track. The need for synthetic brake fluid becomes important in road-racing applications such as this. DOT 5-1 fluid has a much higher boiling point, and therefore is a lot more expensive than stock fluids. Quality brake fluid could mean the difference between successfully making the turn at the end of a long 150+ mph straight, or ending up in the sand. Also, remember to replace your brake fluid after every road race!

common upgrade. We're often asked about the advantages of cross-drilled rotors. Why do small holes drilled in the rotors improve performance? The main reason for using a cross-drilled rotor is that as the wheel turns the rotor, those drilled holes pick up pockets of air, which tend to cool the pads, as well as the rotor itself. A cooler pad and rotor combination should then be expected to

Many aftermarket braking systems can be overkill on street Neons, but for racing applications they will improve lap times. This high-performance rotor/caliper setup is available from StopTech. (Photo courtesy Howell Automotive)

Remember, your tires are also part of your braking system. All components (pads, calipers, rotors, brake fluid, and tires) should be matched in order to get the most out of your system.

Local drag racing events are easy to get addicted to. Going to sport compact days, test-and-tune days, or just bracket-racing events, is a great way to get to know your car and have fun. Don't worry, even if your car is stock, there'll definitely be somebody slower (cough*Honda*cough). (Photo courtesy Chris Malluege)

could also benefit from a fluid that resists boiling.

Regular brake fluid will barely make it to 300 degrees Fahrenheit before boiling, but popular high-performance brands, such as Castrol, will go to about 440 degrees Fahrenheit. The best fluid we tested was Motul synthetic, which resisted boiling up to 570 degrees Fahrenheit. Compare the boiling point of the synthetic fluids in your local parts store to see which is best for your application.

The condition that results when brake fluid boils is called vapor lock. The fluid heats and gives off a gas, which becomes trapped and forms air pockets in your brake lines. Then, when you push on the pedal, the fluid does not compress uniformly, and your calipers may only respond partially, if at all. This is another reason to select a fluid with a high boiling point.

All brake fluids are rated by the Department of Transportation (DOT), and have been assigned grades based on standards for that particular year/period. In other words, a DOT 5-1 fluid has passed all of the latest standards set by the U.S. Department of Transportation regarding brake fluids. That does not mean that a DOT 3 fluid isn't safe. All it means is that it met standards set by the DOT several years ago. Don't choose your fluid by the DOT rating; choose it by the boiling point and/or whether or not you want synthetic or standard. Anything with a rating of less than DOT 3 should be avoided.

Summary

Is a brake upgrade right for you, or should you simply stick with the stock system? Performance pads will certainly improve your stopping distance, but at a cost to your wallet as well as to your rotors. It's all a matter of priorities. Racers often have no choice, but non-racers do. If you don't feel the need to do a brake upgrade, it's probably wiser to spend your money on a better set of tires. But if you choose to spend it on performance pads and rotors, be aware that your tires have now become the weak link in your braking system.

CHAPTER 5

INTAKE SYSTEM

Despite problems we had during the early development and testing of our early ACR, we can say, with confidence, that no other performance bolt-on will give you better "bang for the buck" than an aftermarket intake. The first time we tested an intake on our ACR, the computer didn't seem to like it. But no one was actually making an intake specifically for the Neon back then. It's much different now, as you have several reputable manufacturers from which to choose.

The bang-for-the-buck statement holds true for the permanent high-performance stock replacement filters, engine compartment air velocity intake units, and cold-air intakes. Which system you choose should depend on what you want to do with your car. If you plan on racing your Neon, then first check with the specific rules that govern your class. You may find that they won't allow for anything other than a stock replacement filter.

If you live in a sandy, dusty, or rainy area, then a cold-air intake may not be for you. If you live in a particularly hot climate, and your car's underhood temperatures can become excessively warm, then a standard aftermarket air velocity intake may not perform as well as a cold-air unit. Standard units suck hot engine compartment air, which doesn't burn as well as cooler, denser air. If you take a close look at where most of the warm-air intake systems get their air from, you'll see that it's right above the header/exhaust manifold. For this reason, Neons seem to like the cold-air intake systems bet-

Intakes come in all shapes and sizes. One of the benefits of the Neon powerplant vs. the traditional Honda OHC engine is that the intake faces forward. Open a hole in the hood, and you'll have direct access. (Photo courtesy Gil Diaz)

Installing an aftermarket intake system is probably the best bang for the buck for a Neon 2.0-liter powerplant. The potential for gain is even higher for a 2001–'04 R/T and a 2001–'02 ACR. This is an Iceman intake on a first-generation Neon. (Photo courtesy Patrick O'Hara)

There are a variety of cold-air intakes available from Mopar Performance Parts. This particular model fits 2000-2004 non-Magnum SOHC Neons. (Photo courtesy Mopar Performance Parts)

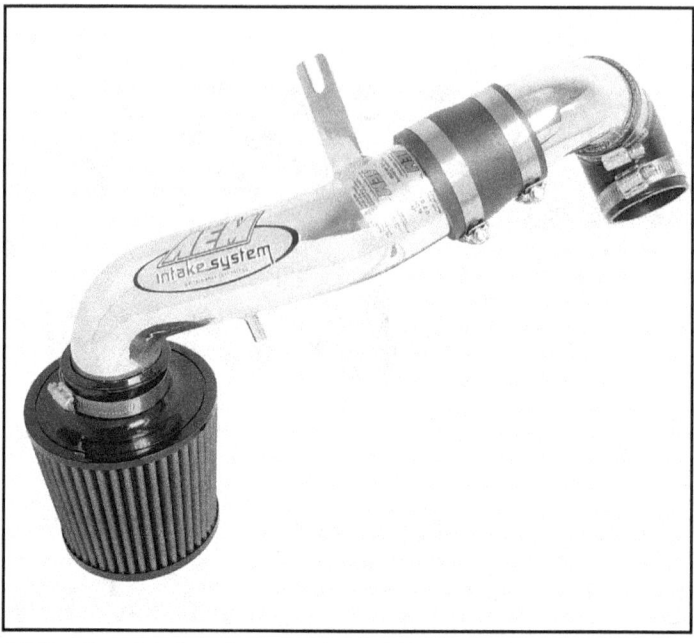
AEM offers intakes for a variety of Neon models. This one fits first-gen DOHC Neons with manual transmissions. As you can see, the air filter is placed outside the engine compartment for access to cool, dense air. (Photo courtesy of AEM)

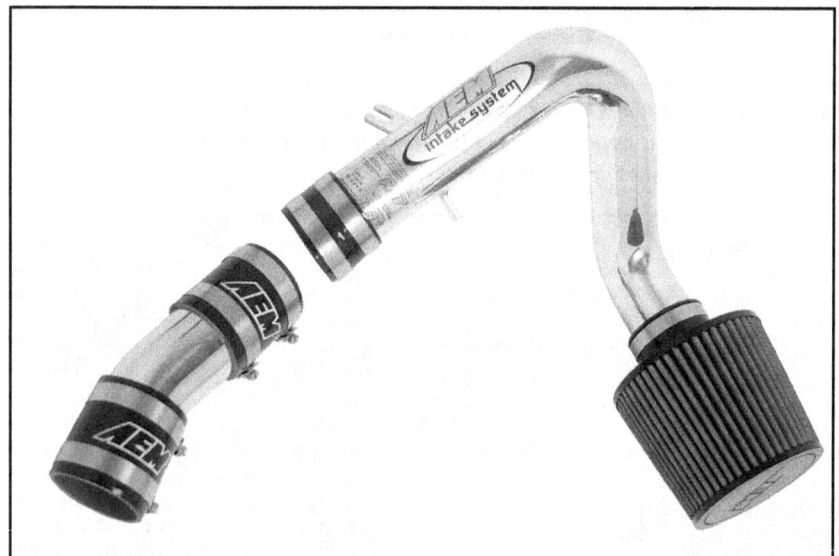
This cold-air intake from AEM fits second-gen Magnum SOHC Neons. AEM intakes are also available powder-coated in red, blue, or silver, and are guaranteed for the life of the vehicle. (Photo courtesy of AEM)

Some cold-kits put the filter behind the factory fog light. You can remove the fog light at the track, giving the cold air a straight shot into your filter. (Photo courtesy Chris Malluege)

ter than the short-ram or warm-air units. The Iceman and AEM cold-air intakes are probably the most popular among Neon enthusiasts. First-generation Neon owners seem to prefer the Iceman, while second-generation owners usually go with the AEM system. Many also make their own using an airbox hose from a Dodge Caravan.

You can probably tell by now that we don't always agree with the aftermarket parts manufacturers when it comes to their claims of "instant bolt-on performance." Frankly, when it comes to product claims, we have been disappointed far more than we have been pleasantly surprised. This isn't the case with mods to the air intake systems. After dyno testing nearly every aftermarket air cleaner on the planet, we've found performance claims to be true – in

Intake System

Above left: Why do aftermarket intakes work so well? Simple: the stock intake that they replace is less efficient. A stock system is designed to be quieter, which is probably the main reason it doesn't flow as well. Finding a way to get direct access to colder outside air is a bonus since colder air is denser and promotes better combustion. Above right: Installing an aftermarket system is rather simple on a Neon, but slightly more complex if you have an aftermarket turbo or if you own an SRT-4. Aren't you glad the intake is on the front of the engine? (Photo courtesy Michael Carpenter)

a sense. We never seem to get the same horsepower numbers on the chassis dyno that you may hear from the advertisements, but still, there are significant gains. We found that to be true with *every* Neon that we tested. Modified or stock, the addition of an aftermarket cold-air intake will likely improve your car's performance.

But we're not letting the parts manufacturers off the hook completely. Let's take a closer look at the numbers. We've found that, on average, you can expect a three to five percent increase in real horsepower, depending on your car. These gains can be achieved by using a product that costs less than $200 and takes only minutes to install. The increase is usually consistent all along the torque curve, not just above 6,000 rpm.

Why do aftermarket intake systems work so well? The main reason is not that these products are highly advanced technological marvels. It's mostly that the stock intake systems they replace are restrictive and inefficient. So why do automobile manufacturers make their stock intake systems so restrictive? The answer could be longer life for the engines, lower insurance rates for consumers, or more business for the factory replacement air filter market. But these are not the reasons – the main reason is noise. The average car buyer wants a quiet car. Why, we have no idea, but a stock intake setup is designed with resonating chambers, much like a muffler, so that noise can be kept to a minimum. If you don't believe that the air intake can be noisy, then you don't already have one of these performance intake systems. The first time you stomp on the gas after installing one, it'll growl like a 1960s sports car.

In reality, an engine is just a fancy air pump. Since stock Neon systems are so restrictive, simply increasing the airflow into the engine will help it breathe better and will usually give you better performance. Sometimes, however, the Neon's computer doesn't know how to manage this increased surge of air and will unsuccessfully try to compensate, resulting in a loss of power. This instance, thankfully, is not the common experience. If it happens to you, just unhook the battery for a while to reset the computer; you should be fine.

So why should you spend money on one of these systems when you could just rip out the existing air filter and box, and put a sock over the remaining plastic intake tube – wouldn't that serve the same purpose? Not necessarily. Usually, anything you do to help the stock system flow better will help. Simply replacing the stock air filter with a freer flowing K&N or Green filter (or removing the filter altogether) will usually net you a couple of horsepower. But you have to understand the theories of velocity, turbulence, and airflow to see why the old "sock over the tube" deal won't give you what these tuned systems offer. We found that out the hard way back in 1994.

Aftermarket intakes work much like a velocity stack on a racing carburetor. When air entering the engine is flowing smoothly and consistently, it can be mixed more uniformly with fuel, allowing for better performance across all cylinders. Most aftermarket intake systems decrease turbulence while increasing the velocity of the air (sometimes as much as twofold) on its way to the injection system. The old "sock" can't do either of these things.

Chapter 5

Often there is little room for an intake if you have a turbo with an intercooler. Keeping out of the way of the intercooler plumbing, not to mention everything else, can make for a tight fit.

Turbo engines crave air. An air intake system will make more of a difference on a turbo than it will on a naturally aspirated powerplant.

Short ram intakes breathe in both warm and cold air. The popular (and probably accurate) theory is that cold air is better for performance. With the cold-air induction systems, cold airflow obviously increases as the vehicle accelerates. However, we are unable to test this theory on a moving vehicle. Our dyno is sort of anchored to the ground – we find it works better when it stays put during testing. Even high-speed fans aimed at the intakes don't net higher horsepower numbers, but we know that cold air is better than warm air.

We had a dyno day featuring the local Supercharged Pontiac Grand Prix GTP club. They came with sophisticated air temperature monitoring equipment and found that the warm air intakes that were shielded from the rest of the engine compartment netted a few more horsepower than the units that had no such shield in place. These heat shields are rather simple and inexpensive to make, and they clearly work for intakes that are drawing warm air from inside the engine compartment. We assume that this effect may be greater for turbo/supercharged Neons, but we have never actually done any testing.

Speaking of fans and intake systems, don't fall for those "turbo" intake systems that give you a fan to install in your intake tube. I have to give them credit – it does sound like it would work. I have seen claims that they will add "turbo-like" performance, and the cost is usually less than $50. They are all over the Internet. Don't be fooled – these systems are absolute garbage. I have yet to find a bigger rip-off in the entire industry. I sent an invitation to the leading manufacturer of these units, but they declined to bring their product to our dyno. We even told them we would allow them to supervise the testing procedure so as to give their units the absolute best chance of succeeding.

There's another new type of product that has shown no significant improvement in the testing we've performed on our chassis dyno. These products use gasses, such as carbon dioxide, to super-cool the intake tube and throttle body. Granted, we have only tested one of these devices (because they are so expensive) and it wasn't on a Neon, but invitations to come to our dyno for a supervised test on our Turbo Neon have not been accepted. We're starting to feel like no one likes us.

Super-cooling is yet another theory that, on paper, seems like it really should work. In fact, a frost coating accumulates on the intake and throttle body when the CO_2 is released. The air passing through the frosty intake must cool down on its way to your engine. Colder air is denser air, and denser air is good for combustion. But for some reason, these $1,000 systems don't seem to work. Again, I am ready to be proven wrong, but for now, I can't recommend

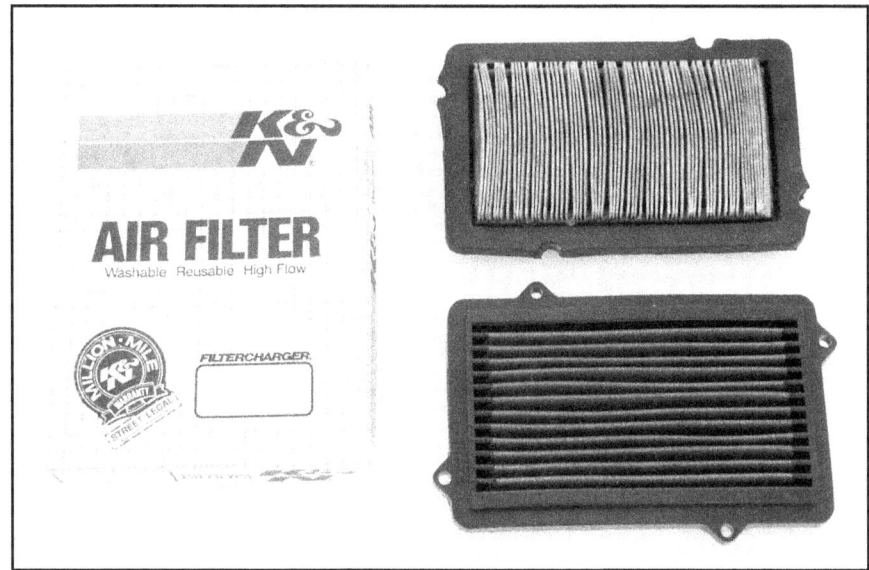

Inexpensive, high-performance replacement air filters are also available from companies such as K&N. Pictured are a stock paper element filter (top) and a permanent, reusable K&N filter (bottom), which can add one to three horsepower over the stock filter.

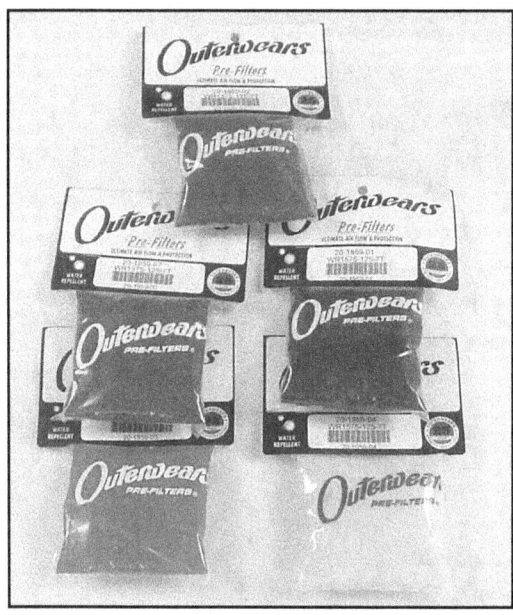

Outerwears Pre-Filters are designed to keep larger particles of street debris such as rubber, dirt, and sand from getting into your air filter. (Photo courtesy Howell Automotive)

spending the cash for these systems. Maybe since the air has to pass though chambers inside these units, the airflow is slightly obstructed, and the cold-air benefit is canceled out. The same is true for air-to-water intercoolers. We had one on our Speednation Neon, and at high RPM, the air is passing through the intercooler so quickly that little cooling is taking place. Air-to-air intercoolers work best.

Hondata makes an intake spacer for DOHC Neons that should help keep the aluminum DOHC manifolds from picking up heat from the head. You won't pick up a ton of power, but it will help keep you from losing power as your engine heats up.

Throttle Bodies

The throttle body is the air gateway to your engine's combustion chambers. It's designed so that a specific amount of air passes through every second. If the opening becomes obstructed, your engine may run too rich. If the opening is too large, then the result could be a lean condition, but if your car is running richer than stock, and if you've updated the rest of your intake system and added a header and exhaust, this step will be worth the money.

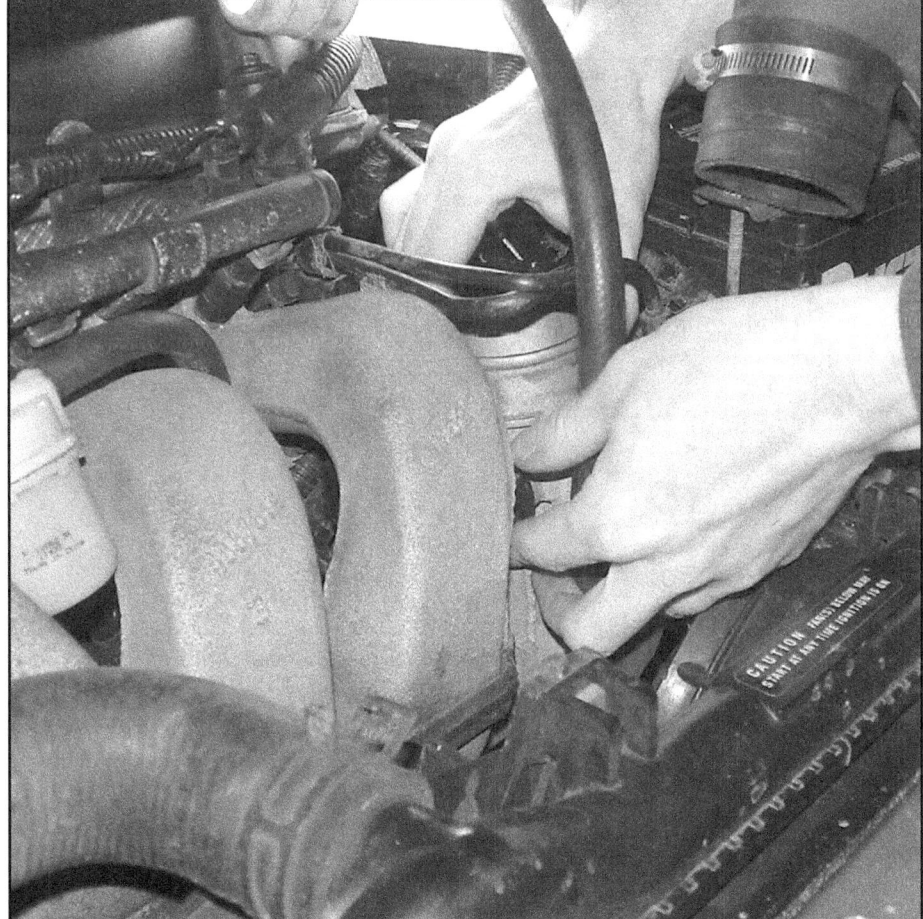

The throttle body is located on the front of the engine in between the intake manifold and the intake piping. Upgrading the throttle body is a great way to improve throttle response.

Chapter 5

This is a 52-mm throttle body from an automatic-equipped first-gen Neon. If you have a manual tranny, your car came equipped with a throttle body that tapers to 49 mm, so swapping on one of these is an affordable upgrade. (Photo courtesy Michael Carpenter)

There is a big difference between the restrictive stock throttle body and this aftermarket piece from Modern Performance. When the larger 55-mm throttle body opens (60-mm is also available), a larger volume of air rushes into the intake manifold. This can rob a little horsepower under 3,500 rpm, but the gains above 5,000 rpm easily make up for it. (Photo courtesy Modern Performance)

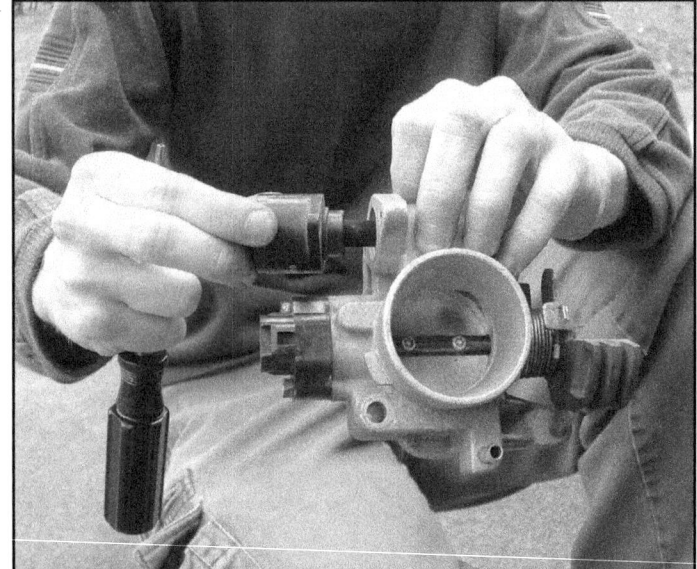

Probably the hardest part of swapping throttle bodies is swapping over your sensors. You will need a set of torx bits or wrenches, and be warned – the factory wasn't afraid to use a little thread lock on the bolts! Be sure to use the correct sensors for your particular Neon. (Photo courtesy Michael Carpenter)

Aftermarket throttle bodies come in all shapes and sizes, and will also give you a few more ponies, especially at higher RPM. This is a 60-mm throttle body for second-gen Neons available from Howell Automotive. Make sure you specify your model year and transmission when ordering. (Photo courtesy Howell Automotive)

Modern Performance makes a trick 60-mm bolt-on throttle body that works well on cars that have been modified to take advantage of that extra rush of air. However, your throttle response may suffer with the larger-diameter throttle body, if it gives you too much air all at once. Going to full throttle as you come out of a turn could give you a bit of a lag under hard acceleration. At the opposite end of the spectrum, when you're at full throttle at high RPM, you'll likely gain a small bit of torque. But if you have a modified powerplant, such as with a ported head and aftermarket cam(s) the throttle body could end up being your weak link. We have one on our Speednation Neon, and it works extremely well.

A popular swap for 5-speed first-generation Neons, which come with a 49-mm throttle body, is to install a 52-mm throttle body from a Neon with an automatic tranny. These pieces look a lot alike, but the 5-speed unit is slightly tapered, and is choked down by three millimeters.

Don't expect too much of a performance boost when going to a larger throttle body. As with most 4-cylinder cars, even a healthy five percent increase in top-end power will only net three to five horsepower at the wheels.

Porting, Polishing, & Extrude Honing

Most DOHC (and a few early SOHC) Neons have intake manifolds that are rather crudely cast. But there are several options available to improve flow through your intake system.

One of the best things to do is send it off to get it Extrude Honed. The casting on the stock intake is very rough, but Extrude Honing will polish the inside like glass by forcing an abrasive goo or gel through your intake. The result is a polished surface that allows air to pass through with decreased turbulence. The improvement from a honed aluminum intake manifold is considerably better than your typical bolt-on modifications (5 to 10 hp) but the cost will be high (check out the Extrude Hone website for current pricing).

In addition to extrude hone, various Neon vendors offer hand-porting services. Some cover the basic clean-up of the casting and port matching, which offers similar performance to the extrude honing. Others take modifying the manifold to the extreme by filling in the injector humps and completely rebuilding the plenum out of sheet metal. The latter is clearly for heavily modified engines, but the results are often impressive.

Indy Cylinder Heads also makes a really trick intake that is only recommended for modified cars. The Indy intake seems to deliver increased torque over the

If you're looking for a larger throttle body for your SRT-4, look no further than these 60- and 70-mm billet-aluminum throttle bodies available from Iceman. (Photo courtesy Iceman)

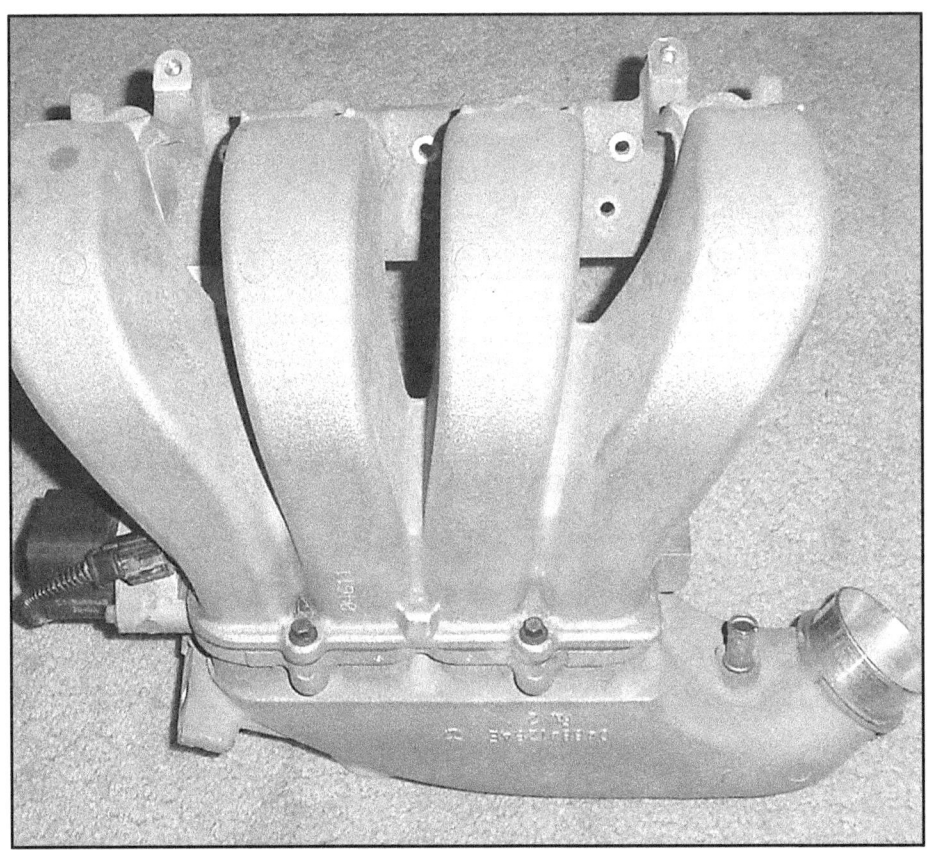

One of the best things about the Magnum engine is this variable-geometry intake manifold. It's one of the reasons why the SOHC Magnum has as much horsepower as the older DOHC motors. The Magnum intake manifold uses longer runners to build torque, then opens some shorter runners for extra top-end power.

Chapter 5

Shortening your intake runners is a neat, but time-consuming project. If you want peak torque at higher RPM, such as for drag racing or road racing, then this trick could help. (Right photo courtesy Chris Malluege)

This is the high-flowing intake manifold from Indy. It's a great alternative to having your stock intake ported, assuming you need all the flow. Many users have gained top-end power at the expense of low-end torque with this intake. (Photo courtesy Chris Malluege)

stock unit when you're running above 6,000 rpm. At approx. $500, this will eat up a decent chunk of your budget, but it's beneficial if you have a modified motor.

SOHC guys can also swap on a 2001-2004 high-output manifold, which is a cheaper alternative. The trick is getting the runners to open up with the first-gen computer. Some enthusiasts have had good luck using an RPM window switch from MSD.

Conclusions

Modifying your intake system is one of the most cost-effective ways to improve horsepower. There are many companies that make aftermarket air velocity intake systems, so which one should you buy? Depending on your car, you may have several choices. It could boil down to a matter of individual preference, price, looks, or color. One brand is not significantly better than another. Even the "no name" generic brands work. We routinely use a number of these systems on both our daily driver and racing vehicles. Additional intake system mods, such as larger throttle bodies, extrude honing, or racing intake manifolds should be reserved for modified powerplants.

Chapter 6

Exhaust System

One of the first things many Neon owners like to do is to replace the stock exhaust system. Keep in mind when considering a new cat-back exhaust or header: although it may sound nice, it may not give you any significant horsepower increase. Neons are lucky in that the factory system is good at doing its job, even though it may not be as cool as an aftermarket system.

Some new cars are being equipped with aftermarket tuner exhaust systems direct from the factory. We recently tested a 2003 Mazdaspeed Protege on the Speednation dyno. It's a nice car – even Neon fans can appreciate Mazda's effort to produce a factory tuner car. The exhaust is supplied by Racing Beat, a premier aftermarket parts manufacturer and tuner. We didn't see a factory-tuned exhaust until the SRT-4.

If you decide to buy a performance exhaust system, one way to think about it is like shopping for a pair of speakers for your stereo. If you have a cheap stereo, buying an expensive pair of speakers will not give you the perfect sound, and you won't hear the full potential of the speakers. The reverse is also true. If you have an expensive stereo and you buy a cheap pair of speakers, you won't realize the potential of your stereo. But sometimes, you buy speakers just for looks, or so you can say you have them.

Putting a wide-open exhaust on your stock Neon may help your performance over 6,000 rpm, but your low-end performance (our favorite kind) could suffer! Don't assume that the louder the system, the more performance you'll receive. On the racetrack, a louder engine equals a faster car only from the spectators' perspective. Any good aftermarket exhaust system will likely help you see a few extra horsepower in the high-RPM range, but, as with stereo components, the new exhaust should be matched to your setup – in this case, your intake, ignition, and fuel delivery systems. Of course, most turbo cars benefit from a free-flowing exhaust system, so if you're driving an SRT-4, there's no need to concern yourself with this warning.

Your exhaust system can be a highly personal item. Both tone and power come into play when choosing an aftermarket system. Thermal's dual tips add a classy look to your exhaust system. Most cat-back systems will give a lightly modified Neon a few more ponies.

When choosing an exhaust system, be aware that with just a few exceptions, they're all about the same (none will give you 15 hp on a stock car). A straight-through canister muffler like this one flows well, but might be too loud for your taste.

High-Performance Dodge Neon Builder's Handbook

Chapter 6

The one misfit in the exhaust aftermarket is the Supertrapp, manufactured by Kirker Performance. Supertrapp mufflers were originally designed for motorcycle engines, but they work just as well on 4-cylinder cars. We have even seen Corvettes using 2 and even 4 Supertrapps on the end of their V-8 system. (Photo courtesy Howell Automotive)

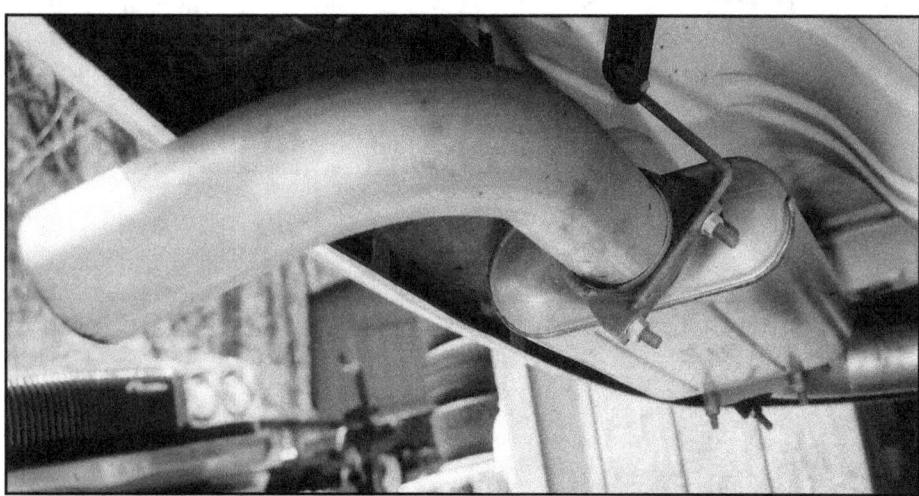

On Speednation's turbo racecar, a 3-inch Edelbrock muffler intimidates the author's 1976 Cosmo, seen in the background. Your exhaust system doesn't have to be flashy to build power.

We did some dyno testing on one of our favorite exhausts, the stainless-steel Supertrapp. Originally designed for motorcycles, it claims to be "the tunable exhaust." We tested a lot of performance products that day (only one exhaust system, however), but the only product that lived up to its claim was the Supertrapp. Our early ACR Neon was the guinea pig for this particular experiment. After getting a baseline, we removed the stock exhaust and installed the Supertrapp. We picked up 2 hp, but mostly above 5,500 rpm. Then we started to play with the diffuser discs. By removing the Supertrapp discs, you decrease the amount of exhaust that can escape from the tailpipe, thus increasing back pressure. The result was a 2- to 3-hp loss above 6,000 rpms, but the reward was a gain of 3 hp at 3,500 rpm. How can that be?

This example serves to illustrate a point about how exhaust systems work and what part they play in your engine's performance. A Supertrapp is an excellent example of how to explain back pressure, because Supertrapps can be tuned to adjust exhaust velocity. At the end of a Supertrapp, you attach a stack of between 1 to 15 diffuser discs. When a high number of discs are used, there are more spaces between the discs, making it easier for exhaust gasses to escape – decreasing back pressure. Most high-performance enthusiasts agree that less back pressure equals more torque in the high-RPM range. And conversely, more back pressure (up to a point) equals better low-end torque.

The tunability of a Supertrapp covers a very small range of torque (plus or minus 1 to 3 ft-lbs). On the other hand, they are relatively cheap (under $200) and work with your stock pipes (replacing the much heavier OEM muffler). When we added all of the 15 discs, the ACR lost the low-end torque gained earlier, but gained high-end. In fact, when we ran the Supertrapp wide open, there was no change in high-end power. The car was louder, however. When we removed the Supertrapp completely before reinstalling the stock system, we did a dyno pull and found no difference between a wide-open exhaust and a Supertrapp with 15 discs. Did we mention it was very loud with no muffler? So there's no advantage to run a wide-open exhaust on a lightly modified Neon, especially since most racing venues have decibel restrictions. Our early Neon project car worked great with this system. Even though we love Supertrapps, Speednation's SSC low-buck Neon has a simple "cherry bomb" glass pack muffler, and our Turbo Neon works well with an Edelbrock. We do have Supertrapps on our Hondas and Solo Formula Vee.

Most quality performance exhaust systems have been tailored to get the most out of your car. But once a standard performance exhaust system is on your car, you have no real options to adjust torque. If you prefer a traditional aftermarket exhaust systems, we recommend sticking with the name brands. Companies such as Mopar Performance, Borla, Flowmaster, Thermal, and Dyno-Max won't let you down. These exhausts will also save you weight over the stock system. The Mopar exhaust we installed was 7 lbs lighter than stock. We've had nothing but trouble with Pacesetter in both Neon and our Honda applications, so we can't recommend that brand. You may have to pay over $400, but when it comes to good exhaust systems, you usually get what you pay for.

Often, a performance exhaust will bring out the best in some of the other engine mods you've made. Once your car is breathing better, you'll begin to reap the benefit from all of your other hard work.

Unlike the aftermarket intake systems, you don't get much "bang for the buck" when it comes to exhaust systems. For most applications, you will be lucky to gain 2 to 5 hp, if anything at all. Some Neons may actually lose power over the factory exhaust system, especially if you jump up to a 2.5-inch pipe. Most people choose the exhaust they want based on the sound, or the look, so decide what your priorities are before you buy.

Headers
by Michael Carpenter

The Neon's exhaust manifold is mostly designed with emissions in mind. The short manifold helps to heat up the large, close-coupled catalytic converter quickly. As a result, Neon headers are somewhat of a compromise. They generally fall into two categories: short tube and long tube.

Most good headers will slightly improve your car's performance and gains can be achieved in both low-end and high-end torque, as well as overall horsepower. Due to increasing concerns about the environment, removing your catalytic converter is illegal in nearly all states. Even with a cat, a header unit will still help your car to breathe by allowing the exhaust gasses to escape more efficiently. Most pure racecars that are only used on the track generally remove the cat and put on a total custom system from the header back.

If the header you purchase doesn't come coated, ship it off to Swain Tech, HPC, or Jet Hot to have it coated inside and out (costing about $200). The coatings even come in a variety of colors. Our HPC-coated header was done eight years ago, and even though the car sat outside in the northeast winters, there is only a touch of rust starting to show. Without one of these coatings, a header

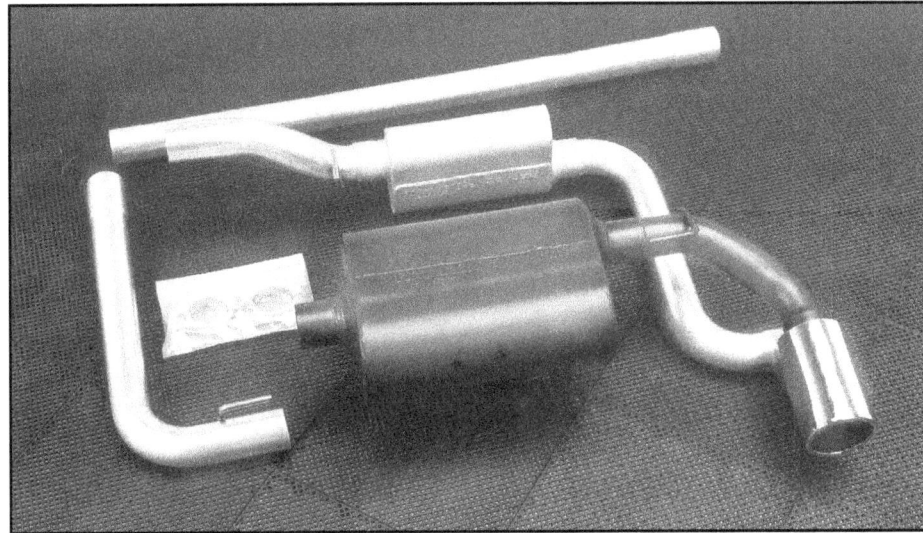

This 2¼-inch aluminized cat-back from Flowmaster fits some first-gen Neons. It includes a resonator and a muffler to keep the sound under control without adding extra backpressure. It also features a 4-inch chromed, stainless-steel tip. (Photo courtesy Flowmaster)

Aftermarket exhaust systems usually eliminate some of the convoluted SRT-4 exhaust piping, but this Borla system retains the dual outlets. If you're wondering, the dual exhaust doesn't flow twice as well as a single exhaust.

will rust in no time. In most cases, it's just easier to buy a header that's already coated to save you the time.

The other benefit of this coating is that it keeps more heat in the header, which decreases under-hood temperatures and increases exhaust velocity. Wrapping your header tubes with a thermal wrap will also achieve this goal.

As we stated earlier, when it comes to exhaust components, you do get what you pay for. We bought a low-cost coated PaceSetter header ($250), but when we matched it to our exhaust ports, we were disappointed. In some places, the header was ⅛ inch off. Holding the factory exhaust manifold gasket up to the header showed us that we'd just wasted $250.

Determined to make the header work, we drafted a welding expert friend to add some material to the inside bottom portion of the header tube, while grinding away material on top in an

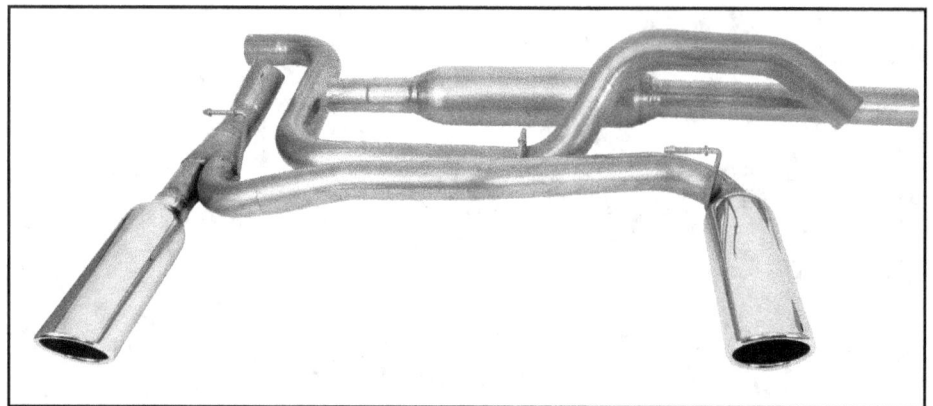

This is the new free-flowing exhaust for the SRT-4 available from Mopar Performance Parts. For a turbocharged car like the SRT-4, having less backpressure allows the turbo to spool faster, making more power. (Photo courtesy Mopar Performance Parts)

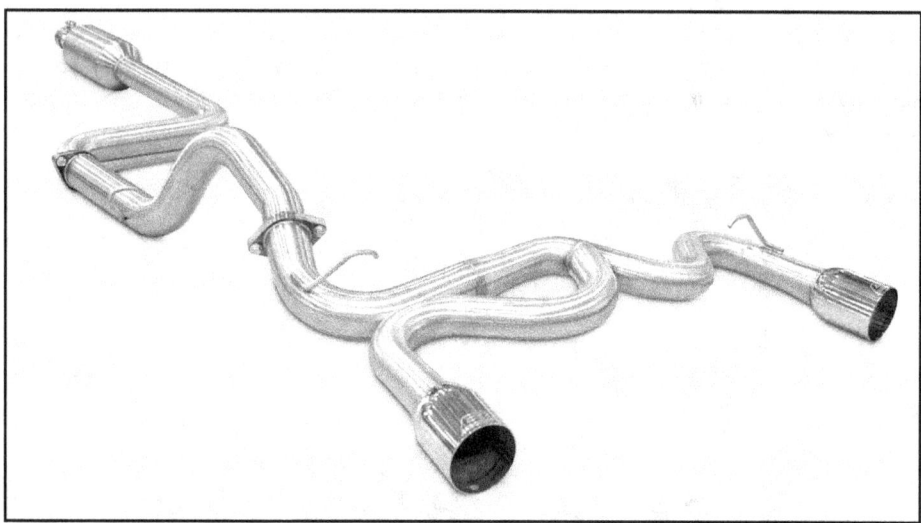

DC Sports manufactures this stainless-steel exhaust system for the SRT-4. It features a 3-inch pipe that splits into 2½-inch tailpipes. It uses a single resonator in the straight section for increased flow. (Photo courtesy of DC Sports)

Solo I Hillclimb legend and expert welder, Rich Rock, is working on a Pacesetter header that didn't even come close to fitting. He had to add material to build up certain sections and grind away other sections that obstructed flow.

effort to port match the header to the head. The grinding could not be done until the original welds were reinforced. To make a long story short, I now owe my welding buddy big time. He put nearly three hours of time in to get the ports to match. I hope he doesn't ask to race one of my cars. But to be fair to Pacesetter, no header comes perfectly matched. Expect to do some port matching if you want to squeeze the maximum power out of your header.

So what did we learn from this fiasco? In the future, we'll buy a good header to start with. Most good headers match up very closely to your head and will increase the overall efficiency of your exhaust system. You may also want to check to see if local emission laws permit their use on the street. Don't expect a huge gain in performance, but with a good header and complete exhaust system, you could pick up 5 to 10 horsepower. As with exhaust systems, even with some of the high-quality headers, you could also lose power, especially if your car is mostly stock.

If your aftermarket exhaust system or header doesn't give your car more power, it will at least save you weight. You can end up saving up to 20 lbs., depending on what header and exhaust you choose. Ask what the components weigh before you buy. And when they arrive, weigh them compared to your old exhaust and header so you know the weight difference. After all, a lighter car is a faster car.

Short Tube

Short-tube headers are designed to work with the factory catalyst. Available from companies like Mopar Performance, Hedman (Chikara), Pacesetter, and Holley, these headers are usually emissions legal. They definitely offer an improvement over the factory manifold. Chrysler even saw fit to install one on the newer high-output SOHC Magnum engine found in 2001 and newer R/T and ACR models. However, gains are usually modest, in the 1- to 5-hp range.

Long Tube

A long-tube header is a no-compromise design for maximum power. Long-tubes put the collector near where the stock catalytic converter usually ends.

This is what a short tube header looks like when it's installed. Most short-tubes replace the exhaust manifold and connect to the factory exhaust (left of photo). (Photo courtesy Chris Malluege)

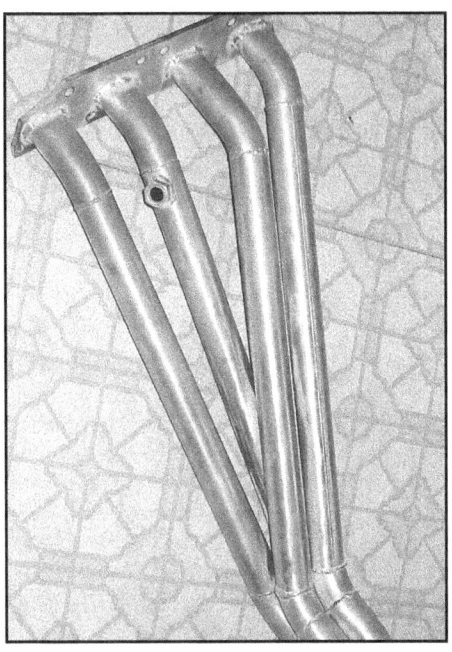

This is a handmade long-tube header from a first-gen Neon. There are usually a few companies out there that will fabricate you a very nice header, if you're willing to pay for it. (Photo courtesy Chris Malluege)

Some fabrication will be required to mate your long-tube header to your factory pipe. Since emissions are a growing concern, you'll want to look into a small, high-flowing catalyst from Magnaflow, Walker, or Catco. Currently TTI, Kirk, and AF/X have long-tube headers available for both first- and second-generation cars. We opted for a Fast Fabrications header on our '98 DOHC Neon, which featured a stepped-tube design. In testing, we found even more power than anyone expected – we picked up close to 10 hp and dropped a good half-second off our quarter-mile times!

Custom

If you fancy yourself as the next Scott Mohler (relatively famous Neon drag racer), off-the-shelf parts for your racecar probably aren't going to cut it! You'll want a lightweight stainless-steel design that incorporates a high velocity merge collector to maximize power while saving weight. Or perhaps you're building an autocross car, where the low-end torque of a 4-2-1 design will help you to blast out of a low-speed corner. Fast Fabrications can design a header with your racecar's needs in mind.

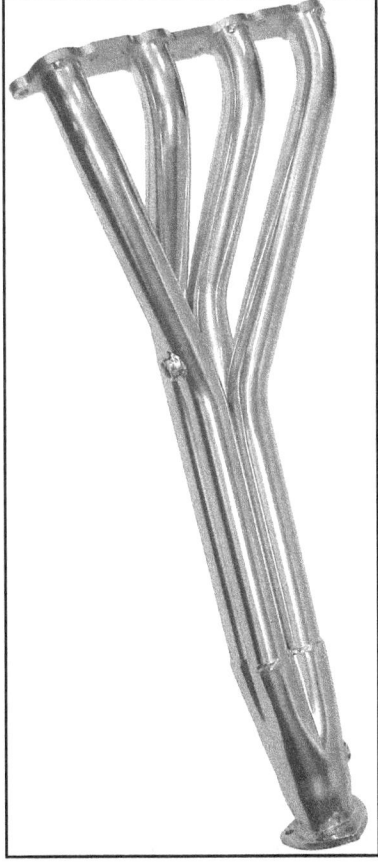

This is the TTI header available from Howell Automotive. It comes in the version shown here and as a short-tube. It is available in nickel-plated and ceramic-coated finishes. (Photo courtesy Howell Automotive)

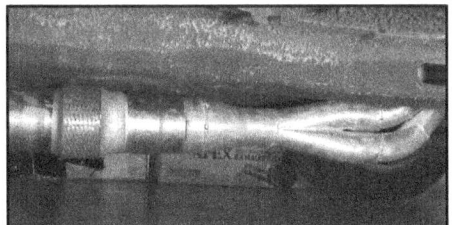

As long as you're getting a custom header for your Neon, you may as well specify that you want a high-flowing merge collector and a flex-pipe. (Photo courtesy Chris Malluege)

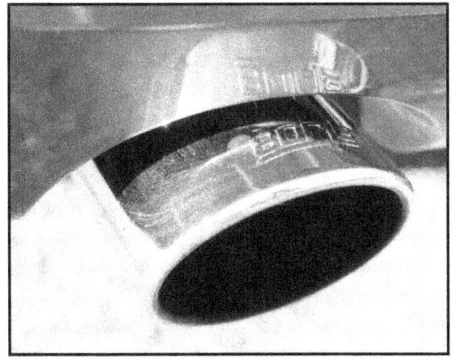

A nice exhaust tip is a fitting touch to your new exhaust system. But just remember, your system doesn't have to be pretty for it to work well. Notice how well this tip fits in the hole in the rear bumper.

CHAPTER 7

IGNITION AND FUEL

There is a lot of mystery surrounding ignition systems, coils, spark plugs, and wires. We've seen claims of mega horsepower gains with the use of certain products. There's unbelievable technology engineered into some aftermarket ignition products, but we couldn't begin to explain much of it to you – we barely understand some of it ourselves. But we have one thing that helps us sort out the myth from reality: our Mustang Chassis Dyno.

In all of the dyno testing we've done over the years, on nearly every ignition product on the market, we can clearly state in simple terms that none of them will add horsepower to a healthy engine. Of course, if your current ignition system is flawed (bad wires, failing coil), then replacing the faulty part with any functioning part (cheap or expensive, stock or aftermarket) will return your engine to normal functioning. That's not to say that you should just skip over this chapter. On the contrary, we want you to be armed with as much knowledge as possible. Plus, there are techniques hidden in some of the paragraphs that will help you add some ponies.

Ignition Systems

An aftermarket ignition isn't necessary to have a fun, competitive vehicle. The stock Neon ignition is an excellent system. Upgrading should only be a priority if you plan on powering a high-performance race engine. Your decision should also be based on the intended use of the car. For example, if you plan on hopping-up a Neon or SRT-4 for the street, you don't need to spend money on an aftermarket ignition. Your money could be spent in better ways. For the track, however, you may want to give it some consideration.

Unfortunately, Neons are ignition challenged in one significant way: you can't easily adjust the ignition timing. At the Speednation dyno, we can usually promise our customers that they'll leave the dyno with at least a few horsepower more than they came with. But we don't make that promise to Neon owners. The chance that a car's ignition timing has been

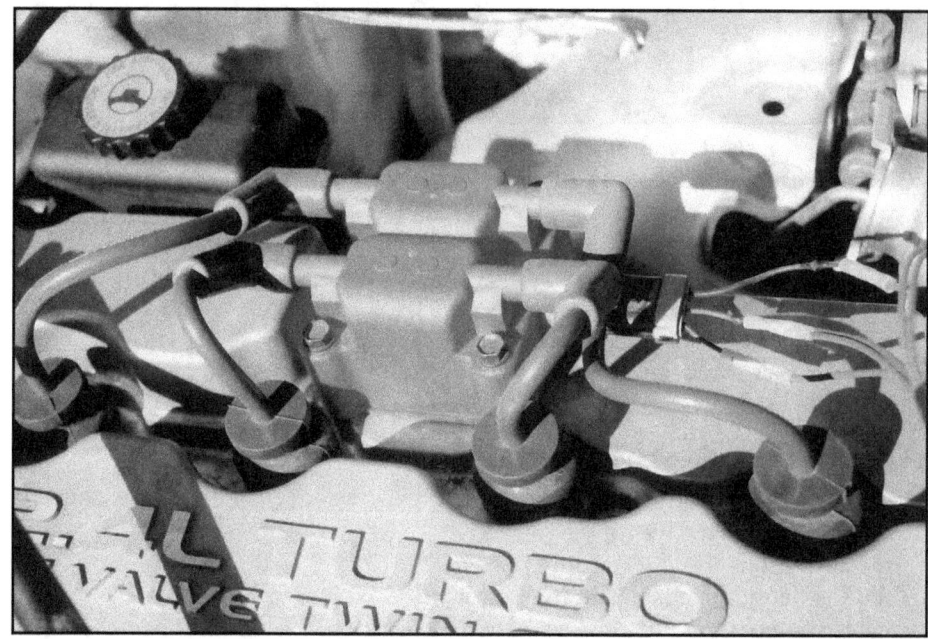

Neons come standard with an excellent ignition system. There is no need for an upgrade unless you plan on exceeding 6,000 rpm for extended periods of time. Highly modified drag cars, aftermarket turbo systems, and serious road racers could consider a performance coil pack.

set from the factory for optimal horsepower is unlikely. Only about 1 in 10 are set to get max power. We pay no attention to what other tuners have done to a car before we get our hands on it. Unless they set the ignition timing on a dyno, they're probably not getting the most out of the engine. The 2.0-liter SOHC and DOHC, and 2.4-liter SRT-4 engines get their spark from a distributorless ignition system. No distributor – nothing to adjust. Even if you install an aftermarket ignition, such as an MSD or Crane, you still can't advance your ignition timing past the programmed factory settings of the stock PCM.

Ignition and Fuel

To install a performance PCM in your Neon, you first need to remove the stocker. It's located on the driver's side of the engine compartment near the battery. Remember to disconnect your battery before starting any electrical work. (Photo courtesy Michael Carpenter)

We've tested a variety of ignition systems over the years, and for the most part, they're the same. Some have different features than others, and if you feel the need to buy one, consider some of those features. For racers, the feature that will serve you best is rev limiting. You can manually select the maximum RPM you want your engine to rev to. If you try to rev beyond that point, the unit will systematically withdraw spark. It will feel like your car is running on three cylinders, which is exactly what is happening. Your car will refuse to accelerate, and you'll have to either back off on the throttle, or shift to the next highest gear. For purpose-built racecars that have no built-in limiter, an aftermarket ignition that keeps you from over-revving your engine could save you thousands of dollars and hours of new parts and labor.

Since the stock Neon PCM has a built-in rev-limiter, you won't need to buy an aftermarket unit unless you have a performance PCM that has raised or eliminated your limit. Even though we didn't need an aftermarket ignition on the Speednation Turbo Neon, we chose to install the MSD DIS-2 (cost: around $325). The reason wasn't that the MSD provides a multiple spark. The multiple spark only works up to 3,000 rpm, and then the system reverts back to a single, more conventional spark from 3,000 rpm to redline. We installed it because of the cool, two-stage rev limiter and timing retard functions. The two-stage rev limiter is great for drag racing, Solo I, and Solo II launches. You can set the first limiter for a low RPM (for your launch), and the secondary limiter for a high RPM (to protect your engine). We played with the launch limiter for several events, and eventually settled on 4,250

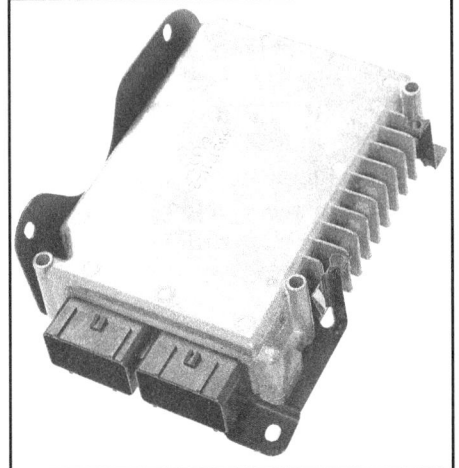

There are lots of great performance PCMs available for Neons and SRT-4s, leaving 99 percent of the people reading this book with no reason to go to a standalone EFI system. Modern Performance, Howell Automotive, and Mopar Performance can hook you up with a great PCM based on what you want to do with your car. (Photo courtesy Mopar Performance Parts)

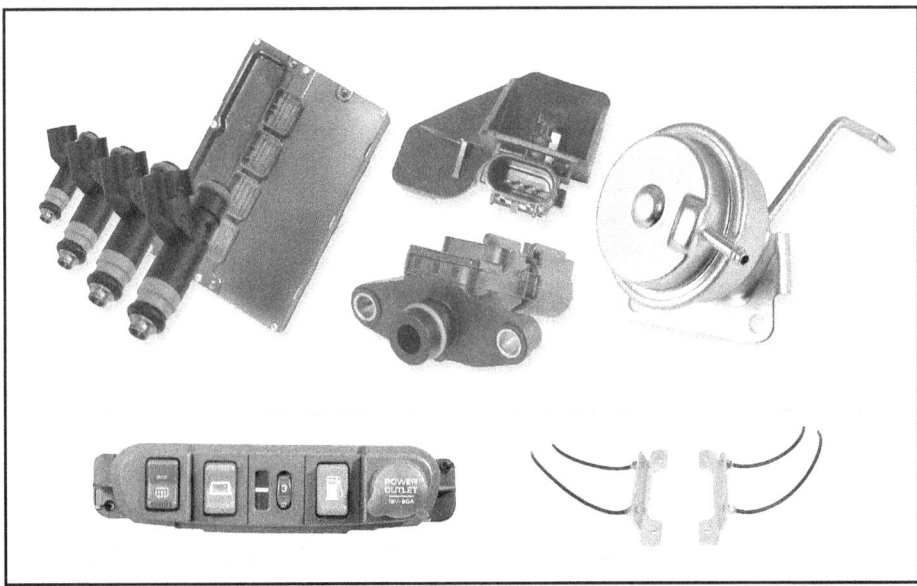

Mopar Performance also has PCM/injector combos for the SRT-4. This Stage 2 kit does the hard work for you, so there's no need to worry about the tune. Adding extra fuel in the right places is especially important for a turbo car, as you're more likely to break parts under boost. (Photo courtesy Mopar Performance Parts)

Chapter 7

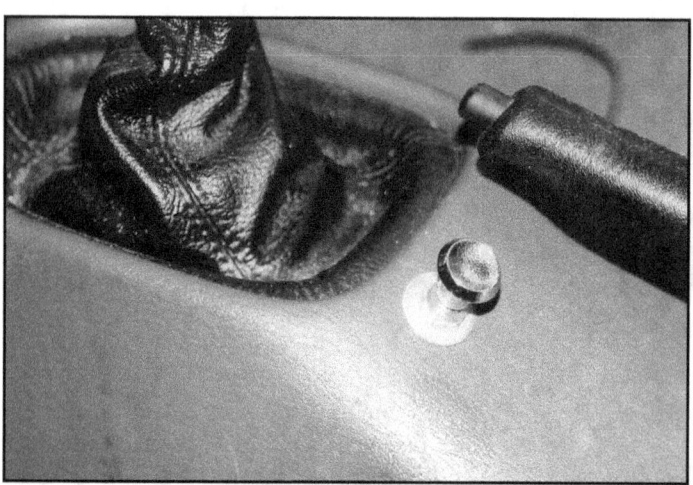

Mark Daddio chose the MSD DIS-2 ignition for his national champion autocross car, but he never took advantage of the cool launch feature. We installed a simple switch so that launches could be better controlled for Solo I hillclimbs. Most of the time, cars are facing uphill waiting for the signal to go, and with the weight transfer to the rear, FWD cars tend to sit in place and spin their tires. This helped.

rpm for the launch. We used a small push/pull switch and set it so that when the switch is pulled upwards, the stage-one rev limit is activated.

Now for the fun. Sitting at the starting line, you floor the throttle, and then let the clutch out – no need to look at the tach. You just put the pedal all the way to the metal. Spectators and fellow drivers alike will come up to you after your run and tell you that your car didn't seem to be running right when you were launching. In fact, that's how the engine sounds as it bounces off the rev limiter at 4,250 rpm. Our turbo car has so much power that even when launching at low RPM, the front wheels would spin. With the launch control engaged, you're basically running on only three cylinders as you let out the clutch. The aftermarket ignition drops the spark on one of the cylinders to keep your revs in check. As you feel the tires start to get traction as you leave the line (it only takes a second or two), you simply push down on the plunger switch and disengage the first stage of the rev limiter. It works great, but it takes a lot of practice to get it right.

Be aware that with all MSD ignitions, you need to install an MSD tach adapter. Be sure to order it with your MSD ignition. There's also a slick harness, MSD part number PN 8883, which plugs directly into the factory coil pack and harness – no splicing or cutting into the factory harness! I wish this was all around when I was ready to shoot my one car over the wiring. You also need a tach adapter with the Neon ignitions that come from Crane Cams.

You may encounter a problem if you spend a few seconds bouncing off the built-in factory rev limiter. Since fuel is being systematically cut off to restrict RPM, your engine is running lean for that period of time. Obviously, that's no big deal if you back off the throttle or shift, which is the response the factory intends you to have. However, depending on the track, sometimes racers will stay on the limiter for a few seconds. If you're entering a turn that requires you to downshift once you get there, and you're already maxed out in your gearing, it may be beneficial (time wise) to stay in gear as opposed to making those two shifts. If it's a second-gear/third-gear shift, then there's a chance you could make a mistake and miss the gear you're aiming for. If you end up having to repeat this ritual several times per lap, and your factory system is still controlling your rev limit, you could do some damage.

Aftermarket ignitions limit spark, not fuel, which means you won't run lean. I probably don't have to tell you what can happen if your engine gets too lean, but I'm going to anyway. My friend drove his Supercharged Honda CRX on the street as if he were on a racetrack. He would hit the factory rev limit all the time, despite having a shift light flashing him in the face well before the factory fuel cutoff. The result: two blown head gaskets. He's actually pretty lucky he never melted a piston. With a turbocharged Neon, the results could be even uglier! So if you plan on spending any time on the rev limit, you should probably consider buying an aftermarket ignition system that has a rev limit feature. Visit a chassis dyno to see exactly where you start losing torque, so that you can set the limiter properly.

Wires and Plugs

Spark plug indexing is an old trick that some drivers employ to get a little extra (and we mean little) bit of power. This trick happens mostly in stock classes, since rules are so restrictive. Most people find plug indexing a waste of time in modified classes, since you can use a powerful aftermarket ignition that could fire a plug that's been in the bottom of your toolbox for the past 10 years. Briefly, the goal of spark indexing is to have the open end of the spark plug facing the intake valves. Make sure you have at least two sets of plugs handy. Mark the position of the open ends of the electrodes on the white insulator covering of the plug so you'll be able to see them when the plugs are installed in the cylinder head. The reason for this, as

Ignition and Fuel

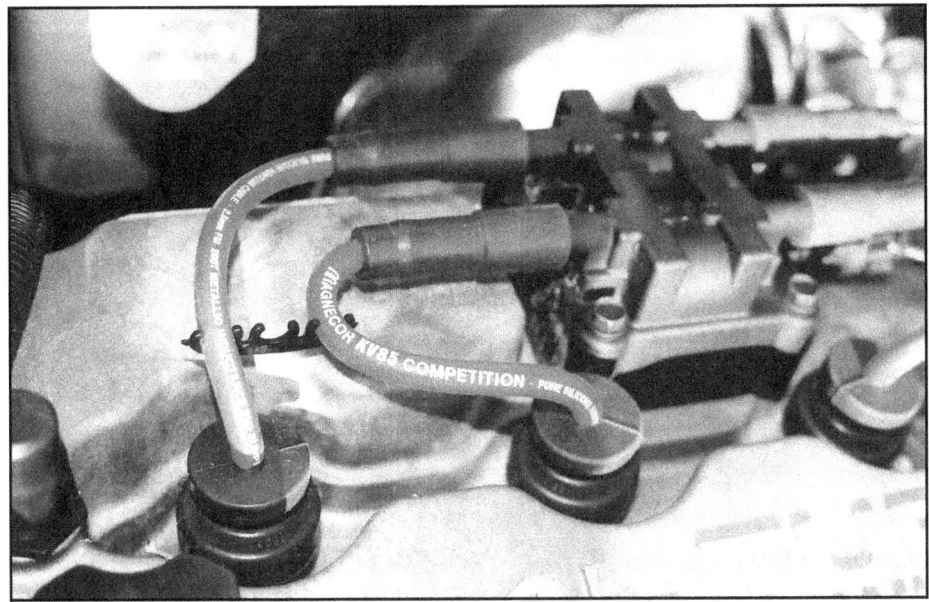

Magnecor is our personal choice if there is a need to replace stock wires. They've proven flexible and reliable. Magnecor makes no claims at improved power (we respect that). They simply claim to be a superior product, which they are.

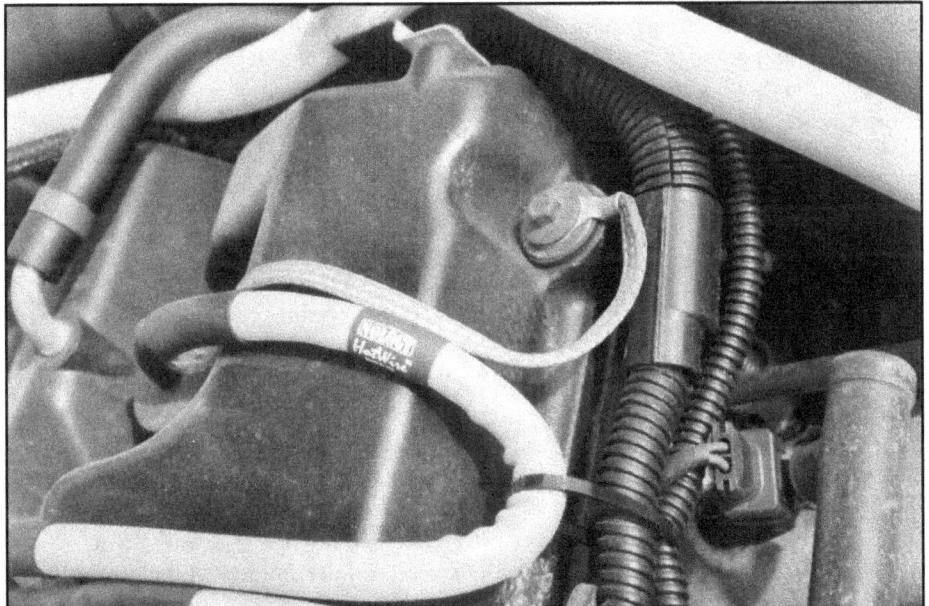

NOLOGY wires are extremely cool, but they don't do anything to improve performance in either stock or moderately modified cars. In fact, no wire can improve horsepower on these engines. Sometimes, however, OEM Chrysler wires can crack and arc when they get old.

increases, eventually causing misfiring. Even with the MSD ignition and a trick aftermarket coil, the factory specified .035 inch was the best for power. The car ran horribly after opening the gap to .065 inch, as the coil manufacturer advertises.

There are ignition products on the market that claim to improve performance in stock vehicles without having to go through spark plug indexing. Although most competition rules do not allow for aftermarket ignition systems, they often allow for an alternate ignition coil, wires, and plugs. We don't use them much, even if we get them for free. Our Neons use stock plugs, stock coil, and Magnecor wires. In dyno testing, we found that even replacing old spark plugs doesn't increase horsepower, unless they are really worn out, fouled, or dirty.

Platinum plugs should be avoided for Neons. First and foremost, they are not a performance upgrade, as some of the manufacturers would have you believe. The Neon's ignition coil essentially fires two of the plugs backwards, which will chew up the center electrode of a platinum plug quickly. Especially the tiny center electrodes on Bosch Platinum plugs. A double platinum plug would prevent this erosion, but they're even more expensive. Platinum is really only used in spark plugs for longer plug life – not for performance.

There are many brands of plug wires available for the Neon. They all more or less work the same – getting the spark from the coil to the plug. The color of the wires or the name brand will be the major selling point for most enthusiasts. I prefer Magnecor for their no-BS advertising. They come right out and say not to expect any extra power. I also like the flexibility of the wires that makes them easy to install.

It's a Matter of Time – Understanding Advance and Retard

Most racers and mechanics know that ignition timing is one of many things that can be adjusted to change how your engine performs. The spark

you'll see, is that each plug has a slightly different orientation. You'll have to try one plug after another until the line you drew on the cover of the plug lines up with the intake manifold (which is where the intake valves are). This usually requires installing and removing several plugs per cylinder before you find one that lines up properly. We don't recommend wasting your time doing any of this, but it is an interesting trick, especially if you're looking for a little edge.

We tried playing with spark plug gap on our Speednation Mustang Dyno. The car would start to misfire and lose power with a gap of more than .040 inch. This is part of why fresh plugs seem to boost power; as the plugs erode, the gap

Chapter 7

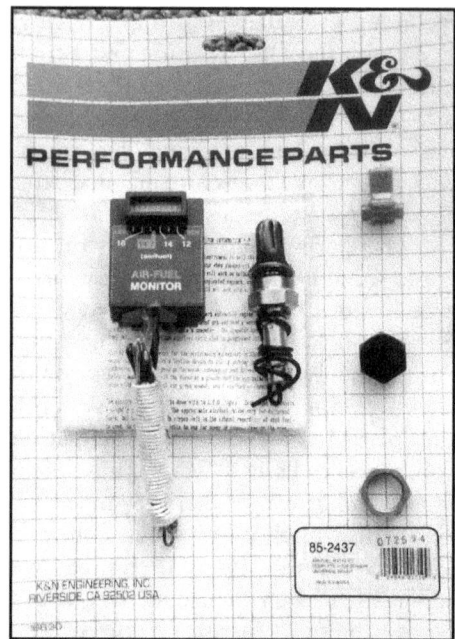

If your Neon is highly modified or is running an altered fuel system, you should think about getting an air/fuel meter. You can go with something as inexpensive as this K&N system, for under $100. A wide-band oxygen set-up is more accurate, but much more expensive.

If you can't seem to get your tune right with any of the available PCMs, you might have to try an adjustable fuel-pressure regulator. Tuning with one of these is quite difficult, and should only be attempted on a chassis dyno with a wide-band oxygen sensor in place. (Photo courtesy Chris Malluege)

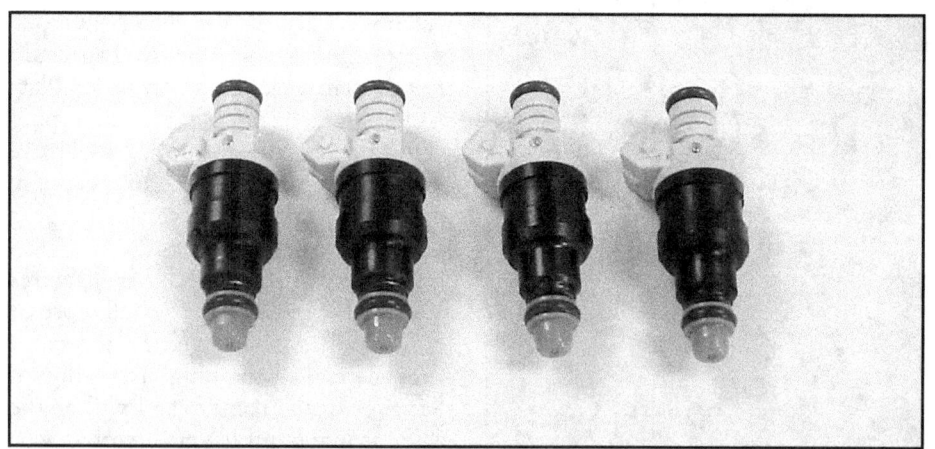

If your Neon is eight or more years old, you may want to think about getting the injectors cleaned. Send them off to someplace like Marren Motorsports that can check the flow and spray pattern for you. Injectors will wear out, and cleaning may not do the trick. If you need new ones, these ACCEL injectors are available from Howell Automotive. (Photo courtesy Howell Automotive)

needs to burn the air/fuel mixture at just the right time to make maximum power. However, the ability to adjust the ignition timing is nonexistent in all Neons – unless you buy an aftermarket PCM. Here's how they work. The computer tells the spark plugs when to fire. There is a small delay between when a spark plug fires and when the air/fuel mixture is ignited. This period of time remains constant (unless you use a different octane gasoline, or are super compressing the mixture). By retarding ignition timing, the PCM is allowing the piston to get closer to the top of its stroke (top dead center) before the spark plug fires and ignites the air/fuel mixture. As RPM increases, the piston travels up toward top dead center (TDC) at a higher rate of speed. Since the time it takes to ignite the air/fuel mixture remains constant, you need to advance the timing at high RPM so that the mixture is ignited earlier, before the piston reaches the top of its stroke. At very high RPMs, the piston may already be on the way down by the time the air/fuel mix starts to burn – this costs you power.

Even if you have your ignition timing set at 10 degrees BTDC (before top dead center), that doesn't mean that all the fuel will burn before the piston reaches the top of the stroke. The spark plug may fire at 10 degrees BTDC, but initially only part of the fuel ignites, which in turn causes the main mixture to explode. During that time, the piston has advanced much closer to (or just beyond) TDC. Where the mixture fires relative to TDC determines how much power your engine makes and where in the powerband it makes it.

Autocrossers tend to be slightly retarded (sorry, couldn't resist) because

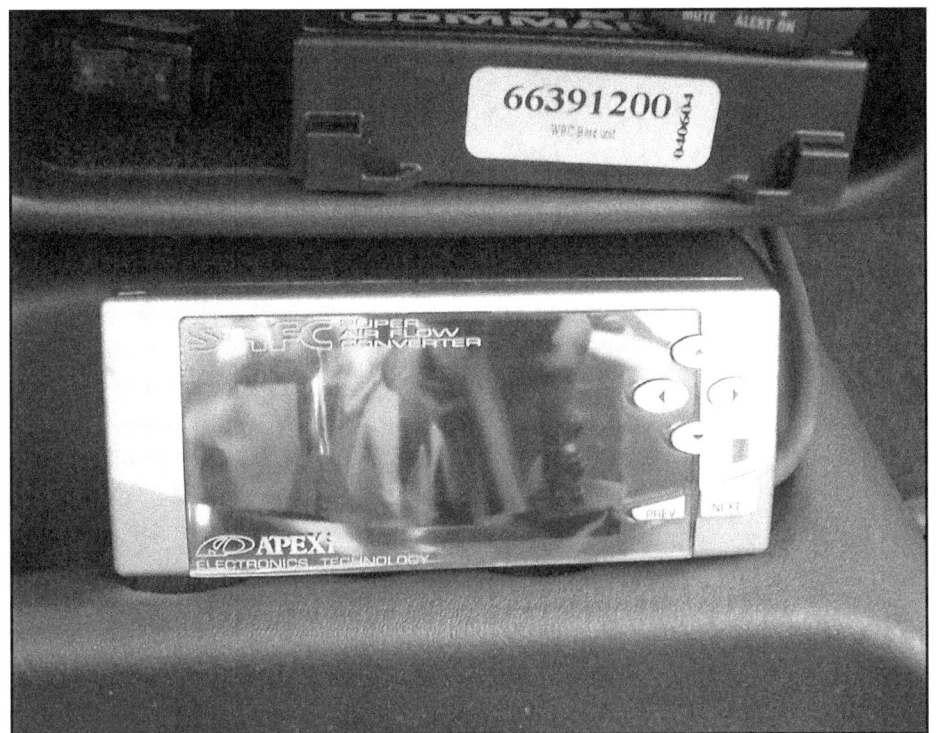

A piggy-back air/fuel controller like this S-AFC from Apexi can help you dial in the correct tune, especially if you're running boost or larger fuel injectors. Again, something like this should be tuned on a chassis dyno with the help of a wide-band oxygen sensor. (Photo courtesy Chris Malluege)

retarding the timing will often increase low-end torque for coming out of a low-speed turn. Depending on the track and gear selection, road racers spend much more time in the higher RPM band and are willing to sacrifice power at 3,000 rpm to gain power at 6,000 rpm. For this reason, they like to have the timing advanced. Drag racers follow the same philosophy.

The Neon's PCM can dynamically control timing. This means that at low RPM the timing can be retarded, and at high RPM it can be advanced. Aftermarket PCMs use more aggressive ignition timing to build more power. The knock sensor manages the timing advance, and retards it when detonation is encountered. On a dyno chart, if your power suddenly drops 2 to 3 hp, it may be the knock sensor at work.

Electronic Fuel Injection Tips

Unlike many of the popular 4-cylinder imports, stock Neon injectors can efficiently handle fuel delivery – even when your engine is pumping through more air and making more power than originally intended. With most cars, adding an intake, header, and exhaust would usually mean you would benefit from bigger injectors to balance out the system, but not with a Neon. However, there are a few tricks that make a difference when it comes to the Neon's EFI system.

If you're serious about making changes to the stock fuel system, you may want to consider installing a wide-band oxygen (O_2) sensor into your Neon's exhaust. The factory O_2 sensor is basically a rich/lean switch for the PCM to adjust the air/fuel at idle and part-throttle conditions – it isn't even used by the PCM at full throttle! With a wideband sensor, you can get precise air/fuel readings, allowing you to set your fuel pressure, or adjust your air/fuel controller correctly and safely. Wideband O_2 systems are available from the aftermarket. A setup including the gauge and sensor will cost you around $500. One example is AEM's UEGO, which will even interface with their new standalone engine management system.

Now that Neons are starting to age (some are already 10 years old), you should consider having your old, worn fuel injectors balanced and blueprinted by Marren Motorsports. Tim Marren explained that after a few years, injectors can lose their ability to flow properly. Even if they are flowing at 99 to 100 percent, the spray pattern may be less than 360 degrees, which will rob low-end torque. Expect to pay $150 to $250 for this service, depending upon the condition of your injectors. If you are a serious racer, the result can be well worth the cost. Don't just buy new injectors at a Chrysler dealer. Call either Marren or Russ Collins of RC Engineering and order from them. They bench test each new injector they sell to insure that both flow and spray pattern are perfect before shipping them out to you.

Many tuners believe you add power by simply increasing the fuel pressure to your current stock injectors. One of the functions of your PCM is to control how long the injectors stay open (longer duration equals more fuel into the cylinder), so by increasing fuel pressure to the injectors, you could make them behave like they're bigger. We've tried adding fuel pressure on a few Neons and it didn't seem to work very well. We probably didn't need the extra fuel just yet – most mild and moderately modified Neons don't.

Replacing your stock fuel rail with an aftermarket rail does nothing unless you're also replacing the stock injectors with higher flowing injectors, which we don't recommend unless you are building a serious turbo or nitrous setup. Remember, it's all about keeping your system in balance.

Stand Alone EFI Systems

If you want complete control over the system (fully adjustable ignition, timing, and fuel delivery), you'll need to install an aftermarket EFI system. This is a major step to take, and requires a major commitment to install and tune. If you decide to go that route, there are many different systems from which to choose. The one from SDS (Simple Digital Systems) is very affordable and simple to use. If money were no object, an Electromotive TEC3, AEM, or MoTeC

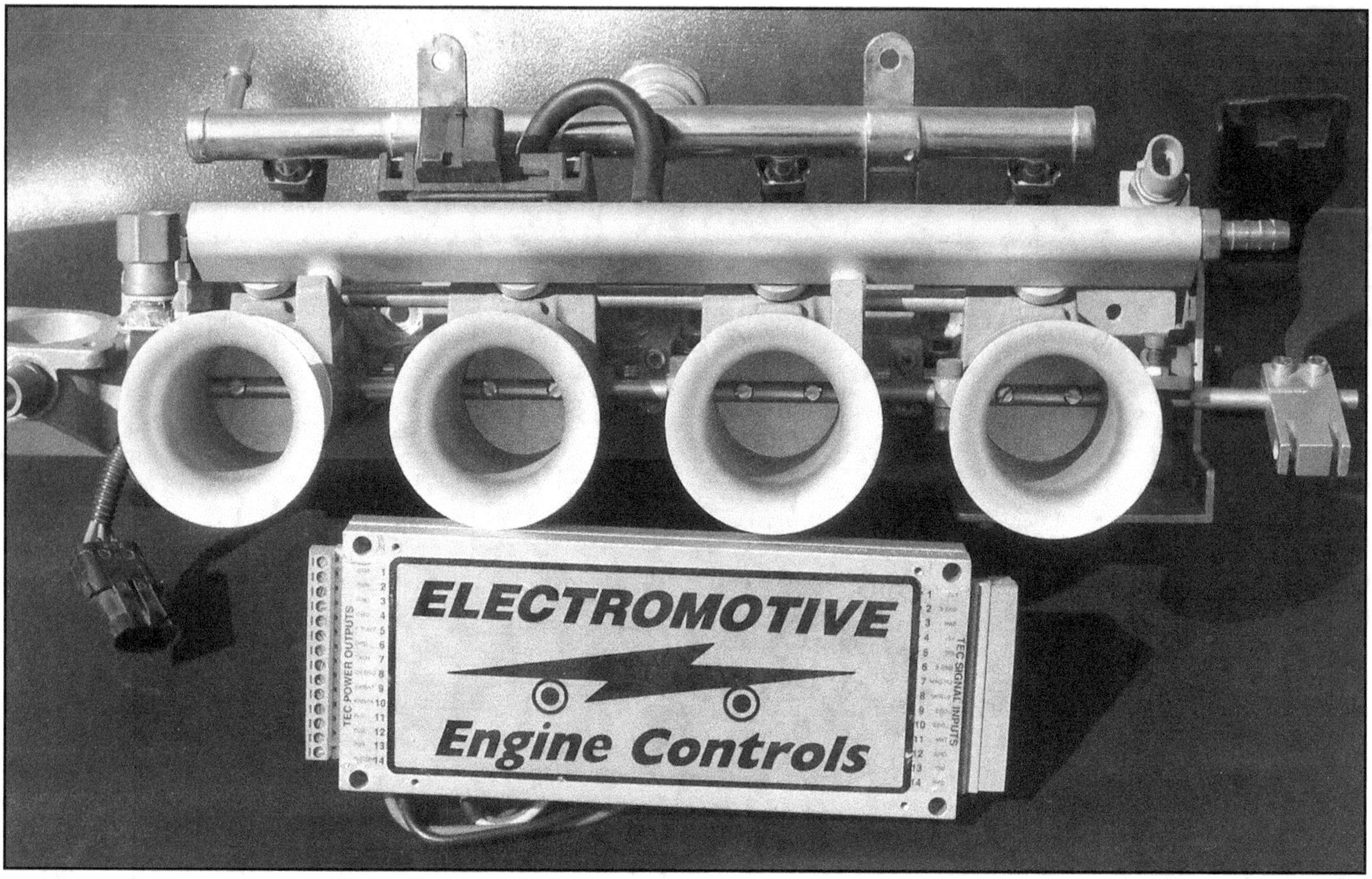

Electromotive makes some of the most advanced engine management systems on the market. Of course, you only need one if you plan on running some very fast times at the drag strip or on the road-race course. This setup comes with its own intake manifold and a set of individual throttle bodies (one for each cylinder). (Photo courtesy Chris Malluege)

unit would be a better choice, but you do need a laptop to tune them. Most systems come with a starter fuel and ignition program to get the car running, but you'll need to take it from there in order to realize the full potential of a programmable EFI system. Even after you get your Neon running well, there are probably a few tweaks that could net you a few more horsepower.

A chassis dyno is your only real hope of getting a system like this dialed in properly, as there are so many parameters to consider. It took us nearly two years to get our first system right, but only about five hours to get the second one tuned properly. Don't even consider getting one unless you have done all of the mods needed to take full advantage of it. Cams, cam gears, bigger injectors (usually included), air intake, throttle body, header, exhaust, high-flow (or no) cat, head work, turbocharger setup, etc., should all be in place first.

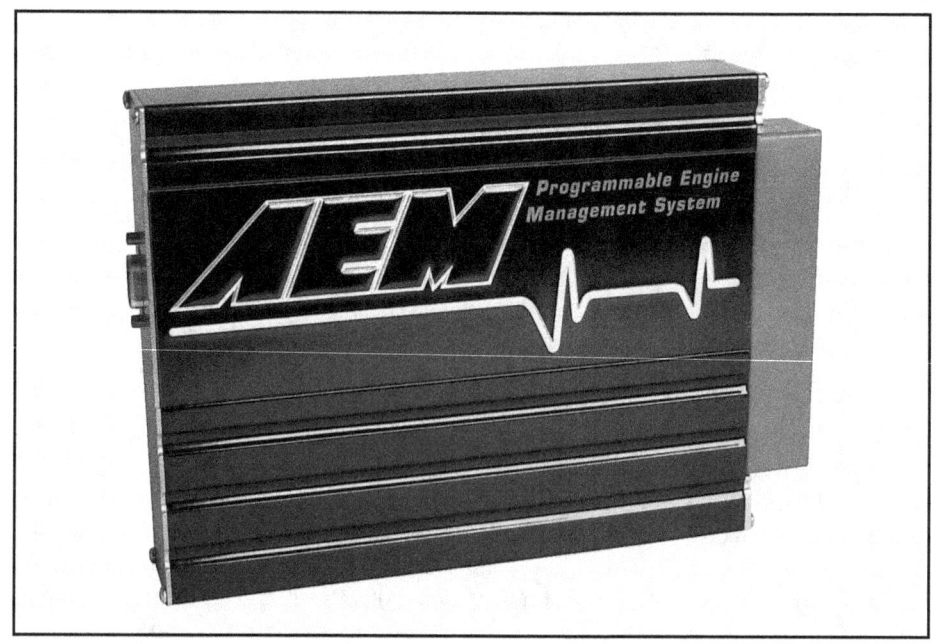

AEM has just released its Plug-&-Play Engine Management system for the SRT-4. The AEM unit works with all your factory sensors, includes a base tune to get you started, and is available with or without a wide-band oxygen sensor. This is something to consider once you've outgrown the factory PCM. (Photo courtesy of AEM)

Chapter 8

Camshafts and Heads

If you've done a lot to your Neon, and it doesn't seem like you're getting the power you expected, the problem may be that your present cam(s) won't let your engine breathe well enough to take advantage of your mods. If that's the case, a cam transplant may be in order. You may want to consider replacing your timing belt and water pump while you're at it. It might also be a good time to replace your timing-belt tensioner, since it's under more stress with the larger cams.

In most cases, adding high-performance cams will increase horsepower, but the important thing to note is where that power becomes available. How much horsepower you'll get is often determined by other modifications made to the engine. On a stock engine, you may simply be changing the shape of the torque curve, and not adding significant power. You may also only see horsepower gains above 6,500 rpm where your present power starts to drop off. The best thing to do before you open your wallet is to check with the experts, or just ask the guys who are racing the same Neon as you, but going faster.

As always, your choice of aftermarket cams should be determined by what you want to do with your car. The more radical you go, the more of a beast your Neon will become on the street. That may sound great as you picture yourself blowing the doors off of a 5.0L Mustang, but those instances are few and far between. The rest of the time, you'll have to deal with poor idle and drivability, bad gas mileage, and emission prob-

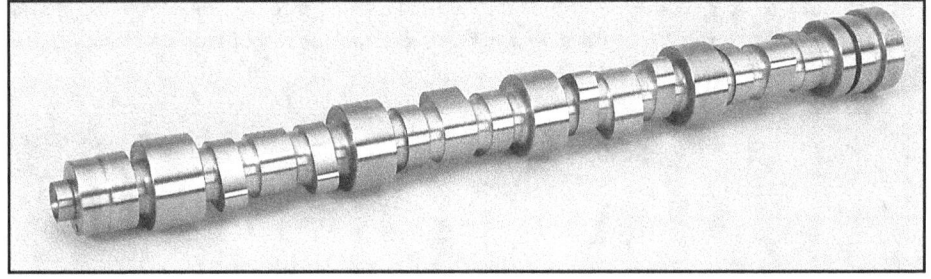

Most 4-cylinder imports don't respond well to cams and cam gears, but Neons do. The more modified your engine, the more you need a cam. Since ignition timing is unadjustable on a Neon, an adjustable cam gear can give you a little control over your torque curve.

lems. Also, the more radical the cam, the more money you need to spend to actually take advantage of that cam's potential. If your car is destined to spend most of its time on the street, you need to have some restraint when selecting cams. It all comes down to a compromise. If you want to go really fast, you have to spend a lot of cash. If you build a racecar, it will remind you every time the tach falls under 2,500 rpm.

All Neons, including the SRT-4, have 16 valves: two intake valves and two exhaust valves per cylinder. The main difference between the heads is that some have two camshafts, while others only have one. The DOHC setup devotes one cam to the intake valves, and one cam just for the exhaust valves. The SOHC design controls all the valves with a single cam, therefore requiring twice the number of lobes per cam (16) as its twin cam counterpart.

But before we go any further, we should probably spend a minute explaining cam specifications. For our purposes, the two main specs that Neon drivers need to understand are duration and valve lift. Let's take a look at an entry-level street cam manufactured by Crane for SOHC Neon owners. The 158-0010 cam has 196/200 degrees of duration. This figure tells us how long the intake/exhaust valves will remain open in terms of degrees of crankshaft rotation. This particular cam holds the intake valves open for 190 degrees of crankshaft rotation, and the exhaust valves open for 200 degrees, which is slightly longer than stock (192/198).

Increasing duration is helpful at high RPM, but not much at low RPM. The extra degrees of open valve time in high-RPM engines gives the air a little more time to get in or out of the cylinder. These cams are designed for periods when the pistons are frantically moving up and down the cylinder walls, and the rest of the engine is trying to keep up that pace. However, at lower RPM, increasing duration will either do nothing or actually decrease horsepower

AEM Tru-Time Cam Gears are great for engines with milled heads, forced induction, or that use aftermarket cams. Adjustable cam gears enable users to dial in their cam settings by advancing or retarding the cam profile in one-degree increments. It would be a good idea to set your cam gears on a dyno to see the results of your changes. (Photo courtesy of AEM)

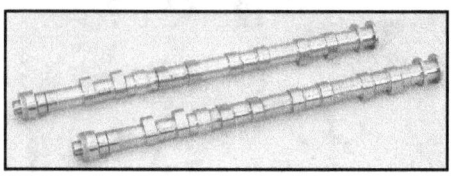

DOHC Neons can also net 10 or more horsepower by installing cams and cam gears. The amount of power you gain is usually directly proportional to what else you have done to your engine.

since the valves will be open at a less than ideal time to maximize power.

The 158-0010 cam also has .335/.315 inch, or 8.50/8.00 mm of intake/exhaust lift, which is a significant increase over the stock cam, which has .309/.275 inch lift. Lift is a little easier to visualize, and simply tells us how far the valves will open. The wider they open, the more air can get in or out of the cylinder. But with Neons and every other car on the planet, opening the valve past a certain point will not increase the flow. Once a valve is open to the point where the maximum amount can get in, there is no benefit from opening it further.

With our mild Crane street cam, the intake valves open 8.5 mm, the exhaust valves open 8 mm, and they stay open for 190 and 200 degrees (respectively) of crankshaft travel. As long as everything is timed properly and lift/duration is properly matched, whenever you move more air in and out of your cylinder, you will get more power. We recommend sticking with proven cam packages designed for your Neon by Crane, which can be purchased at aftermarket dealers such as Modern Performance and Howell Automotive.

Since Neons come with roller camshafts straight from the factory, lobe wear is practically nonexistent. This is a great luxury, as a racer friend of mine needs to replace his conventional flat-tappet cam frequently to get that last horsepower. If you choose to run a used cam, we recommend it be checked out before installation to be sure that it's within spec.

Any time you install a performance cam, you should also get performance valvesprings. Performance valvesprings are stiffer to help withstand the increased lift and duration your new cams will be delivering. Depending on your application, Crower, Crane, and Mopar Performance all sell valvespring sets. Crower and Crane also offer titanium spring retainers, which are probably overkill for most applications. There is a lot of talk about the Mopar Performance springs being unreliable. We personally have not seen this at Speednation, but we have been in contact with several people who have installed the Mopar springs and had them break.

If you plan on turbocharging your Neon, or you have an SRT-4, Crane turbo grind cams incorporate a feature that helps reduce turbo lag. These cams have more valve duration and lift on the intake profile. This helps to reduce the restriction on the intake side of the motor, allowing the turbo to come on sooner. The smaller exhaust profile keeps the effective RPM range from moving up too high.

SOHC Neons

The SOHC cylinder head is somewhat limited in camshaft selection. This is due to the fact that the head is cast as one piece, so the cam must slide through the bearing journals. Because of this, the maximum valve lift and duration is dictated by the cam bearing size.

For the SOHC, Crane Cams and Comp Cams both offer a variety of camshafts. Most cams are advertised based on the RPM range at which they make their power. Choose carefully, as using a cam that works best beyond your factory rev limiter would be an expensive mistake! Expect to pay between $250 to $300 for a camshaft for your SOHC Neon.

While the Neon is somewhat undercammed from the factory, you'll be disappointed with some of the hotter camshafts if your car lacks the basic modifications. Crane also makes bigger custom cams than the ones you'll find in the catalog; they require the use of lash caps due to the base circle being reduced to fit the cam into the head. Custom cams like this are rather impractical for most applications other than serious engine builders. The more horsepower you covet, the more you have to build an engine that is on the edge, and the more unreliable that engine becomes. A good racer is one that can finish the season without breaking.

Another way to get a little extra boost of power is for SOHC owners to use the slightly hotter 2001+ Magnum cam. On a stock motor, you'd likely find a few ponies; but you'd get more with other modifications. Another budget trick that will net a few horsepower for 1996–1999 cars is to use the cam from a '95. It's cheaper than an aftermarket piece, and it's available right at your local salvage yard.

The valvesprings from the 2001+ Magnum SOHC are an inexpensive alternative to other aftermarket springs for the SOHC. They seem to work well with all of the commercially available cam grinds. If you happen to have a 2001+ ACR or R/T, you already have these springs, so save your bucks. If you already have the Magnum cam, the Crane #14 cam is the only real upgrade.

DOHC Neons

The DOHC has a selection of cams available from both Crower and Crane Cams. As with the SOHC, careful attention to the RPM range is important, based on the type of driving you plan on doing. Expect to pay about $400 to $500 for a pair of cams for your DOHC. There seems to be a difference in how the cams are designed. Assuming comparable cam "stages" – with Cranes, you get a bit more duration, while with Crowers, you get a bit more lift. They seem to work equally well, and the difference could very well depend on your cylinder head, such as if it is ported or has oversized valves or not.

The DOHC head has removable caps, so the cam lobes can be much larger than with a SOHC. While this is not a huge deal if you're building a street car, it's a fairly important consideration if you plan to build an all-motor racecar.

With a 2.4-liter swap, you can generally run the higher stages that you might not consider for your street 2.0. The longer stroke and extra displacement helps to keep the idle quality and the torque quantity up, even with larger cams.

SRT-4

You may want to consider looking at a complete upgrade Stage 1, 2, or 3 package before you buy some cams for your SRT-4. Places like Modern Performance can hook you up. The packages will give you all you need to reach the horsepower level you want. Installing hotter cams in an SRT-4 is a waste of time because the extra power won't materialize unless you can rev past 6,500 rpm. But as you probably know, your stock PCM won't let you get that high.

Adjusting cam gears on a DOHC head is a little more complicated than with a SOHC, but the result could be to move your power band to optimize either low-end or high-end torque. As with ignition timing, you usually won't find gains at both ends.

Cam Timing

In the old days, cam timing was rarely adjusted, except by serious engine builders and racers. In general, cam timing is much more precise than ignition timing. For instance, you can move your distributor from one end of the spectrum to the other, and most engines will usually still run. On my 1976 rotary-powered Mazda Cosmo, the engine will still run even if you put the distributor in 180 degrees off. But move the cam just a few millimeters in any direction, and your engine will get real angry in a hurry. That's because the camshaft controls when the valves open and close, which determines when the air and fuel get in, and when exhaust gasses get out.

Although you are powerless to adjust the ignition timing on a Neon or SRT-4, you can adjust cam timing. You'll first need to spend $100 to $200 on an adjustable cam gear or gears and swap onto your engine. For our testing, we used a set of AEM cam gears. This is an easy change to make, as it usually isn't even necessary to remove the timing belt. But before rushing out to buy an adjustable gear(s), be aware that you will likely not gain any horsepower if you have a stock cylinder head, intake, injectors, and exhaust. The exception to that is if your cam timing is incorrect as it is. Your engine can only breathe as well as the air you are letting in and out. Fuel also needs to be considered as you strive for a balanced system. The best you can hope for by adding cam gears alone is to fine tune exactly where you want your power, by moving the powerband up or down. As with ignition timing, if you are able to dial in a few more horsepower at 5,000 rpm, you'll likely lose a couple horsepower at 3,000 rpm. However, if you have increased compression, aftermarket cams, or other serious modifications, then you will probably be able to find some additional power.

The reason for this is simple, and can best be illustrated by reviewing a less complicated, SOHC application. The cylinder head on our original '95 SOHC project car was shaved slightly (as are many competition heads), a condition that naturally retards cam timing. This is because the distance between the cam and the crank decreases due to material being removed from the bottom of the head. An adjustable cam timing gear will allow you to advance the cam back to the factory setting (or any other spec), to pick up any power you may have lost from it being slightly retarded.

When working with cam gears, always use a torque wrench! We've seen cases in which the cam gear was not torqued properly, the center bolt came loose, and BOOM – the valves crashed into the pistons. This happened to a motor one of our friends had spent over $1,500 on, and believe me, you don't want that to happen to you. It's also common to see the adjustment bolts get over-tightened, stripping the aluminum and ruining a nice $100+ gear.

The other thing to consider is that as precise as the factory is, your stock cam gears can be as much as a quarter of a degree off. If you can find your way to a chassis dyno, you'll be able to precisely

There are many ways to port a head. This head features a pattern machined into the combustion chambers (in the shape of a cloverleaf) that increases swirl and improves combustion by creating a more turbulent airflow.

dial in the exact torque curve that fits your needs, and you may find some improvement over the stock setting due to the fluctuations at the assembly plant.

For DOHC cars, you can adjust the intake and exhaust cams separately. Most Neon owners have found some benefit by slightly retarding the exhaust cam. At Speednation, we do this all day long. There is a single setting that works right every time. Get your car to a dyno, and make sure that you have a pen and paper handy. Start by moving the exhaust cam gear slightly toward the negative, one degree at a time, and then record what the dyno says. Trust me, you can't do this on a Dynojet machine as it is not sensitive enough. The Mustang Dyno is the one to look for. We get no money from Mustang to say this; in fact we had to pay for our dyno even though we were offered a Dynojet for free. Older dyno designs also can't account for all the extraneous variables present in the drivetrain (referred to as parasitic), so even when you make no changes between dyno runs, the graphs don't always match up. We can do a dozen pulls with our Mustang Dyno, and as long as no changes were made in between runs, when you compare the graphs only one line will be visible. All the other runs will be buried under the initial curve. This happens a lot with adjusting cam timing or making small changes to your fuel delivery system. If the dyno says that nothing changed, then whatever you just did obviously didn't work.

Anyway, don't be discouraged if you see no real change. Just keep retarding the exhaust cam one degree at a time until you start to lose torque, then go back to the setting that was best. You won't know that you have found the perfect setting until you go too far and see that you've lost power. You will likely find that the exhaust cam works best between two and four degrees retarded. Then move on to the intake cam and do the same thing, but start by advancing it. Let the dyno guide you. You'll probably end up back to zero, but every engine is different and it all depends on what else you have done. Just play around until you get the information you need – but don't go too far too fast.

Cylinder Heads

When it comes to Neon cylinder heads, there is good news and bad news. The bad news is that unlike many of the import cars on the market, Neon heads are a little rough around the edges. The castings aren't perfect, the edges aren't smooth, and the ports don't match as well as on a Honda motor (some Honda motors are even worked over from the factory). The good news, however, is that there is a lot of room for improvement. There isn't much those import guys can do when it comes to their heads. It isn't worth the money spent for the small gains they receive. But with a Neon head, you get what you pay for. Remember, Neons were designed as affordable grocery getters. If you already have the basic intake/header/exhaust/PCM mods, you can get in the neighborhood of 15 hp and 9 ft-lbs of torque with some decent headwork on a DOHC motor.

One of the most popular head builders in the Neon community is Nick Riley of Nrgy Heads in Gilbert, Arizona (623) 204-9717. He comes highly recommended by subscribers of the Neons.org forum. His website (www.nrgyheads.com) also explains things in much more detail than we are able to do here. Howell Automotive also offers several stages

If you decide to do some head work, you may as well dress up your valve cover. You can get one to match the color of your SRT-4. (Photo courtesy Howell Automotive)

of head porting and polishing. Of course, I still need to repeat that if all you do to your car is to get the head done, you won't get that much of a gain. It's all about balance. A ported and polished head will flow much better, so you'll need more air and fuel going through the head in order to get the best possible results.

You could also try porting your head yourself, but companies like Nrgy and Howell Automotive have done a lot of research, so they have a pretty good idea of what works and what doesn't. We recommend that you have them smooth the casting, blend the valve seats, and match all the ports. For some extra cash, they'll do a full race port, which includes reshaping the ports and combustion chambers to further maximize power. For even more flow, you can also get a 3-angle valve job, which will also ensure your valves seal perfectly with the seats. Most places that port heads will require a core (your stock head), or they will use one of theirs for an extra fee.

For around $1,500, Howell will also sell you a full CNC-ported Indy cylinder head with Crane valvesprings and Indy oversize stainless-steel valves already installed. Just bolt it on and go – as long as you have all the other mods to

CHAPTER 9

BODY AND INTERIOR MODIFICATIONS

We all spend a great deal of time in our cars. Whether you're driving to work, or just cruising around, it's important to be comfortable in the cockpit. No matter how nice your car looks on the outside, you can't admire it when you're behind the wheel.

From a racer's point of view, a dent in the side of the car is a battle scar that tells a story of how you overcame adversity to eventually win the race against the non-Neon-driving competitors. Many racers don't care as much how their car looks from the outside, but the interior is another thing. Just like a fighter pilot, the racecar driver relies on gauges to help determine how the car is running and the proper driving position to be comfortable. Road racers who remain behind the wheel lap after lap will tell you how much of a workout it is. The constant g-forces wear down even the best athlete. Even Solo I, II, and drag racing can take a lot out of you. It's important that your cockpit is comfortable, and driving position is essential to success. If you aren't in the proper position to turn the wheel and perform multiple upshifts and downshifts or heel/toe braking, you probably won't be on the podium at the end of the day.

Most of us have spent a great deal of time and money on performance enhancements and engine modifications. Even though Neons and SRT-4s have

At Speednation, we're racers and tuners and mainly interested in functional modifications, but we can still appreciate a cool-looking Neon. By the time their owners are finished, some Neons don't even look like Neons anymore.

well-equipped dashboards, we often need more information about how our car is performing than what the factory has provided. Let's face it – the majority of people who buy Neons are not gear heads. We've all heard the story about the driver who heard a funny noise coming from the engine compartment and dealt with it by turning the stereo up louder. In any event, the standard warning lights and gauges on Neons are not adequate to meet the needs of most of us hop-up types. Depending on how you use your car, there's certain information you need to know.

Gauges

Neons are missing one critical gauge that helps avoid engine damage: the oil pressure gauge. Those of you who have driven other people's cars that are simi-

High-Performance Dodge Neon Builder's Handbook 75

Chapter 9

An oil-pressure gauge is a must-have for modified engines.

The owner of this SRT-4 has added some essential gauges. From left to right: a boost gauge, a wide-band air/fuel ratio gauge, and a shift light. (Photo courtesy Chris Malluege)

lar to yours have surely noticed that all temperature gauges are not created equal. Some register a normal operating temperature by moving the indicator halfway between cold and danger. While others, even though they are the same make, model, and year, record "normal" as being about one quarter of the way to the top of the scale.

And then there's the tach. Who did they have in mind when they designed the factory tach? Certainly not us gear heads. Even the larger aftermarket tachs are only useful if you can sneak a look at them before you shift. Drag racers, Solo I racers, and road racers don't always have time to watch the tach, which is why the shift light is one of the best inventions to date. When racing in time trials or at the drag strip, there is no room for error. If you make even the slightest mistake that results in lost time, that run is ruined. I prefer to use a shift light that is so bright,

I can still see it even if my eyes are closed. Shift lights are also very beneficial to road racers, but they spend so much time behind the wheel, they can probably tell you exactly what tone corresponds to 6,500 rpm. That is, if they can hear the engine. Even unmuffled Neons are quiet compared to a Mazda RX-7 with a straight pipe. Not only can you not hear your own engine when passing an unmuffled rotary car, you can barely even think. From a distance, it's a beautiful sound, but up close, it can make your ears bleed. For those occasions, a shift light becomes invaluable. In my last race, I was trying to pass a first-generation RX-7. I never had to look at my tach more in my life (no shift light, unfortunately). But with all the fuel this RX-7 was spilling out of its fill nozzle onto the road in front of me, I needed to concentrate completely on the track to keep from slipping on the mess. I didn't get to check my tach as much as I would have liked until the RX-7 was in my rearview mirror.

If you've added a turbo, you'll require additional gauges, such as a boost gauge. With a boost gauge, you'll be able to tell if your engine is making too much, or too little boost. It's also imperative that you install an exhaust temperature gauge. Since turbocharged

The SRT-4 gauge array is both functional and informative. All turbo engines should have a boost gauge, and the SRT-4 comes with one from the factory (right). Besides showing you how much boost you're making, boost gauges also show you the boost you don't have (when something breaks!).

High-Performance Dodge Neon Builder's Handbook

Body and Interior Modifications

Investing in an aftermarket tach isn't necessary unless you're racing your Neon. If you are racing, we recommend getting a tach that also has a shift light indicator. The shift light will help you keep your eyes on the road, not on the tach.

If your Neon racecar doesn't have the gauges you need, adding them is no big problem. You just have to put them somewhere you can see them. This Neon has gauges on the A-pillar, the steering column, and where the stereo used to be.

cars use exhaust gasses to power the turbo unit, exhaust temperature is a very important thing to know, especially during cool down (before you shut off your engine). As you know, coolant stops flowing through an engine once the engine is shut down. Shutting off a turbocharged engine before it has properly cooled can damage the turbo. There are systems, such as a turbo timer unit, that will continue to run your engine (even after you turn off the key) until proper cooling has been achieved. Knowing your exhaust gas temperature is also useful when tuning the air/fuel ratio, as too high or too low of an exhaust gas temperature indicates that the engine is running too rich or too lean, respectively.

Cockpit Comforts

Aftermarket seats come in all shapes and sizes, depending on the purpose of your vehicle. You can even buy brand-name racing seats mounted on casters for your office. They make great gifts for weekend racers who experience withdrawal and have a hard time making it through the work week. Neons don't have the greatest seats for racing, since they weren't designed to be pocket rockets. If you plan on doing any racing, and competition rules permit, you may want to consider installing an aftermarket driver's seat. Even the strict Showroom Stock SCCA road racing class allows for this modification. You can't run an effective race if your driving position changes through each turn because your butt is sliding around. Racing seats also weigh less than a stock seat. If the seat you plan to buy is not 50 percent lighter than your stock seat, it's not a racing seat. Check with the race seat manufacturer to find out the exact weight of a seat before ordering it. Don't assume that a "racing" seat is lighter than the factory unit. Racing seats range from about 10 pounds to as much as 40 pounds, depending on features (reclining, head rests, etc.). As you saw in the corner weighting section, the most weight you'll ever put in your car is your body, so anything you can do to offset the weight in that area will be beneficial.

Some aftermarket seats will bolt right on to your present rails, but others will require some fabrication. Another problem that drivers run into is that some aftermarket seats will reduce headroom. Many Neon owners who have limited headroom with their factory seats purchase an aftermarket seat to increase the distance between their head and the headliner. As far as myself, my goal is to get as low as possible in my racing seat. I want as much distance between my noggin and the top of the roll bar. The day I put my Neon upside down, I will really appreciate that planning. Of course, even though I'm over six feet tall, I look like a little kid when I'm behind the wheel. Be careful not to put your seat too low,

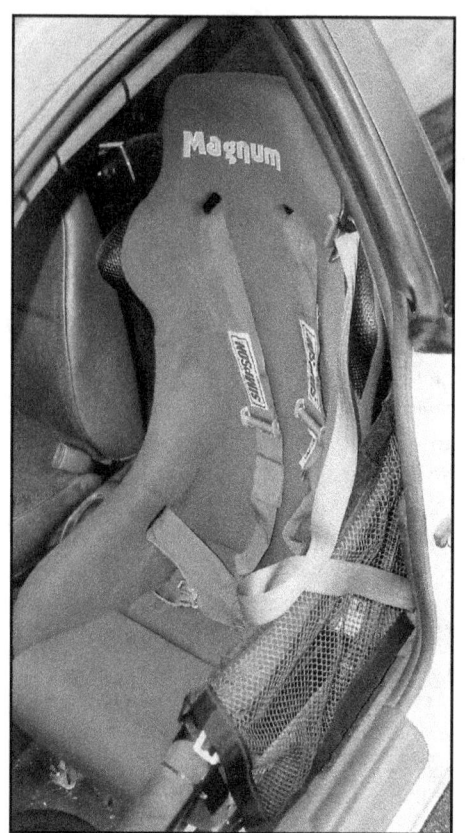

All interiors are designed to serve a purpose. Racecar drivers need a seat that keeps them firmly in place despite the g-forces. A harness, roll cage, and window net are designed to keep the driver inside the vehicle in the event of a mishap.

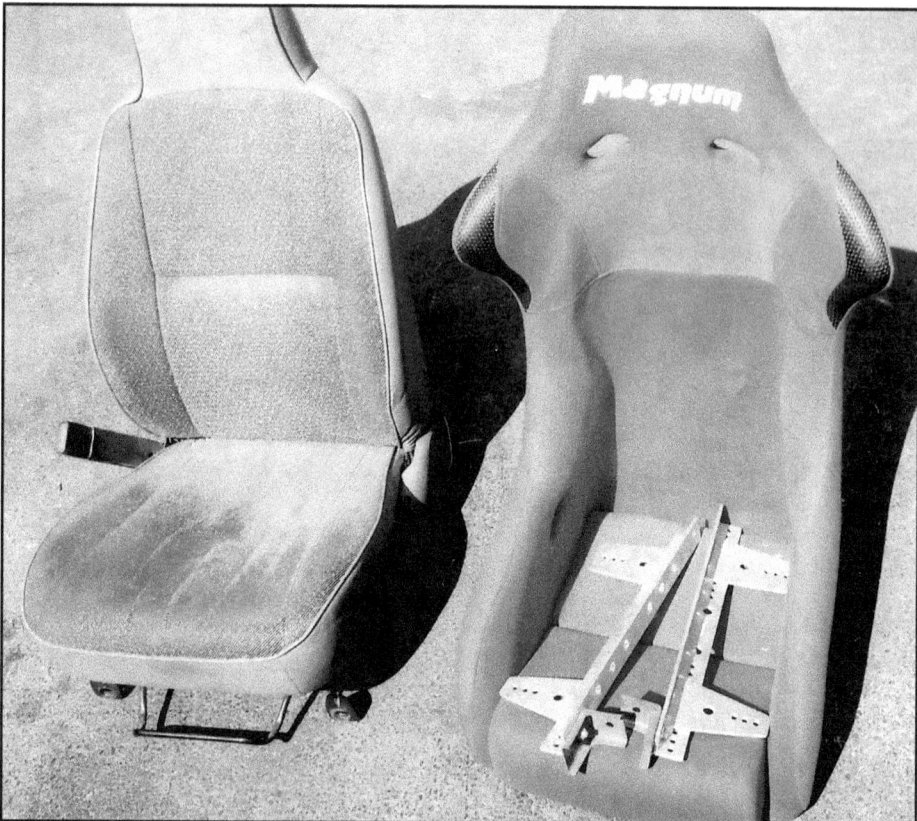

There is a huge difference between a stock first-gen Neon seat and a racing seat. Rigidity, side-to-side stability, and seating position are all improved. Racing seats also lower the center of gravity and weigh much less than stock.

however. For autocrossing, the seat in my SSC Neon is too low, but it doesn't keep me from winning. For hillclimbing, since you're always looking up anyway, a lower seat is great. The center of gravity is also lower.

Seats are a personal choice, just like wheels. That's why it's important to sit in a seat before purchasing it. Don't assume that since a seat fits in your friend's Neon that it'll fit in yours. They may have spent the entire weekend getting it to fit properly, and just aren't telling you.

Weight Reduction

Obviously, the lighter your Neon, the faster it can go, the better it can handle, and the quicker it can stop. Removing weight from your car's interior can be a daunting task, but usually it's a lot of fun. The best thing about it is the cost

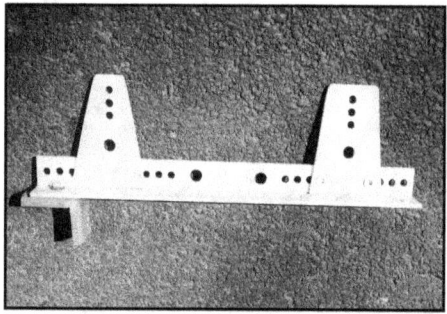

Aluminum seat brackets for your racing seat will save a great deal of weight. Since the seat can't be adjusted on the go, you need to establish the proper seating position before you do the final installation. If you're on a budget, you can make your own brackets out of angle iron. Having a lower seat moves your head even further away from the roof and roll cage, which could come in handy in the event of a rollover.

– it's free (except for a few cuts and scrapes, and your time). You must plan things out before you start. Don't even think of removing or cutting something before you see if competition rules per-

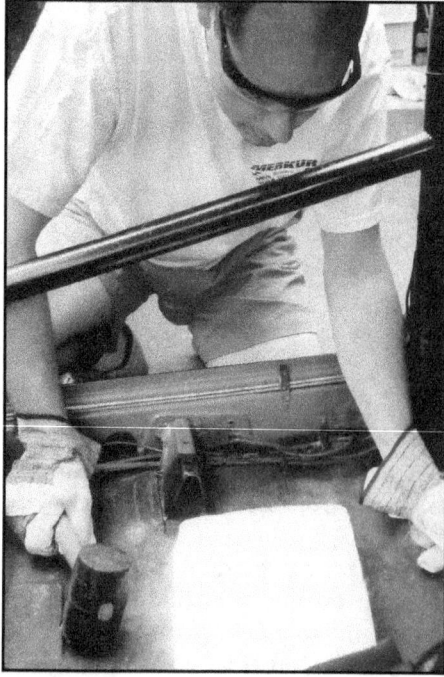

Saving weight is like adding horsepower. Look for weight reduction everywhere you can. We routinely use dry ice to remove interior insulation on the floorboards. Be careful!

Body and Interior Modifications

If you are serious about speed, then get into the habit of weighing everything. Don't put anything on your car unless it's a safety requirement or it makes you faster. (Photo courtesy Michael Carpenter)

For tricked-out street Neons, there are other considerations for interior space. It's all up to individual taste. (Top photo courtesy Howell Automotive)

mit it. If the rule book doesn't say you can do it, then you can't. You'll be protested and lose your podium finish, and "the rule book never specifically said that I couldn't do this," is not a good excuse.

The weight you can get out of your Neon's interior can really add up. A few pounds here and there end up equaling 100 pounds before you know it. One of our favorite things to do is to take out all the seats and carpeting to expose the bare floor, and then get some dry ice, and have at it. Don't even try to chip away the insulation material sprayed on the floor of the car without the dry ice. It will take forever. You'll need at least 10 pounds of dry ice, a pair of work gloves, and safety goggles. Don't ever touch the ice with your bare skin, and if you get any in your eyes, well, never mind. I don't want to talk about it. Make sure that the floor is as clean as you can make it, and then work on one section at a time. Cut off a chunk of ice and smash it up into little pieces right on the area you want to strip. Wait a few minutes (you can even add a little water, but be careful), and then smack the floor with a rubber hammer. Again, be careful, and don't let any ice get into your ears. I don't want to talk about that either. You

A smaller-diameter aftermarket steering wheel allows you to make quicker turns with less hand movement. Installation is not difficult. You could use a special steering wheel puller tool, or just get a buddy to pull it off for you. If it's your car, you probably won't be able to pull it by hand yourself. You need to find someone who won't care, who'll just yank the crap out of your stock wheel until it comes off.

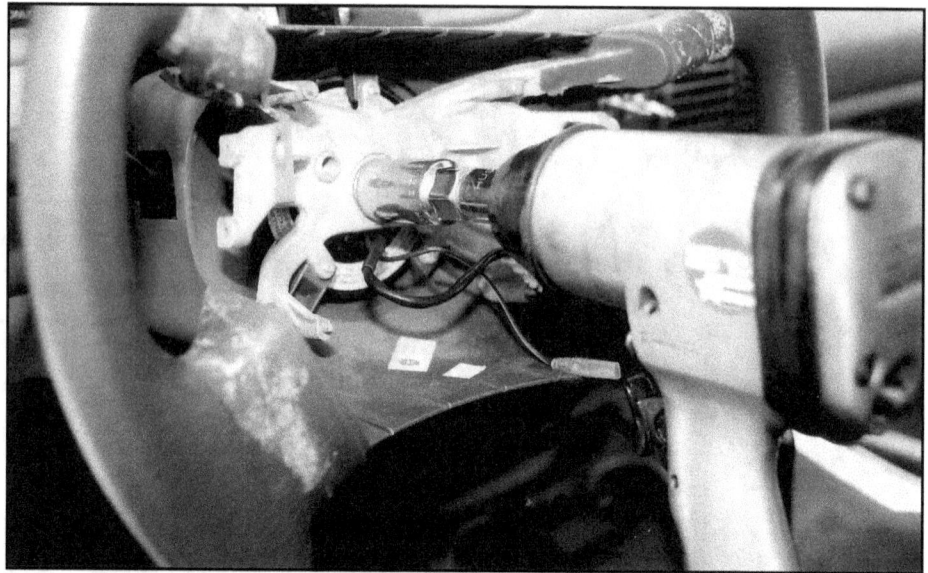

may need to help it along a little with a scraper, but you won't believe what happens when that hammer hits the floor! We ended up getting over 30 pounds of insulation material out of our Neon.

Cutting out door panels will also get lots of weight out of your car. Depending on how much you cut, you can save 40 pounds per door by also removing the glass and cranking mechanism. The blower/heater is also a small weight savings, but a lot of work. Each time you take out a piece and weigh it, it's disappointing, but at the end of the day when you add up the totals, it'll surprise you. We recommend using a bathroom scale and keeping a log as to what each part weighs. The first 100 pounds is relatively easy, but then it gets very hard and you start thinking about drilling holes, which isn't recommended due to structural integrity. The next 50 pounds can be expensive and time consuming. Let's see, if I get those $300 lightweight racing wheels, that will be another four pounds, times four – that's 16 more pounds! Quick, how much does this shift knob weigh?

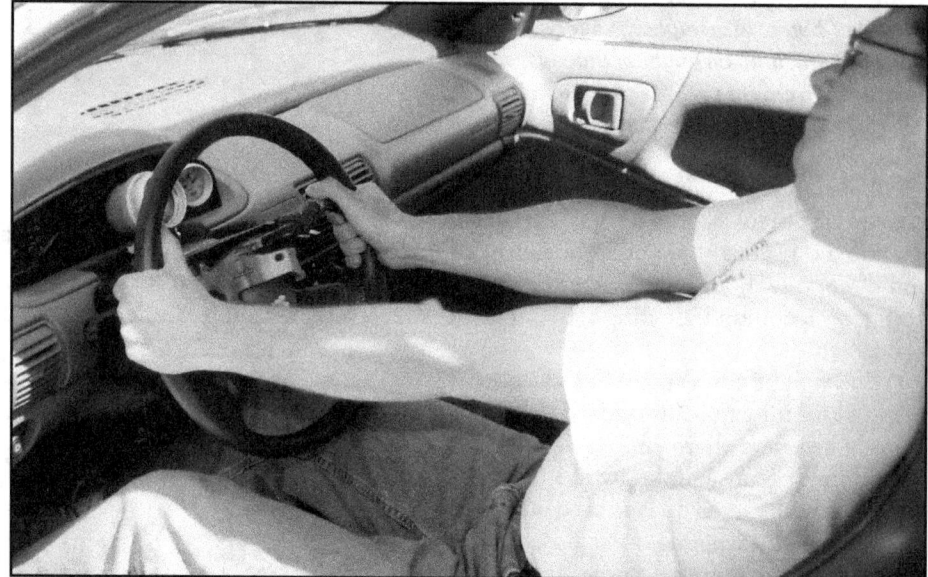

Steering Wheels

Though they're very important to many racers, an aftermarket steering wheel is mostly a luxury item. Since Neons are equipped with air bags, it doesn't make sense to replace the steering wheel if you're driving your car on the street. But for racing, it may not be an option. For SCCA road racing, you have no choice but to dump your airbag for obvious reasons. Many rulebooks allow you to use a racing wheel. Prices range from under $75 (Grant GT-type wheels) to more expensive items, like those from Sparco or Momo. Racers

Body and Interior Modifications

who need to turn the steering wheel while racing can benefit from a steering wheel that isn't a perfect circle. The flat spots help the driver determine which way is up. Autocrossers find that a smaller-diameter wheel makes it easier to dart in and out of the pylons. If you do plan on competing some day, check with the rules first to see if it's legal to replace your factory wheel. If you buy from a racing catalog, such as through Racer Wholesale, they'll tell you exactly what models will fit your Neon. But if you want to get a cheap wheel through your local parts store, then there won't be a listing for your Neon due to the air bag situation. You'll need to get a hub adaptor kit to make it fit. It seems that the Chevy S-10 kit works for Neons. When we installed ours, we had to put the hub on backwards, with the side that's designed to face the dash facing up toward the driver's seat. Once we figured that out, most everything else fit just fine.

Last but not least, high-power stereos, shift knobs, and drilled aluminum pedals can really personalize your vehicle, but all fall into the category of fun, nonessential items. Of all the fun interior modifications we've seen over the years, none can hold a candle to the car owners who've installed their own onboard Sony PlayStation. Think about it. What better place to play Gran Turismo than from the cockpit of your (parked) Neon?

Exterior Modifications

Let's get one thing out of the way right up front. Unless you are competing at speeds of over 100 mph, a body kit or rear wing is not considered a performance improvement. Wings and body kits add weight to a car, and most racecar drivers would rather go faster than throw a boat anchor in the back seat. But if your goals don't include faster speed and improved handling, then performing exterior body modifications can make a real statement. Is it vain to want a good-looking car? Maybe so, but people often judge you based on how your car looks. Have you ever had anyone write "wash me" on your car by scraping off dirt?

Installing a roll cage is a two-person operation. One person needs to hold the bolt in place while the other person torques down the nut. Always install your cage so that the bolt heads are on the bottom of the car. This gives you more ground clearance. A cage adds 80 to 90 pounds to your Neon, but it also adds some structural rigidity.

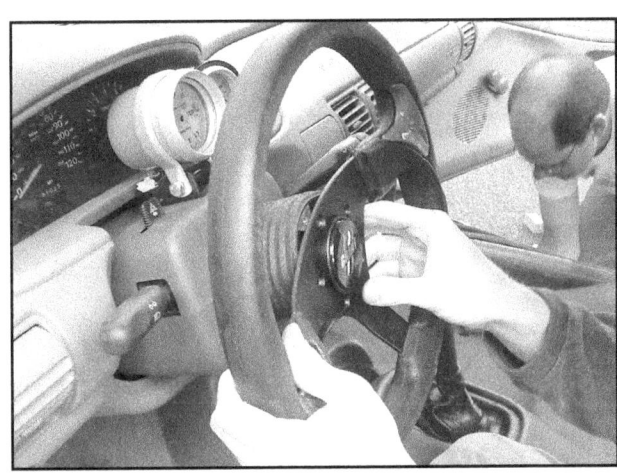

Since most aftermarket wheels are not designed for cars that came with air bags, you'll have to improvise. We used the hub adapter for a Chevy S-10.

Of course, you can simply remove your air bag and retain the original wheel, if you can stand to look at it. Apparently it didn't bother Mark Daddio, as this is what the cockpit of our Turbo Neon looked like when we got it.

Chapter 9

Tim Kish's R/T is one nice-looking ride. With nitrous on tap, it's also pretty fast. There are many body kits on the market. Just remember – you get what you pay for in both fit and finish.

Wings come in all shapes and sizes, but they all add weight to your car. They're an appearance-only item, since they aren't functional at regular speeds (most aren't even functional at top speed).

to do with speed and handling. Wings and air dams may make a car look cool, but unless you're racing at very high speeds, the downforce created by these wings will make little difference in your car's performance and will in fact make it slower.

There seem to be two basic types of automobile owners: Those concerned with form first and function second; and those who feel that function should be the priority, and form comes in a very distant second. Okay, I'll admit it. I have a bias toward function, but deep down inside I want to have a clean, cool-looking car. But I take the opposite approach with my racecars; I never even wash them. I want to have the ugliest car on the track that runs the fastest times. The reason for this is clear – I'm lazy. It takes a lot of time and energy to keep your car clean. If you hit a tire wall, it'll hurt all the more if you just added a new coat of paint or wax.

Back when I started racing, we didn't have a lot of choices. Function was the priority because the go-fast parts were usually homemade and not very pretty. Due to the recent interest in sport compact performance, manufacturers are now building functional parts that will also enhance the good looks of your Neon. For the enthusiast who wants their car to be unique and also reflect their radical personality, this is the section for you.

Body Kits

There are many aftermarket body kits available for Neons, and it seems that new kits are turning up every week. But be careful, because quality varies. Often you have to spend big bucks just to install a body kit since most don't line up correctly. Watching a "tuner" TV show recently, I was shocked to see a body shop installing a Silvia Veilside brand body kit on a US version Nissan 240SX. The kit was from a reputable manufacturer, but the body guy did not seem to be phased as to the amount of modification he had to do just to get it to fit: shaving the door joints, installing supports under the panels, and seriously cutting and patching nearly every fit

How about when you see a car you wish you had, but there's a dent on the fender, and you say to yourself: "I'd fix that immediately." And finally, have you ever seen a nicely detailed older car, even one that you have no interest in, but you notice it because the owner has taken a lot of time to restore it to original condition? Then you find yourself thinking: "I respect a guy who takes good care of his car." Let's face it, we judge people based on how their car looks.

On the other hand, if racing is your thing, the look of your car has nothing

The rear wing on an SRT-4 is stylish, and it's at least partially functional since it was designed by Chrysler engineers especially for this particular application.

Of course, sometimes less is more. This SRT-4 looks very smooth with its wing removed. Hey – it's lighter too. (Photo courtesy Chris Malluege)

your carbon hood shows up at the front door. It looks so great when you take it out of the box, but fit tends to vary greatly, and the hinges can also be a pain. Then just try to get it to stay shut. But with some perseverance and help from a friend or two (one to hold you back from the car while the other grabs the hammer from out of your hand), you will get through it.

Another problem many people have faced is when the new exhaust system they purchased won't fit without banging against their rear sway bar, or worse yet, won't fit through their rear ground effect. Always ask a lot of questions before you buy a body kit, or an exhaust, for that matter.

Functional Body Modifications

The only time a racecar driver will add anything to his or her car is if it performs some valuable function, or if it saves weight. Racecars can often reach speeds high enough to where lift becomes a factor, causing your car to lose traction, resulting in a decline in handling, or worse. This is the only time that air dams will actually perform a function.

Formula cars sometimes use large wings that have a high degree of negative lift, so the car is literally pushed down on the pavement, maximizing friction across the tire patch. Lighter open-wheeled formula cars with big wings are, therefore, able to generate downforce at significantly lower speeds than street cars. My favorite example of this occurred one day when I had finished my runs up the Duryea hillclimb and hiked down the trail to watch some of my friends navigate through the most famous turn on the hill. It's a high-speed kink that separates the men from the boys (also, the women from the girls). To do it correctly, you need to stay floored at 100+ mph around a left-hand turn. The trick is that the mountain is on your left, so your view of the turn's exit is obscured. It took me several years to get up the courage to drive it correctly. As expected, only a handful of competitors made

point. Then, after many hours of work, he declared: "overall, the kit seemed to fit rather well." If that kit fit well, then I would hate to see how much time you would have to spend on a poor-fitting kit. You may save money up front when buying a lower-priced body part, but you'll spend more time and money getting it to fit. You nearly always get what you pay for when it comes to aftermarket body components.

There are chin spoilers, carbon fiber hoods, rear spoilers, fender flares, and more. Wings West and Xenon are reputable companies that will support their products, but there will always be some fabrication needed. One of the biggest headaches you may experience is the day

Chapter 9

Hoods come in all shapes and sizes. Some are designed to just look good, while others serve a purpose, such as having an air intake or cutting major weight. Whatever hood you choose, at least try to find one that weighs less than the one you have.

What would you do if you had a couple of junk Neons sitting in your yard, some extra time on your hands, and needed a good way to promote your Neon performance business? I'm guessing the long wheelbase smooths out the ride on the highway, but doesn't help any in the twisties. (Photo courtesy Howell Automotive)

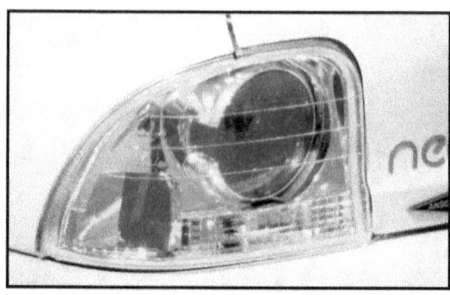

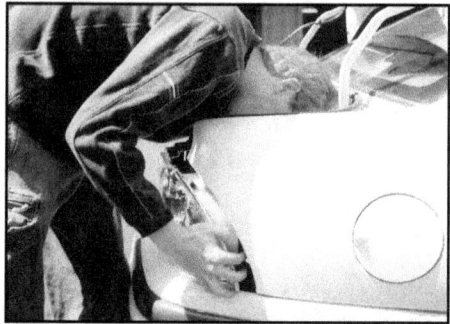

Clear taillights are all the rage, and can really change the look of your Neon or SRT-4. If you're going for a stealth look, just keep your OEM lights. It may look like Michael Carpenter is getting sick in the trunk, but he's actually replacing the clear lights with OEM lights. We sold the clear taillights on eBay for $75.

it though the turn without letting off the gas or using the brake.

An SCCA Solo I hillclimber's motto is: You lift – you lose. One of the cars that blasted through that turn at full speed was driven by Barry Griffith, who competes in Formula Continental. When I saw him in the pits at the end of the race, I told him that he was the man. What he said back to me will forever stick in my mind, and serves as a serious example of downforce technology. Barry explained that he never used to go through that turn at full speed, but once he mustered up the nerve, he realized that the faster he went, the better the car stuck to the ground. So whenever he's having trouble negotiating a turn, he just pushes the throttle to the floor. That concept still blows my mind.

In the early 1990s, there was a movement in the autocross world in which big wings were coupled with "sucker" devices that actually worked like a vacuum cleaner to literally suck the car down to the pavement. One such sucker car even won the *Road & Track* skid-pad g-force contest several years ago. These systems, when they failed, would cause a car to instantly lose traction, making it difficult to control. The sucker cars were outlawed a few years later.

Just as formula cars benefit from negative-lift technology, so do Neons, especially when traveling at high speeds. A front-end air dam or spoiler will serve to keep air from getting under the car, thus defeating lift. Most racing sedan bodies utilize air dams that nearly scrape the ground and completely surround the car in order to keep air from getting underneath, even when cornering. There are functional spoilers available for Neons, but don't get them from a shop that specializes in form. Refer to a trusted name in racing design, or else make it yourself.

CHAPTER 10

TURBOCHARGING, SUPERCHARGING, AND NITROUS

If you feel intimidated by the technical aspects of forced induction, you're not alone. I've tried to read technical articles and books, but it seems that the more I read, the more I realize how much I don't know. But, if you keep in mind that your Neon's engine is just a fancy air pump, you're on your way to understanding how turbos and superchargers work.

In a standard intake system, air enters (or is drawn into) the engine through the intake manifold. If there's a cold-air or ram-air intake in place, the air entering the intake manifold will be cooler and have less turbulence. The effect is usually slightly increased horsepower. A forced-induction system takes this theory a lot further. Simply stated, turbocharging and supercharging are just more effective ways of getting air into the intake manifold.

So, what's the big deal about forced induction? Well, with a naturally aspirated engine, you rely on atmospheric pressure to fill your cylinders with air. With forced induction, the air is compressed and crammed into the combustion chambers at a higher rate than the atmosphere would force it in. This is measured in psi, usually called boost. In unscientific terms, you're able to fit more air in

Turbo systems are very popular additions to normally aspirated Neons. Various configurations are available, and you can use an air-to-water intercooler (shown) or an air-to-air unit (like the one that comes on the SRT-4).

the cylinder (actually it's just more dense). When you add extra fuel to go with the extra air, you get extra power.

Turbocharging

So how does a turbocharger go about compressing air? In a turbocharged engine, the turbocharger is positioned in the exhaust, just after the header or exhaust manifold. As the exhaust gasses are forced out of the engine, the hot gasses are pushed through the turbocharger. The gasses spin the turbine wheel before flowing out through the exhaust. The turbine wheel is connected

High-Performance Dodge Neon Builder's Handbook

Mounting a wastegate can be a bit of a challenge. You have to make sure that it's adjusted properly so that the valve is fully closed (no leakage) when the system is under boost.

A blow-off or pop-off valve makes a distinctive noise during upshifts, which is why so many turbo enthusiasts like them. But they also serve a valuable purpose: Keeping the boost up during shifts.

to a compressor wheel, so when the turbine wheel spins, so does the compressor wheel. The spinning compressor wheel forces the air into the intake, compressing it and building boost.

The size of the turbo and the speed at which the turbo spins work together to determine how much boost is made. Are you already worrying about how much boost is too much? Well, that depends on your engine. The more boost, the more horsepower – period. To what point? The point where your engine blows up. The more your engine can take, the higher the horsepower.

Since you don't want your engine to blow up, you have to somehow control how much boost is made. This is where the wastegate comes in. A wastegate is a relatively simple device that bypasses some exhaust flow around the turbine section of the turbocharger to limit boost. Under normal conditions, the wastegate is held shut by a spring inside the unit. It controls the amount of boost your turbo develops by opening when the turbo spools up and builds a certain amount of boost, thereby releasing the extra pressure. The basic turbos that you'll find in most kits have the wastegate built into the exhaust housing. On more advanced setups that require more exhaust to be bypassed, the wastegate is mounted to the exhaust manifold or header separate from the turbo.

Don't confuse a wastegate with a blow-off valve. When your engine is at full boost, you have a lot of compressed air traveling through the throttle body. When you shift gears or otherwise let off the gas, the throttle body snaps closed, and all that air will have no place to go. If there were no way of relieving this pressure, it would either back up in the system and damage the turbo, or blow out through the weakest link in the turbo system (hoses). The blow-off valve is located in the intercooler piping between the intercooler and the throttle body. Having a blow-off valve takes pressure off of the turbine wheel, allowing it to keep spinning as you shift through the gears, reducing turbo lag.

You can also control the amount of boost with a boost controller. By installing a boost controller, you can increase boost pressure to the threshold of your turbo's capacity, or decrease it to the threshold of your wallet. A blown engine will cost a lot of cash, so I let my wallet dictate how I set the boost controller. This is where a boost gauge comes in handy. You may have set your controller at 10 psi, but a boost gauge can tell you if you're getting more (or less) than you expect. Of course, an SRT-4 already has a gauge. Most boost controllers are fairly accurate, but it's nice to be able to check. Mechanical boost controllers are more affordable, but electronic boost controllers are easier to deal with.

Turbocharging, Supercharging, and Nitrous

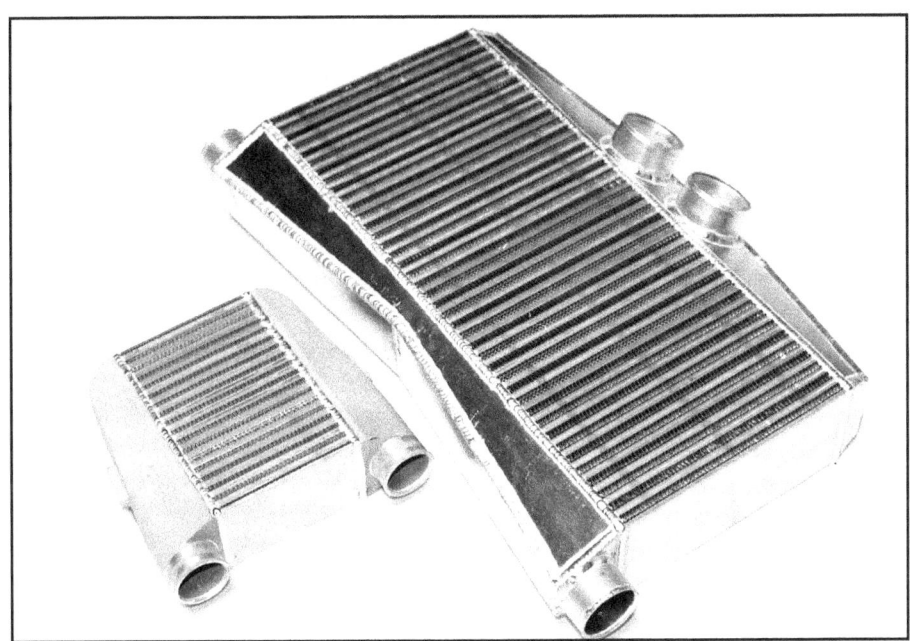

The most popular intercoolers are air-to-air units. Intercoolers cool the hot, compressed air before it enters the intake manifold. These Spearco units from Turbonetics can be ordered specifically for your application.

The SRT-4 comes from the factory with a front-mounted air-to-air intercooler. One of the performance upgrades available from Mopar Performance is a water sprayer that keeps the intercooler cool.

If you have added a turbo to your Neon, be aware of the heat buildup in your turbocharger. If you're used to shutting your car off right after your autocross or quarter-mile run, then you need to develop a new routine. The exhaust gasses used to power your turbo will heat it up, and the longer you remain under boost, the hotter it will get. When you're driving, the turbo will cool down quickly when you get off the throttle, but when you just shut off the engine, there's no water or oil flowing through it to cool it down. If you fail to cool the turbo before you shut off the engine, you'll likely do some serious damage. You could buy a turbo timer unit, which automatically keeps your car running for a few minutes until your turbo is cool, or save the cash and get into the habit of doing a cool-down lap or waiting a few minutes before turning your key off.

Dense Air – Good; Heat – Bad

The laws of physics dictate that as air is compressed, heat is generated and the density of the air is decreased. A heated incoming air charge is not really what you want in your engine. Increased temperature of the incoming charge means less power. A general rule is that an 11-percent increase in air temperature equals a one-percent power loss. A hotter intake charge also increases the chance of unwanted detonation. Detonation occurs when the mixture of fuel and air ignites before the plug fires. Depending on the frequency and severity of detonation in your engine, an expensive rebuild may be in order.

Intercoolers are the answer to high incoming air temperatures. Intercoolers are really nothing more than glorified radiators, but instead of cooling your water, they cool the incoming air charge. Intercoolers go in between your turbocharger and your throttle body. There are two basic types of intercoolers: air-to-air and water-to-air. To maximize your power output, you want to chill the incoming air as much as possible. Air-to-air intercoolers can operate at up to 80 percent efficiency, whereas air-to-water intercoolers can easily operate at this level or higher. Air-to-water intercoolers are a little more complex than the air-to-air type, due to the need to add a pump and a tank to circulate the liquid through the system, but the payoff comes in more potential power from the engine. Inserting an intercooler between the turbo and the throttle body does cause a restriction for the intake airflow, but this is more than offset by the increased density of the cooler intake charge.

Autocrossers or drag racers can get by with air-to-water intercoolers because they only have to supply ice water to the intercooler for one to two minutes. After that, all of the ice melts and there's nothing but hot water to circulate

High-Performance Dodge Neon Builder's Handbook

Chapter 10

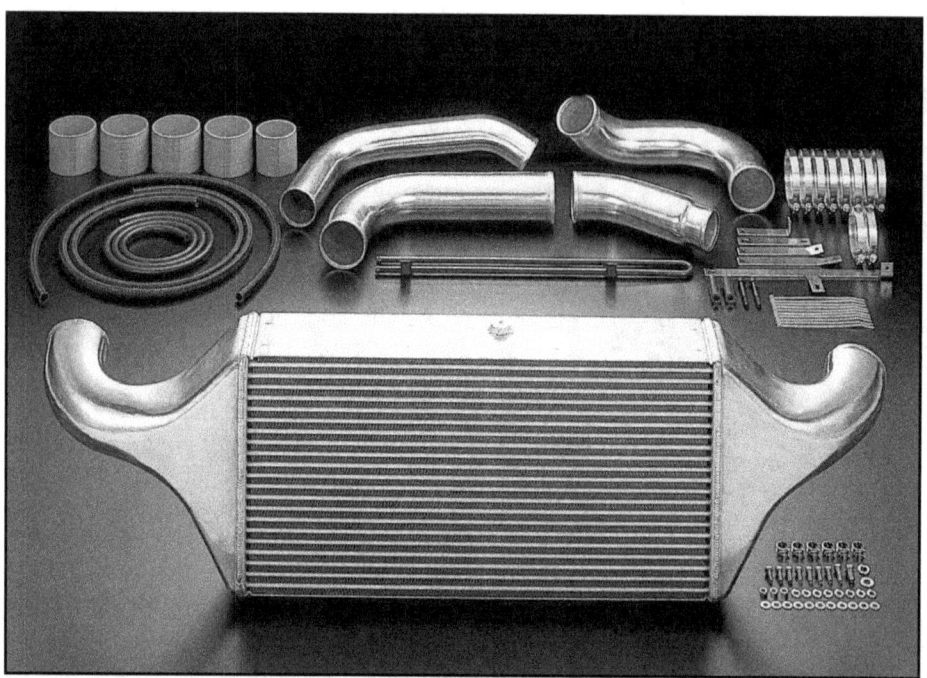

HKS has been in the intercooler and turbo business for years, and an SRT-4 application is promised in the near future. A thicker intercooler core, like the one shown, does a better job of cooling the intake charge.

If you are using an air-to-water intercooler, it helps to install a cool can somewhere. The trunk seems to be a good choice – it's away from the heat of the engine so the cold ice water will last longer.

through the system. Obviously, efficiency is decreased.

PCM and Fuel Injection

Unlike the SRT-4, regular Neon PCMs were never designed to compensate for increased airflow provided by a turbo, so you'll have to figure out a way to provide increased fuel delivery under boost. The incoming air must be properly mixed with a precise amount of fuel to ensure maximum horsepower and torque, and to keep your engine from running lean and melting pistons. Depending on the amount of boost you plan to run, an additional computer can be piggy-backed onto the stock unit, or a stand-alone aftermarket unit can be used in place of the existing factory computer. By tuning the fuel pressure with an adjustable-rate fuel pressure regulator that adds a certain amount of fuel pressure per pound of boost, you can generally get a safe air/fuel mixture up to about 250 hp. The turbo kits available from Hahn Racecraft and Chill Factory tune in extra fuel in this manner.

Another issue with the Neon's PCM is that the MAP (manifold absolute pressure) sensor doesn't recognize boost. When pressure in the manifold goes positive, the PCM essentially will freak out for a moment. You can eliminate this problem by preventing the MAP sensor from reaching the maximum voltage. The "missing link" method is to insert a one-way valve between the sensor and the manifold so that the sensor physically only sees vacuum. The "black box," available from Hahn Racecraft, tricks the ECU by altering the signal from the MAP sensor.

Modern computer-controlled cars are tuned for minimum emissions and maximum fuel economy. The parameters set at the factory constitute a compromise that ensures a safety margin built into the system. In general, factory computers try to achieve a stoichiometric ratio of 14.7 parts air to 1 part fuel. This is the point where the least amount of emissions is generated and the car will still perform in an acceptable manner. This may be fine for running at a steady pace down the interstate, but if you want real power, you need more fuel. At full throttle, the PCM generally runs a richer air/fuel ratio to build extra power, but it's nowhere near what a turbocharged engine demands. If you turbocharge your engine and fail to provide additional fuel, your engine will run lean and melt pistons. You need to figure out a way to enrich the fuel mixture as boost increases. This can be accomplished through the computer system or by using a fuel pressure regulator to increase the fuel flow relative to increasing boost. Additional injectors and/or larger injectors may also be added. But don't just add larger injectors and trust that things will be okay. You should tune your new injector/fuel pressure regulator setup on the dyno to make sure your air/fuel ratio is safe.

Running your air/fuel ratio a little rich may fowl your plugs, but will otherwise do no harm. However, if your fuel-delivery system comes up short, creating a lean condition, major engine damage will occur. We strongly recommend installing an air/fuel ratio gauge (along with a boost gauge) so you can make sure your engine is getting a proper dose of fuel. Monitoring your boost and air/fuel ratio while on the dyno will allow you to make any changes to your car before you blow it up on the strip or the street.

For a selection of the available turbo kits, check out Howell Automotive and Modern Performance. They have experience with their kits, and should be able to give you advice on what's right for your car.

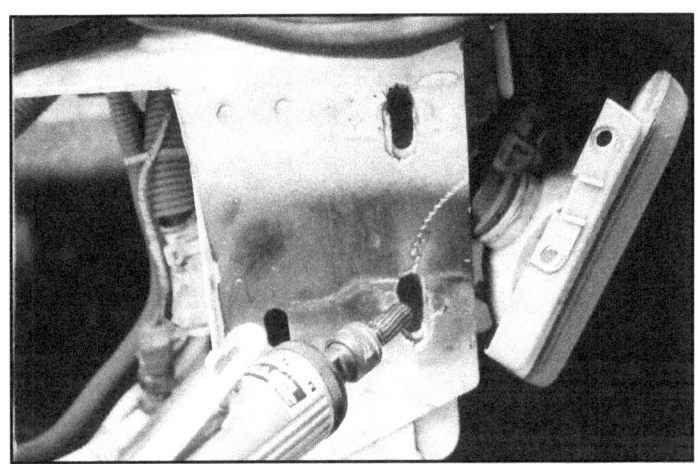

We chose to replace the air-to-water intercooler on our turbo Neon since it was designed to operate only for 60 seconds at a time. After that, all the ice would melt and the water became very hot. We wanted to locate the Spearco intercooler under the front bumper. That required cutting a big piece out of the bumper, and then cutting an access panel to allow for the intercooler inlet and outlet plumbing that reached back to the throttle body. We slotted the mounting holes so that it could be positioned just right after it was installed.

Superchargers

Supercharging achieves the same effect as a turbo but in a somewhat different manner. The energy used to turn a turbocharger comes from the spent exhaust gasses and would otherwise be lost to the atmosphere. On the other hand, a supercharger gets its power from a belt running off the engine, much the same way as a power steering pump or air conditioning compressor does. Since this belt is turned using some of the power of the engine, running a supercharger technically does result in a small power drain on the engine. Of course, the supercharger will build more power than it consumes, which is why people use them in the first place. Superchargers in general are a little more compact and a little easier to install than a turbocharger since they require less plumbing. Most aftermarket superchargers will come with everything you need to make instant power. The problem is, as of this writing, there are no superchargers available for the Neon or SRT-4.

Nitrous Oxide

If you don't want to go to the trouble of installing a turbo or supercharger, you can still blow the doors off of those Mustangs and Camaros by installing a nitrous oxide system. Even if your car is already "charged," you can still give it some gas (N_2O), if your engine can take it. These systems are affordable and relatively easy to install, but before getting out that MasterCard, you had better be sure your Neon can handle the extra strain. An older engine with worn bearings or rings may not hold together very well when exposed to turbocharger, supercharger, or nitrous systems.

Nitrous oxide is mixed with air and fuel in the combustion chamber. The result is an air/fuel mix that is super-combustible, due to the extra oxygen contained in the nitrous oxide. As with a turbo or supercharger, you need to be sure you have enough fuel to mix with the extra oxygen, or you'll run lean and melt parts. The resulting explosion will force your pistons down harder than normal, thus building more power. This will put a great deal of strain on your

The Stage 1, 2, and 3 upgrades are bolt-on, no-nonsense, reliable systems for the SRT-4 engineered by Mopar Performance. You can sometimes spot a Stage 2 or 3 car by the emblems.

If you add a turbo to your Neon, make sure you use high-quality, extra-strength hose brackets, such as this one on an SRT-4. Under the pressure of a turbo, typical hose clamps can fail and hoses can pop off.

bearings and connecting rods. A newer Neon can usually take this abuse, but one with very high miles may not. Even if your engine is healthy, you don't want to go above 75 hp on stock internals.

There are two basic types of nitrous kits available: dry and wet. A dry nitrous system injects only nitrous into the intake. Dry kits either rely on your factory computer to add extra fuel at wide-open throttle, or trick the computer into adding extra fuel. A wet kit will add nitrous and fuel at the same point and time.

Bottle Heaters

Nitrous systems are designed to work best with a bottle pressure of 900 to 950 psi. Nitrous isn't pumped into your engine; the system relies on the pressure in the bottle to force the gas into your engine. The pressure will change based on both temperature and the amount of nitrous remaining in the bottle. If you're serious about getting the most out of your N_2O system, then it's a good idea to use a bottle heater. Bottle-heater kits are thermostatically controlled to keep the bottle near 85 degrees Fahrenheit, which will provide correct pressure.

Since nitrous gas is very cold when it is discharged, you can also use it to give your intercooler an occasional squirt to help keep it cool. In some smaller turbo systems utilizing less than 8 psi, often an intercooler may not be used, but running a small shot of nitrous can keep your intake charge as cool as it needs to be. A nitrous system is not legal for SCCA racing, but most of the fastest Neon drag cars don't leave home without one.

The SRT-4

It's best to discuss the turbocharged SRT-4 separately, since there are specific aftermarket performance parts designed to work with it. These upgrades work best when purchased as a set. For instance, any time you install or upgrade a turbo, you need to address ignition timing and fuel delivery issues, or you could end up running too lean. The packages described below were designed by Dodge and are available from Modern Performance and several other retailers. Prices are relatively the same at most of the retailers, so purchase your package where you'll get the best technical support. That is the advantage of buying them from companies such as Modern Performance. These three packages are designated and organized into performance stages. The higher the stage, the greater the gains. They are all engineered to deliver more torque and power, and to deliver that power with less lag.

Stage 1

In this stage, a re-tuned wastegate control is offered for better turbo response. There is also a wide-open throttle-hold

Turbo cars are not as effective as they could be on an autocross course unless the course allows you to be under boost for an extended period of time (left). Many local clubs only have access to smaller parking lots. In that case, a lightweight, all-motor car is best (right). However, the larger the parking lot, the more a Turbo Neon can be successful.

control, so that when you shift gears, lag is minimized. The kit also includes a reprogrammed computer and bigger fuel injectors. With the Stage 1 kit, you can expect to achieve 240 hp at 5,200 rpm.

Stage 2

The Stage 2 kit can net 260 hp at 5,200 rpm and 280 ft-lbs of torque from 3,600 to 4,400 rpm. To develop this additional peak power and torque, the boost is increased during wide-open throttle conditions. The boost is also raised for part throttle conditions to enhance drivability. The wastegate control is similar to the unit in Stage 1. The reprogrammed PCM increases the engine's redline from 6,240 rpm to 6,500 rpm. This kit also includes a wastegate actuator, 3.0 bar MAP sensor (to monitor the higher boost pressures), 3.0 Bar TIP (throttle inlet pressure) sensor, and 30 percent bigger injectors that flow up to 682 cc per minute.

Stage 3

For maximum power and torque, the Stage 3 turbo kit is the ultimate upgrade for your SRT-4. This package boosts power to 310 hp at 5,600 rpm and 325 ft-lbs of torque from 3,200 to 4,800 rpm! You also get the 6,500-rpm rev limit increase as in Stage 2. The Stage 3 kit includes a reprogrammed PCM with block-off connector and a bigger turbo with a 16 percent larger compressor wheel diameter to flow and compress more intake air and a 19 percent larger turbine wheel diameter to flow more exhaust gas and reduce back pressure. The turbine wheel is made of titanium aluminide for significantly less rotational inertia than the standard Inconel steel unit. As for the fuel system, the Stage 3 kit includes a high-flow fuel pump, a fuel rail assembly with returnless regulator and hose kit, and the larger injectors, TIP, and MAP sensors included in Stage 2.

Other Goodies and Add-Ons

SRT-4s already have a great turbo system and front-mounted intercooler in place, but they can benefit from installing a larger intercooler for even better intake-charge cooling. Turbonetics manufactures several different units that work very well and can net up to 20 more horsepower. The trade-offs include more turbo lag, and possibly having to remove the crash bumper to make room for the intercooler. Use your head before taking this step on the street.

You may also consider an intercooler sprayer. With the Mopar Turbo Toys setup, a sprayer can increase the efficiency of the intercooler and reduce charge air temperature, resulting in increased engine performance. My Subaru STi autocrosser pal, Larry Fine, has many national Solo II trophies on his mantle and just loves the sprayer function. When he comes out of a hard turn, and hears his engine start to knock, he simply presses the button and water sprays the intercooler. The knock goes away, and the STi takes off without having to back off on the throttle or downshift. You can add a sprayer to any of the above packages, or to any Neon that has been turbocharged. Make sure to use distilled water to keep the sprayer nozzle from clogging due to impurities in tap water.

We discussed boost controllers earlier in the chapter, but a specific unit is available for the SRT-4. This "dial a boost" controller, also included with Mopar's Turbo Toys package, can manage boost on demand by adjusting a four-position thumb wheel that corresponds to four different boost settings. Believe it or not, there are times when you don't want full boost, especially in 2003 SRT-4s that had no limited-slip differential (LSD). Charging out of a hard turn will toast your inside tire without

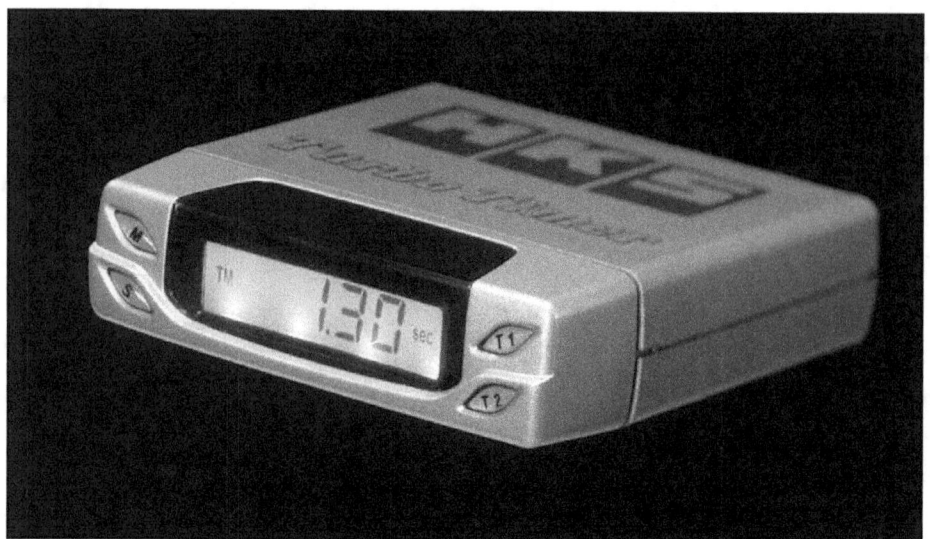

A turbo timer can help save your turbo. According to HKS, their Type-0 is a basic turbo timer that features an auto mode that adjusts engine idle time according to the most recent driving pattern and includes multiple preset times, audible alarms, and a volt meter. The Type-1 (shown) offers all the features of the Type-0, plus several monitoring and measurement tools. Vehicle speed and RPM can be displayed on the Type-1's LCD monitor, and a speed warning level can be set. A two-stage RPM warning can also be set and used as a shift light. When a warning level is reached, the Type-1's LCD monitor will switch from blue to red and an audible beep will sound.

The HKS A/F Knock Amp is an electronic monitoring device that displays two of the most vital engine conditions for tuning: engine knock and air/fuel ratio. Engine knock usually occurs when there is too much timing, not enough octane, or too little fuel. It can rob power, reduce engine longevity, and even lead to catastrophic failure.

an LSD to give you traction. Add in maximum boost, and you will cord your race tires after just a few laps. Keeping the boost down is great anytime there may be reduced traction due to a lack of an LSD, your OEM tires, or compromised track conditions.

The Turbo Toys package also offers a high-octane fuel switch that can be ordered with the Stage 2 or 3 packages. If you use 100+ octane unleaded fuel, the switch will tell the reprogrammed PCM to increase spark advance and adjust the fuel flow to take full advantage of the high-octane fuel, which results in increased horsepower and torque. Even during this high-octane operation, the PCM can prevent detonation via the OEM knock detection system.

Words of Caution

Make sure you discuss your plan with tech support personnel before you make your final purchase. If you decide you want to add a few of the above "toys" to your car at a later date, they may not be compatible with one of the lower stages' ECU. This book has hopefully taught you to create a budget based on what you want to do with your car. Changing your mind down the road, especially when it comes to an SRT-4, will cost you some cash. For instance, you can't simply upgrade from a Stage 1 to a Stage 2, or Stage 2 to Stage 3 without buying a complete kit (you can't just trade up). Also, installing one of these kits will likely void your factory warranty.

Another issue is that these kits are not legal for pollution-controlled vehicles. If your state has emissions testing, you may run into problems. On our Turbo Neon, the state's computer went crazy when the inspector plugged into the ECU. If you recall, it was the ECU out of a Razor. The testing system's computer looked like it was going to crash, so technically, the car is not legal for the street.

You'll need to provide your SRT-4 vehicle identification number (VIN) in order to keep the SKIM (Security Key Immobilization Module) functional. Each kit is programmed specifically for the your SRT-4 using your VIN. This also means Dodge will know if one of its kits have been installed on your SRT-4.

Finally, whenever you add more power, some of your stock components could become a limiting factor in getting maximum performance from your upgrades. Consider installing a high-performance clutch to handle all that extra torque. Mopar also makes a better blow-off valve for the SRT-4. If you haven't installed a more efficient exhaust system by the time you get to Stage 3, your stock system will definitely become the weak link in your SRT-4.

CHAPTER 11

TRANSAXLE TECH
by Mike Ancas and Michael Carpenter

Neon Transmissions

In general, Neon transaxles are very strong, lightweight, and reliable. Designed and built by New Venture Gear for Chrysler, the transmission is a split-case design that weighs in at only 80 pounds. Even drag racers with turbocharged engines cranking out well over 400 horsepower rarely develop problems. The same goes for road racing and autocrossing. Axles will snap, clutches will break, but the trannies have a reputation of holding together under extreme conditions.

Neon transmissions are strong units that can handle a turbo upgrade with no problem. However, you may want to consider installing a limited-slip differential if you plan to do some racing.

High-Performance Dodge Neon Builder's Handbook

There are several choices you can make regarding clutches. The stock Neon clutch (left) is still okay even after 100,000 miles. Since it was already out, we replaced it with a PT Cruiser clutch that has easier pedal effort and more holding power. The PT clutch is also a cheaper option than an aftermarket clutch.

Mopar Performance Parts offers a kit to help you install a modular clutch assembly in place of your traditional clutch and flywheel assembly. Once you install a modular clutch with this kit, installing another modular clutch is as simple as swapping it in.

The only real weak link is the differential, which does not like excessive wheel spin. But we should take a closer look at the different gear ratios and final drives to see just which tranny may be best for your project.

I've got nothing against Chrysler automatic trannies. Unless you're content to keep your Neon on the street, a car with an auto tranny is not the best car to start with. We've seen people spend literally thousands of dollars on all the bolt-on modifications, only to run about the same times at the strip that they would have with a manual transmission in a stock car. Of course, you can swap out your auto for a stick, but why bother? Neons are cheap, and the ones with automatic transmission are worth more on the used-car market. The real exception to this is if you are serious about turbocharging your car. The automatic works great for drag racing a high-torque car, as traction is easier to manage, and the auto helps keep the car in boost.

It may seem that there were a lot of different 5-speed configurations from 1995 to 1999, but in reality, there were only a few. Actually, from 1995 through 2000, all manual trannies had the same gear ratios from first through fourth gear. From mid 2000 on, first and second gear changed slightly. First went from 3.54:1 to 3.50:1, and second went from 2.13:1 to 1.95:1. The earlier cars had slightly lower gears, which means they got off the line with a little more gusto.

The first-generation cars basically had two different trannies. The base SOHC cars had a lower final drive (3.55:1) than all of the other cars. The lower final drive acts like a multiplying factor, and in this case makes it harder for a car to get off the line. Using this transmission is like pedaling your bike up a steep hill in fifth gear instead of first. But if you think about it, the base cars are light and the SOHC motor has great low-end torque, so when actually driving the car, you really couldn't tell much.

All DOHC cars had a higher final drive of 3.94:1, which compensates for the small amount of low-end torque they give up to the SOHC cars. If you want to take full advantage of the low-end torque produced by a Neon powerplant, then the SOHC ACR is your best choice. They have the 3.94:1 final drive mated to their SOHC engines. For many local autocross courses that have a lot of turns and fewer straightaways, the SOHC ACR is your best choice. Even in road

Aftermarket clutch discs and pressure plates typically help your tranny hook up better. Depending on what you want to do with your car, there is a perfect set-up out there for you. For street driving, you shouldn't get too wild since the more radical the clutch, the harder it is to push down the pedal and the harder it will engage. (Howell Automotive)

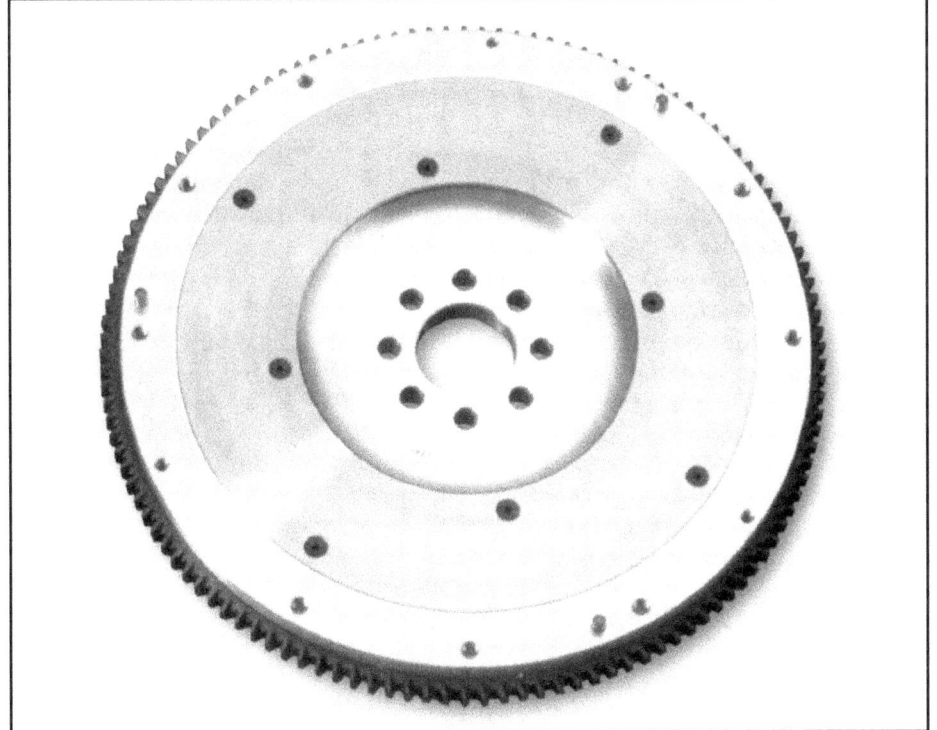

Lightened steel and aluminum flywheels should also be reserved for racing purposes only, as they can be a pain to deal with in a daily driver. But the lighter the flywheel, the less torque is required to get it to turn.

gears. The 2001–2003 SOHC Magnum cars have the best final drive for autocross, 3.94:1, while the 3.55:1 is found in all of the other cars.

If you turbocharge your Neon, or own an SRT-4, then all the recommendations made so far need not apply. The best final drive for you may not be the higher 3.94:1. Turbo cars don't have a problem with low-end torque, so you may want to take advantage of a tranny that will keep you in gear longer. A lower final drive takes better advantage of gearing, but then you run out of gear sooner and have to shift. First-gen turbo cars can benefit from using the 1995–99 SOHC base tranny with the 3.55:1 final drive. SRT-4s come stock with a 3.53:1, which seems to prove this point.

For many Neon owners, it may not be worth buying one tranny and swapping it into your current Neon in order to gain any kind of advantage. There are a few instances, however, in which you may want to consider doing a swap. First, if you're competing for a Solo II National Championship where the difference between a top-three trophy and a tenth-place finish is measured in one or two tenths of a second, then you may want to check your class rules and get the perfect tranny for your setup. The same applies for serious drag, Solo I, and road racers.

Second, you may want to consider a swap if the tranny that is in your current Neon blows up. Since you have to replace it anyway, you may as well get something good out of the process. Whenever any part on any of my cars breaks, I see it as fate, and look for a way to come out of it ahead in some way. Otherwise, you've spent time and money, and you aren't any faster than you were before the break. Even if all you can do is clean the area surrounding the part you are replacing, do something just to make yourself feel better.

Aftermarket Clutches

The Neon has a very robust clutch setup from the factory. Your stock clutch will likely hold up to any and all bolt-on mods you can throw at it short of nitrous and turbocharging. But that

racing, when a SOHC and DOHC car are battling for a position and it comes time to shift into a higher gear, the SOHC car will get a slight lead just before the DOHC car catches up and passes it (not that I have ever experienced that).

All second-gen SOHC trannies also share the same first through fourth

Chapter 11

Once you've raced a Neon with a limited-slip differential, you'll never go back. The 2004+ SRT-4 comes with one standard. You can add one to your car, but they can be expensive – up to $1,200, not including installation.

doesn't mean that a good aftermarket clutch won't improve performance. There is a big difference between a standard clutch and one that has been engineered for high performance.

Aftermarket high-performance clutches have a much better holding capacity compared to stock clutches, and will "hook up" or grab, much more dramatically. If you've never driven a car with one of these clutches, it'll take a little practice to keep the car from bucking when you start out. The higher the horsepower and the heavier the clutch, the harder it is to drive on the street. Don't pick just any high-performance clutch. For example, SPEC offers four different clutches, including a special lightweight pressure plate option. However, the basic Stage 1 clutch is likely more than 98 percent of the people reading this book will ever need.

You may also want to consider the clutches from Clutchmasters. They'll handle just about anything you can throw at them. The FX300 unit is recommended for cars with less than 300 hp. If you're pushing more than that, you may need the FX400. Once you've addressed your clutch situation, your tranny or axles may take over as the new weak point.

If you're on a budget, you can consider upgrading to the PT Cruiser clutch. The Cruiser clutch is inexpensive and can hold up to 180 hp, which takes care of most basic turbo or nitrous setups.

Many Neons come with a modular clutch assembly, which is a pre-assembled clutch pressure plate, clutch disc, and flywheel. It was designed to bolt right up to the drive plate used by the automatic-transmission cars, and you don't have to worry about aligning the clutch disc inside the pressure plate. Dealerships love them because they save disassembly and installation time. We love them because they're so simple to install. You simply replace the entire unit with a new one when any of the parts become worn out. If your car was manufactured at the Belvedere assembly plant, then you probably have the modular clutch. The aftermarket has caught on to the modular clutch, and many of the performance clutches are available in modular form, often with a lightweight flywheel.

If you decide to install a high-performance clutch, then be sure to select the one that's right for your particular needs and horsepower. If you can, break in the new performance clutch with a few hundred miles of stop-and-go driving before you take it racing. With any new clutch, keep any oil or grease away from all contact surfaces during assembly.

Lightened Flywheels

Anytime you find yourself removing your old clutch and pressure plate, you have another decision to make: What should I do with the flywheel? You have to get it resurfaced anyway, so should you take one step further and get it cut before you put it back in? You can reliably remove about 8 to 10 pounds of surface from your flywheel by having a machine shop reduce its thickness. You could also just buy a new aluminum flywheel, which will be the same thickness as your stock unit, but half the weight.

Does your Neon really need a lightened flywheel? That depends on your application. If you are doing a lot of stop-and-go driving with a high-horsepower Neon and a performance clutch, then a lightened flywheel could make your commute to work a tortured experience. Letting out that clutch a few dozen times every mile will aggravate you. The flywheel alone will be no big deal, but in the combination mentioned above, you'll start leaving your cool Neon in the garage in favor of your wife's minivan.

Another thing about lightened flywheels is the lack of momentum. Yes, it takes less effort (and more finesse) to get a lightened flywheel turning, but once a heavy flywheel is moving, its momentum (inertia) adds to your low-end torque coming out of a turn. A lighter flywheel will help your engine rev more freely, facilitating acceleration. In general, I recommend a lightened flywheel for drag racing. For autocross, it's probably not a huge advantage. Fidanza makes a great flywheel for your Neon and SRT-4, as do a few other manufacturers.

Limited-Slip Differentials

With all of the suspension and engine tweaks discussed in the previous chapters, the problem many Neon drivers will have is a loss of traction when accelerating out of the turns. On especially tight

Transaxle Tech

This Short Throw Shifter is available from Mopar Performance Parts. It shortens your shifter throws for quicker, easier shifts. (Photo courtesy Mopar Performance Parts)

turns, thanks to their great low-end torque, most Neons and especially 2003 SRT-4s will have a difficult time controlling wheel spin without a limited-slip differential. This traction loss equals slower track times, and since the inside wheel is spinning, the tire is being worn away. The same is true if you burn rubber leaving a red light. When you see the patch left behind, that's rubber that used to be on the tire. Say goodbye to your expensive soft-compound racing rubber and say hello to cord. This is the most common way Neons wear out their race tires prematurely. You can minimize this problem if you can find a way to more efficiently transfer your Neon's power to the pavement. You'll go faster with less tire wear – it's a win-win situation.

If you want to compete in a stock class, you won't be able to install a limited-slip differential, but most rules will allow you to add a large front sway bar. A larger front bar will keep the car flatter in a turn and can help the inside wheel stay in contact with the pavement for a longer period of time. If you don't own an ACR, look for an ACR front bar in a local junkyard; they're much bigger than the stock bars found on non-ACR Neons. There are also a lot of choices in aftermarket front sway bars on the market. The best thing to do is to find out exactly what setup the winning Neon drivers have, and just copy that.

Now let's get serious. The best performance improvement you can do to improve traction is install a limited-slip differential. Unless you know what you're doing or enjoy tearing apart transaxles, here's our advice: take the tranny and your new LSD to a tranny shop and have them install it. You would be surprised how many little parts are packed into that little tranny, and how difficult they are to get back together properly. We tried it once, and failed.

LSDs are available for all models. The good ones, like a Quaife, will cost $1,200, but it does have a lifetime guarantee. Don't even think about getting a phantom grip – you'll be wasting $275. A good LSD senses which wheel has better grip, and smoothly biases the power to that wheel. In straight-line acceleration, this results in a near 50/50 power split to both drive wheels. When accelerating out of a turn, the Quaife biases power to the outside wheel, reducing inside wheel spin. This allows the driver to begin accelerating earlier, exiting the corner at a higher speed.

Starting in 2004, the SRT-4 came standard with a Quaife LSD. First-year (2003) SRT-4 drivers could look for a 2004 tranny in a junkyard and transplant the whole unit, but it will likely be expensive, and not many new SRT-4s are in junkyards yet. You may be better off just installing an aftermarket Quaife.

The other thing that putting in a Quaife will do for you is to rectify one of the only problems encountered with stock Neon trannies. The large pin inside the differential is prone to failure. In most cases, the roll pin that retains the pin will exit stage right through the bellhousing. Hardcore folks have even exploded the whole deal, sending spider gears every which way. The main cause for this is extended wheel spin. By doing long peg-leg burnouts, the lubricant is burned off of the spider gears, which then grind away at the pin. The Quaife makes it more difficult to spin the tires, which reduces the chance that your tranny will explode.

Another fix enthusiasts have come up with is to have the differential pins welded on both sides. This will prevent the pin from exiting the case, but you can still encounter catastrophic failure.

Chrysler's solution to this problem is straightforward and simple. Inexpensive brackets will help keep the differential pin and spider gears in place. If you have to open up your transmission for any reason, you should contact your local dealer and get a pair of these brackets fitted. The tops of these brackets may need to be trimmed if they interfere with the speedometer gear. Of course you could just avoid all this, and go faster, by buying a Quaife.

So is an LSD worth it? As you have seen, a lot of what is being marketed by performance parts companies is more hype than help. But this is one situation where it's all worth it. There's no way to be competitive on a national level unless you have an LSD. And if you've turbocharged your Neon, you'll go through enough tires to eventually pay for an LSD. Not to mention that your autocross times on a 60-second course will decrease by as much as three seconds. An LSD is everything that it's cracked up to be, and the more powerful your engine, the more you need one.

Driving With an LSD

If you think an LSD will instantly translate to faster lap times, then you're mistaken. Successfully driving a racecar with as LSD is completely different from driving a car without one. The first time you race a car with an LSD, be prepared for plowing (understeer). If you were used to throwing your car into a turn to induce some oversteer, you'll likely take the scenic route through the first hairpin turn you approach. Keep the windows rolled up so that your friends don't think you're crazy when they hear you yelling at your Neon to "turn!"

An LSD tends to drive the front wheels further into the turn (especially if you are moving a little too fast). Entering a turn too fast is a common pre-LSD habit that can be hard to break. Drivers without LSDs expect the front wheels to slide a little, which they often compensate for by left-foot braking. When done with skill, this will cause the rear end to slightly rotate, resulting in a controlled four-wheel drift. But with an LSD in place, the front wheels maintain traction as you turn the wheel, which is what you got the LSD for in the first place. If you go in too hot, the result is understeer. You'll need to slow down when entering the turn. This will pay off big time on the way out since power can be applied earlier and with more gusto, resulting in much faster exit speeds.

Fine tuning the front suspension to match your individual driving style can be accomplished by experimenting with negative camber, toe, sway bars and sway bar bushing material, shock and strut stiffness, and the easiest of all to adjust: tire pressures. If you've done a lot to your suspension prior to installing an LSD, you may need to make some changes. Before you re-setup your suspension, try to get used to driving like we've described above. Slow in – fast out. If your Neon is still plowing, then you may want to loosen your front sway bar a little. If that doesn't work, you should try to stiffen the rear a little more. If all that doesn't work, you may need to go back to a smaller front bar. If you still have stiffer springs on the front than the back, that could also be your problem. A fully set-up Neon with an LSD will benefit from stiffer springs in the rear.

Gear Oil

It seems like everyone is using synthetic fluids nowadays: Mobil 1 in the engine, Castrol in the brake lines, and RedLine in the tranny. But is there really anything to putting synthetic gear oil in your transaxle? For the most part, if your car is only a few years old, you don't need to stray from the owner's manual. Just stick with the specific semi-synthetic fluid available at Chrysler dealers.

There are several reasons to go with synthetic gear oil. First, if you've installed a limited-slip differential, then a good synthetic gear oil, such as Redline, will help the differential to "hook up" more smoothly. Overall wear will be reduced, as is the case with most synthetics, so you will be able to get the most out of your diff over time.

Another good reason to go with full synthetic is if you have a lot of miles on your car. Once a tranny gets a little worn, synthetic gear oil will make shifting a little smoother. We've tested RedLine in our older cars, and they respond noticeably.

Lastly, if you're racing, a good synthetic will help ease some of that extra strain on your gearbox. Road racers especially will see benefit, as downshifts can be less troublesome.

As for the cost, the price is worth the benefit if you fall into one of the three categories above. Synthetic gear oil is about five times more expensive than regular oil, but it's not like you change it every 3,000 miles.

Don't just dump any old gear oil in your Neon's transaxle! We've found that running conventional gear oils can cause shifting problems with the synchros. You'll want to look for a product like RedLine that is specific to modern transaxles.

Conclusions

The different Neon 5-speed trannies are more alike than they are different. The only reason to replace the one in your car is if it is failing or if you are a serious national-level racecar driver. All of the trannies are strong, lightweight, and durable enough to handle all the power your bolt-on modifications will make.

But no matter how much horsepower you have at your disposal, it won't do you any good unless you can get the power to the ground. Since weight shifts to the rear every time you accelerate, a RWD car can put down that power better than FWD Neons and SRT-4s. We have the advantage of having the front tires pull us out of a turn, but we lose out at the starting line. The more horsepower your Neon car has, the harder it is to keep the inside wheel from spinning.

Chapter 12

ENGINES

by Michael Carpenter and Mike Ancas

Several different engines found their way into Neons over the course of production. But looking at the big picture, they were more similar than different. The main difference could be found in the cylinder heads. The 132-hp single overhead cam (SOHC) motor was introduced in the first Neon sedans (early 1994), and the 150-hp dual overhead cam (DOHC) motor made its debut later that same year in the 2-door coupe. The DOHC was discontinued after 1999 and was never offered in a second-generation Neon. In 2001, a 150-hp high-output version of the SOHC engine was added and was known as the Magnum. All three configurations shared the same 2.0-liter block. These engines powered Neons' 0-60 times of approximately 8 seconds and quarter-mile times of less than 16 seconds.

If you're an SRT-4 owner, much of this chapter should be read for amusement purposes only. With the bolt-ons discussed in earlier chapters that could give you well over 300 hp at the wheels, there's no way we would ever consider doing any kind of engine swap on an SRT-4. If you added another 50 horsepower on top of that 300, you probably wouldn't be able to get it all to the ground anyway, so it wouldn't be worthwhile to do as a project. Chrysler doesn't currently have a better 4-cylinder motor than the turbocharged 2.4.

First-Generation Powerplants: 1995–1999

2.0-liter SOHC: 132 hp at 6,000 rpm and 129 ft-lbs of torque at 5,000 rpm

One good feature of the SOHC engine is that it only requires regular 87-octane fuel. In fact, adding premium gas doesn't build any extra horsepower; it just costs money. Running 87 has saved us a significant amount of money over the years.

The SOHC changed slightly over the years. The '95 used a slightly hotter camshaft and a different valve cover and airbox. Holes were drilled in the front of the block for the oil separator box and PCV setup. The '95 block also had different notches for the main bearing tangs, which can make replacing the main bearings a bit tricky. Finally, in '95 there was a shortage of the plastic intake manifold, so aluminum ones were cast to fill in. From '96 to '99, blocks and heads were fundamentally common with one another.

The SOHC was also available in TLEV (low emissions) form in California and Massachusetts. This engine had different pistons that reduced the

One of the best 2.4-liter powerplants ever can be found in the SRT-4. With 250 hp and 230 ft-lbs of torque, this engine is hard to beat, even in stock trim.

compression ratio from 9.8:1 to 9.3:1. Power was down to 129 hp.

2.0-liter DOHC: 150 hp at 6,500 rpm and 132 ft-lbs of torque at 5,500 rpm

On paper, both the DOHC and SOHC have similar statistics. The bore and stroke are common, at 87.4 mm and 83 mm, respectively. The DOHC head has a slightly larger combustion chamber, so the pistons have a small dome to bring the compression ratio up. The main difference in powerband between the first-gen 2.0s is that the DOHC version has 18 more horsepower up high, right where most racers need it.

Although mid-grade fuel is recommended for the DOHC, you'll want to use the premium in your area for maximum performance. While we haven't seen it with the 93 octane available here, folks who only have 91 have told us the computer will pull back the timing at high RPM, reducing power. With the DOHC setup, the PCM advances the timing when you're turning high RPM, so to take full advantage of what the DOHC can do for you, give your engine the high octane. High-RPM performance is the big advantage that the DOHC has over the SOHC, so it's the motor to have if you don't want to take any crap from those pesky VTEC Honda drivers who like to run up near the redline. DOHC Neons should be able to leave most of those Hondas in the dust.

There were no significant changes made to the DOHC throughout the first production generation, excepting the main crankshaft bearing change mentioned above. There was also no difference between an ACR, R/T, or a regular DOHC, so any Neon with the DOHC engine will have roughly the same power to start with.

The Second Generation Powerplants: 2000–2005

2.0-liter SOHC: 132 hp at 5,600 rpm and 129 ft-lbs of torque at 4,600 rpm

The 2.0-liter SOHC saw some minor changes in 2000. The main differences were in the intake manifold, throttle body, and airbox. The new intake setup was redesigned to give the car more low-end torque, as the second-generation cars were a bit heavier. The new airbox featured a high-flow conical filter,

The first-generation powerplants were chock full of torque, 129 ft-lbs, which was enough to convert many import enthusiasts. Add an air intake and a few cheap, simple mods and you had a car that was much quicker than most other sport compacts on the market in the mid to late 1990s.

Neon's DOHC motor was introduced shortly after the SOHC motor debuted in 1995. With a lot more horsepower on tap (150 vs. 132), racers became very interested in these cars. (Photo courtesy Patrick O'Hara)

and a shorter, straighter path into the manifold.

Regular SOHC Neons all began using the 9.3:1 compression ratio pistons, same as the TLEV, in 2003. Horsepower

Engines

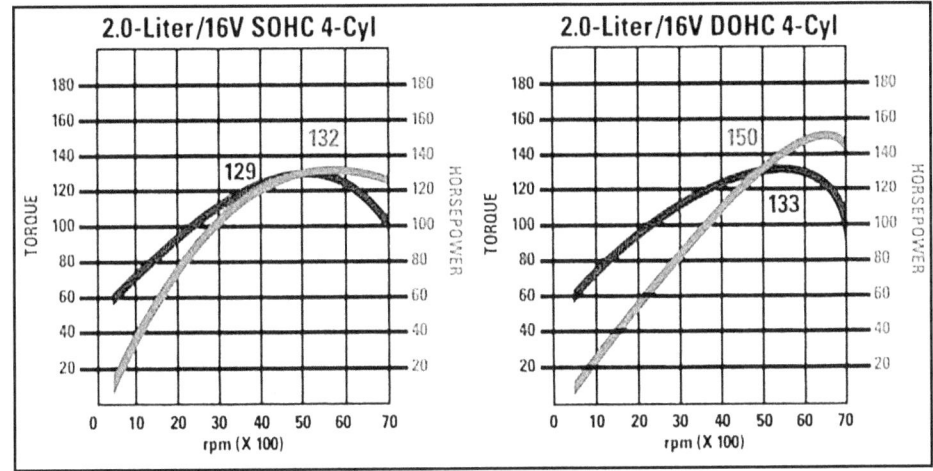

Both engines performed similarly under 5,000 rpm, but the DOHC motor was superior when the revs started to climb. (Photo courtesy Patrick O'Hara)

The 2.0L Magnum gave Neon enthusiasts a choice over the standard SOHC motor. Domed pistons created higher compression and horsepower numbers similar to the old DOHC powerplants. (Photo courtesy Matt Wiggins)

ty of the new Magnum engine isn't necessarily in the peak numbers, but in the fact that it has a better torque curve than the previous engines below 4,000 rpm.

2.4-liter DOHC Turbo
2003: 215 hp at 5,400 rpm and 245 ft-lbs of torque at 3,200 rpm
2004+: 230 hp at 5,300 rpm and 250 ft-lbs of torque at 2,200 rpm

The 2.4-liter turbo represents the next generation of Chrysler turbo engines, far surpassing any 4-cylinder produced to date. This engine had been used in Mexico for years, and has finally come to the rest of North America under the hood of the SRT-4 and PT Cruiser

ratings are the same, so one can guess that Chrysler tweaked the PCM to bring the power output back to the same level. The crankshaft and block are slightly different from 2003-on to accommodate new electronics.

2.0-liter SOHC High-Output Magnum: 150 hp at 6,800 rpm and 135 ft-lbs of torque at 4,800 rpm

The Magnum is the high-output version of the SOHC engine. The blocks are the same as other 2.0 SOHCs, but the pistons have an anti-friction coating on the skirts. The cylinder head remained unchanged on the intake side, but is heavily revised with larger ports on the exhaust side. The factory also included a hotter cam, aggressive PCM,

Before the SRT-4 even showed up in showrooms, Sport Compact Car did some magic to their project car. The most popular ways to squeeze even more power out of the 2.4-liter turbo powerplant are Stage 1, 2, and 3 upgrades available from Mopar Performance. (Photo courtesy Howell Automotive)

and a shorty header. Finally, the Magnum featured a unique variable runner intake manifold. The manifold has two sets of runners, one short and one long, and a set of throttles that open or close to maximize performance across a wide RPM range.

The 2001 engine is the one to look for, as it had a slightly hotter cam. In 2002+, that cam was re-profiled with slightly less intake valve lift to decrease strain on the valvetrain. As with the standard Neon, crankshaft and block are slightly different starting in 2003 to accommodate new electronics. The beau-

GT. The turbo short block is vastly different from the regular 2.0 and 2.4s. It has a bigger water pump, bigger oil pump, an oil cooler, piston oil squirters, and the list goes on. The rods are heavier duty than the standard 2.4 rods. The turbocharger is a compact Mitsubishi unit that is unique in that it's cast as one piece with the exhaust manifold. The intake manifold is unique as well.

The turbo engine itself remained the same for 2004, but it uses larger injectors and a recalibrated PCM to achieve a slightly higher power level similar to the Stage 1 upgrade.

The 2.4-liter (right) is not simply a stroked-out 2.0 (left). It uses its own unique engine block, which is one inch taller deck height than the 2.0. (Photo courtesy Howell Automotive)

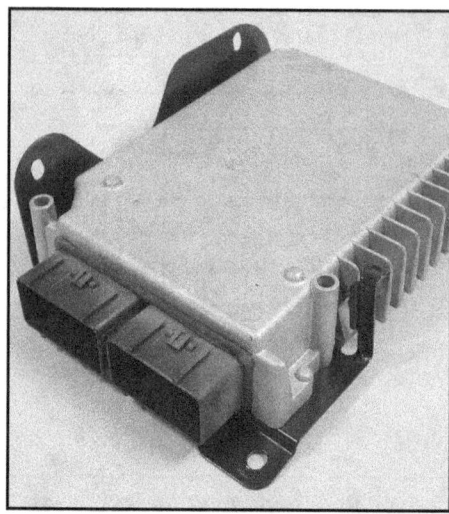

There is more power to be found in your computer. The OEM unit is designed for performance and economy, but if you want more performance and less economy, then you need an aftermarket Mopar Performance computer. (Photo courtesy Modern Performance)

Blocks

Chrysler's 4-cylinder engine blocks (both 2.0- and 2.4-liter) are made from cast iron, and feature a bedplate where the block is essentially split open to install the crankshaft. The crankshaft is fully counterweighted, and is also made from cast iron. There's no need for re-sleeving or block girdles here; the closed-deck design is rugged enough to handle over 600 hp!

PCM Tech

Powertrain control modules, or PCMs (Dodge's name for ECU, or engine control unit), control all of your Neon's engine management systems. The PCM receives a signal from a knock sensor and will retard the spark timing if detonation occurs. However, the controller will not advance timing beyond the factory setting, so keep that in mind if you're considering adding an aftermarket ignition. If you want total control over your timing, you have to install a stand-alone EFI system. Thanks mostly to enthusiasts like you, there are excellent choices available for aftermarket PCMs that can give you more ignition timing at high RPM, add some extra fuel, and give you a few more hundred RPM to play with. Increasing the rev limit is one of the best things you can do for your Neon if you plan to get involved in any form of racing.

Note that the PCMs varied over the years, and break into the following groups:

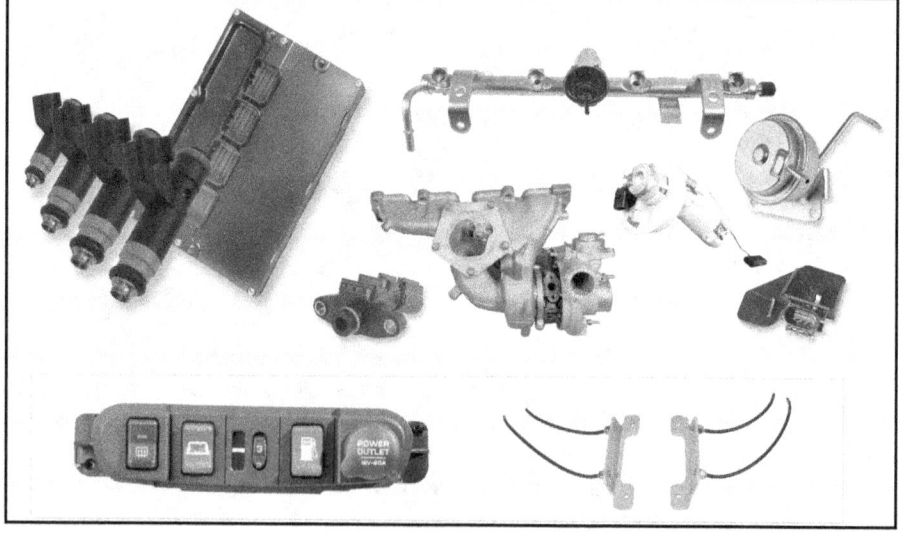

Mopar Performance Parts offers 3 stages of SRT-4 performance upgrades. This Stage 3 kit comes with everything, including a revised PCM, a larger turbocharger and exhaust manifold, a high-flow fuel pump, a fuel pressure regulator and fuel rail, and a set of high-flowing injectors. This photo also shows the Turbo Toys package, which includes the intercooler sprayers, an adjustable boost switch, and a high-octane switch. (Photo courtesy Mopar Performance Parts)

1995 / 1996 / 1997–1999 / 2000 / 2001 / 2002 / 2003+

As you can see, early first-generation PCMs do not interchange, and second-generation PCMs are different every year as well. Physically and functionally they are all more or less the same from 1996 to 2002, but differences

Engines

You can have the power of an SRT-4 in your older Neon chassis. One way is to swap the whole engine, but another is to find an SRT-4 head/manifolds/turbo and swap it all onto your 2.0.

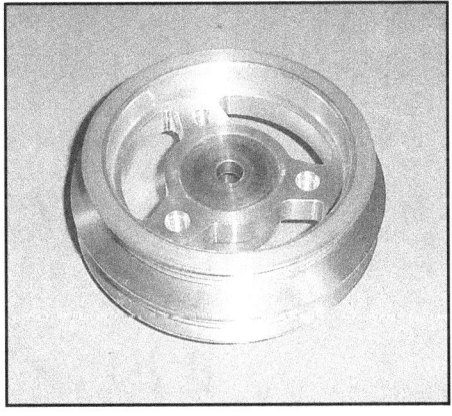
Lightweight underdrive pulleys will create less drag on your motor and save you a few horsepower – power that you can use to drive the wheels harder. Many choices are on the market, like this one from the Howell Automotive. (Photo courtesy Howell Automotive)

This is the Unorthodox Racing pulley as installed on our turbo Neon. You need to get the correct balancer puller before attempting the installation.

in pinouts and programming prevent them from interchanging correctly.

The 2003+ PCMs are uncharted territory, as they represent Chrysler's new PCM setup. Engines from 2003-on were changed with new crankshaft triggers. While they allow for far more precise ignition and fuel mapping, they don't work out so well for enthusiasts with older Neons looking to swap engines.

First-Generation Swaps

The car I used to race, which started its life as a 1996 DOHC ACR, is a good example of the interchangeability between the various Chrysler engines. Mark Daddio (I just love dropping his name, it gives me credibility) swapped a head and turbo from an SRT-4/PT turbo on to the 2.0-liter short block before we got our grubby hands on it. The only real reason for doing a swap like this is so that the exhaust ports line up with the inexpensive SRT-4 turbo manifold.

2.4-Liter

You also can swap an entire 2.4-liter DOHC engine into a DOHC Neon. This swap gives you extra displacement (.4 liters, to be exact!), along with more horsepower and lots more torque (25+ ft-lbs). Nearly all the accompanying original parts can be retained if you start with a DOHC car. You'll need to swap on your DOHC intake and exhaust manifolds. Some of the accessories, such as the power steering and air conditioning, may be difficult to retain when swapping to a 2.4.

The reason we don't recommend using a SOHC car to start with is because there's a lot of rewiring (can you tell I don't like wiring?) required to make it run properly. It has been done, but the SOHC uses different sensors due to manifold clearance, so you have to rewire the throttle position sensor and IAC on the throttle body. You can use a PCM from a 2.0-liter DOHC as long as you get the wiring right, but it's just easier to start with the right car. Let's face it – old Neons are cheap. Just go out and buy a no-option car with a blown DOHC engine, and do the swap.

Going with a 2.4 will give you more torque and give you a higher baseline to build on. Even if you're only doing bolt-ons, you'll easily surpass what you would get with your 2.0. The same is true with serious build-ups and turbos – just look at the SRT-4.

You will need to find, modify, or fabricate an engine mount spacer for the passenger side of the new 2.4-liter block. There are a few kits you can purchase to help make this an easy swap. JLM Motorsports (jlmmotorsports.com, formerly Neonparts.net) makes the one we saw, and the price is right at approximately $400. You get a new right-side motor mount, and modified left and front motor mounts. You can even get a more comprehensive kit that includes the fuel system for under $800.

Chapter 12

The Neon's motor mounts are one of the weakest points in the entire car. For normal street driving, there's no real problem, but even if you're an occasional autocrosser, your motor mounts will start to wear out. Road racers often need to replace their mounts several times during the racing season. Aftermarket mounts really solve the problem, but many racing classes prohibit them. (Photo courtesy Matt Wiggins)

Taking good care of your engine is essential to long life and good performance. We use Mobil 1 synthetic oil in our Neon and really like it. There may be better lubricants out there, but expect to pay a lot more for Royal Purple, Red Line, and Amsoil. (Photo courtesy Travis Thompson)

Magnum

Do you feel lucky, punk? The SOHC Magnum head is the most powerful Neon head in the world. Okay, enough with the Clint Eastwood routine. But there's something special about the Magnum engine found in second-gen R/Ts and ACRs. The Magnum swap is becoming a popular and relatively inexpensive swap for many first-generation SOHC owners. If you choose not to swap the entire engine, there are quite a few desirable bits from the Magnum cars that can be worthwhile to have on your Neon. The camshaft and valvesprings are especially popular among enthusiasts. Should you choose to swap the intake manifold and throttle body, you'll also need to get the second-gen starter, which is slightly different because of clearance issues.

Second-Generation Swaps

There's no need to buy special aftermarket engine mounts to swap a 2.4-liter into these cars. The 2.4 was used in the SRT-4, and for that reason, a 2000-2002 2.4-liter engine bolts right into 2000-2002 Neons, and the 2003+ 2.4-liter engine bolts into 2003+ Neons (remember the difference in PCMs!). You'll just need a

Howell Automotive has seen it all in their years of building motors and blowing them up racing. You have to blow a few motors up before you can learn where the limits are. Then you can fix the problem so the limits can be extended even further. Any powerplant you get from Howell comes with a lot of motor-building experience behind it, which will help keep problems like this from happening to you. (Photo courtesy Howell Automotive)

Engines

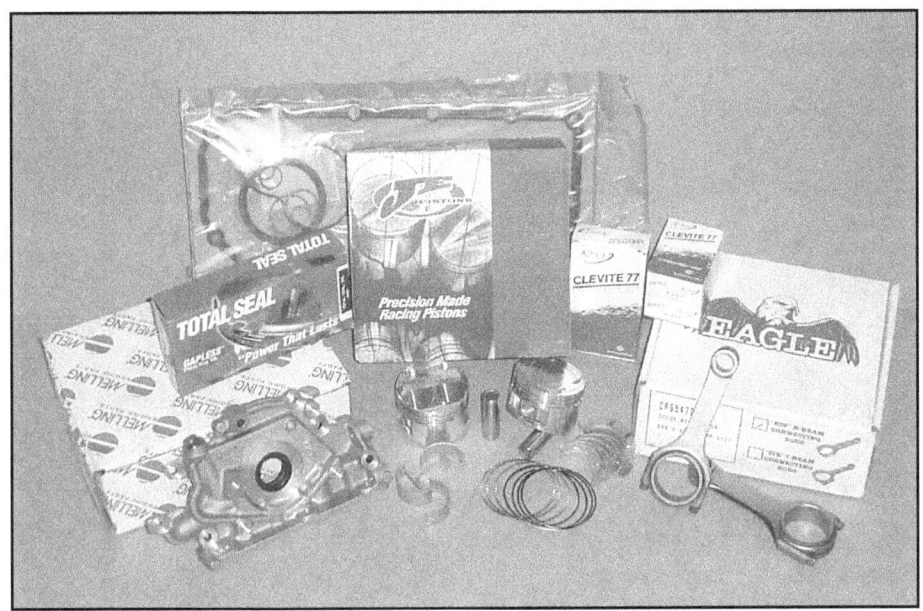

If you want to build a motor that will stand up to nitrous and turbocharging, then you need to spend some money on your short block. Howell Automotive can hook you up with all the best parts to meet the needs of how you plan to use (or abuse) your engine. High-quality pistons and seals are all well and good, but often the weak points are the connecting rods and rod bolts. Valves can also break at high RPM. Make sure you get high-quality hardware. (Photo courtesy Howell Automotive)

There is no sense spending a fortune on a new engine without keeping a close eye on how it is running. At the absolute minimum, you should have gauges that monitor (left to right) water temperature, oil temperature, and oil pressure.

set of SRT-4 engine mounts from your local Chrysler dealership. The big issue at this time is what PCM to use. Most people say that the SOHC PCM can run a stock 2.4 with some fuel pressure tweaks, but a seriously built motor may run lean at high RPM. A Magnum's PCM may be the solution in that instance.

SRT-4 Swaps Into non-SRT-4 Neons

I'm sure everyone can agree that the 2.4-liter turbo motor found in the new Chryslers is appealing to swap into your current Neon. If you consider doing this, realize that it's a truly HUGE project. For second-generation Neon owners, it is possible, although it requires you to rewire the entire engine bay. For first-generation owners, this is a much harder swap. The engine itself will fit like other 2.4s, but the crankshaft trigger is so radically different that the car's existing electronics are useless. With a standalone EFI system, this swap would certainly be possible. Once these engines start to become a little more common and available, more info on this swap will surface.

Underdrive Pulleys

We've already discussed most of the basic modifications you can do to your Neon's engine, intake, exhaust, etc. There are a few other bolt-ons that you may want to consider.

Underdrive pulleys are not all that expensive, but they can be a real pain to get on and off without the proper Chrysler puller. An underdrive pulley can give you a tiny bit of torque and improved engine response. The performance boost is the result of having less reciprocating mass (lighter pulley), and a reduction in parasitic loss from the alternator, water pump, and power steering pump. If you have a car with A/C, then you will get even more benefit. The beauty of the underdrive pulley is that since you aren't changing the airflow characteristics of the engine, as with some mods, you don't have to give up torque anywhere.

When considering any mod, such as an underdrive pulley, you should look at the big picture. Every little bit can add up. For instance, it might not be worthwhile for you to waste your time and money doing a pulley swap if that's all you are planning to do. But if you add an exhaust, intake, high-flow cat, PCM, cams/am gears and bigger injectors, it can all add up to a significant gain. Neons with ALL the popular bolt-ons can see anywhere from 10 to 25 horsepower more at the wheels over a stock Neon.

Motor Mounts

The stock Neon motor mounts are soft and flexible, designed to help reduce vibration and noise. Normal street use

Chapter 12

Mopar Performance Parts offers this stiffer front motor mount for first-gen Neons. It really reduces wheel hop – just stomp on it and go. You can also use it in conjunction with motor mount inserts for an even stronger setup. (Photo courtesy Mopar Performance Parts)

There are various motor mount inserts on the market. You can install these into your current motor mounts for extra control over your engine. They will reduce wheel hop but increase vibration inside the car. (Photo courtesy Chris Malluege)

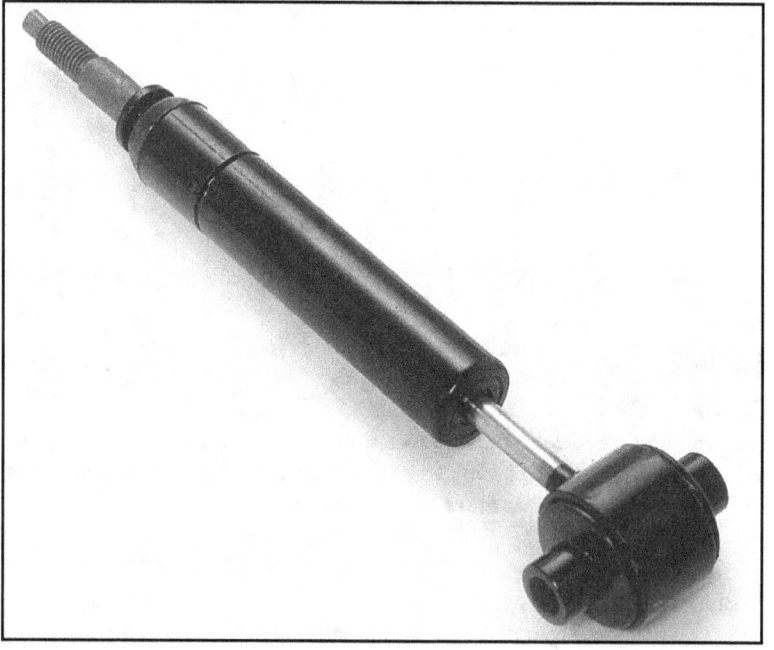

After you've beefed up your front motor mount, the next weakest link is the bobble strut in between the engine and the body. It uses its resistance to help hold the engine in place to reduce movement and wheel hop. Be sure to reuse your factory rubber-coated washers to keep vibration down. (Photo courtesy Mopar Performance Parts)

really presents little problem for the stock mounts until your Neon has been around the block a few times. Even living a pampered life in a street car, motor mounts can wear out and need to be replaced. If you're road racing, motor mounts should be replaced a few times per year. Autocrossers are smart to get new ones installed during the off-season, as should occasional drag racers.

One of the biggest problems autocrossers, hillclimbers, and drag racers experience is wheel hop. If you're stuck in a stock class, then you may just have to learn to live with it. On warm pavement, once you've got a little heat in your tires, wheel hop is barely manageable, even with some practice. But if you experience excessive wheel hop, then it's likely you need to replace either an engine mount or two, or a transmission mount. The more you induce wheel hop, the faster you'll wear out your mounts.

Believe it or not, installing a limited-slip differential doesn't solve the wheel-hop problem, but replacing the front motor mount with a stiffer or solid mount will. This is actually one of the top modifications we recommend. There are polyurethane inserts available that will strengthen your stock motor mounts and reduce wheel hop. Some vendors, such as Deyeme Racing, offer a service where the original motor mounts are filled with a hard urethane compound. We've found these mounts to be less harsh than the ones with inserts – we even run them in our daily-driven Neons. Remember that any modification to stock mounts is not allowed by most stock competition rules, but that doesn't keep it from happening.

Another potentially problematic mount is referred to as the bobble strut. It's located near the bottom rear of the engine and extends from the frame to the motor. The bobble strut pushes on the back of your engine to help keep it from rocking back and fourth. Much like the struts in your suspension, the bobble strut can wear out over time and lose its effectiveness. We've cut polyurethane sway bar bushings, inserted them around the strut rod, and then secured them with a hose clamp. Usually, two is all you need. You can also get an aftermarket solid bar, which is nice if you need to tweak the engine up or down to fit an aftermarket header, or you just want to make sure there's as little movement as possible.

Engine Care and Lubrication

The lubrication industry is a multi-billion-dollar business. I just watched a show on TV where they dyno tested an oil additive. It was not an infomercial – those should be viewed for entertainment purposes only. This one was part of a real test to determine whether it delivered increased horsepower. And, according to the dyno results, it worked.

Another claim I see on TV is how a particular motor oil, for example, Castrol Synthetic, is better for your car. In a Castrol ad, I got the impression they were saying their synthetic oil was better than all other oils. But actually, I noticed the statistics they quoted were actually comparing their synthetic to conventional oils. They have a great marketing strategy. The ad is worded so well (give that ad guy a raise) that even a skeptical viewer could assume that their oil was the best synthetic on the market, and that is not the case.

Whether you tackle an engine swap or decide to hop up your present engine, you should be sure that you are properly caring for the engine. Always refer to

One of the most affordable and rewarding upgrades you can give your Neon is a stiffer front motor mount. If you really want to do it on the cheap, you can remove it and fill the empty space with something hard. This mount has been filled with 3M windshield urethane, which costs about $13. (Photo courtesy Travis Thompson)

your owner's manual or factory workshop handbook for routine engine maintenance, such as changing the oil every 3,000 miles. So which oils seem to be better for your Neon? Most racers and enthusiasts swear by high-quality synthetic oils. Test results indicate that Mobil 1, Havoline, and Castrol Synthetic well exceed the SG/CD ratings, and any would be a good choice. They also beat 95 percent of all of the other conventional and synthetic oils on the market. That is not to say standard motor oil is no good. Many mechanics swear off synthetic and will only use a multi-grade conventional lubricant. Some people speculate that many synthetic oils have recently changed their base oils over to a cheaper type, and that Mobil 1 is the only one that has remained unchanged, but that's just what I've heard. I can tell you from experience that Amsoil, RedLine, and Royal Purple are also excellent synthetics. At this point, I will only consider adding Mobil 1, or these other three smaller-market synthetics into my racecar engine crankcases.

Many sources strongly believe that if you use synthetic oil, you can forget the "change your oil every 3,000 miles" rule. According to most owner's manuals, the recommended oil change inter-

To keep your motor from rocking back and forth, and to control wheel hop, you may consider strengthening your stock motor mounts with these urethane inserts, available from Howell Automotive. Remember to check first to make sure they're allowed by your class rules. (Photo courtesy Howell Automotive)

val is 7,500 miles, but if you read the fine print, they indicate that the oil should be changed more frequently when you operate your vehicle under extreme conditions. That doesn't mean driving your mother-in-law to Bingo on Fridays. It refers to city driving, autocross, drag racing, off-road racing,

Chapter 12

The Moroso Racing oil pan has ended up on nearly every racing Neon we've ever seen. It's not a bad idea, since this unit is specifically designed to keep oil flowing even through those long, sweeping carousel turns. These pans have been known to leak a little, so take great care when installing one to insure a tight seal to the bottom of your block.

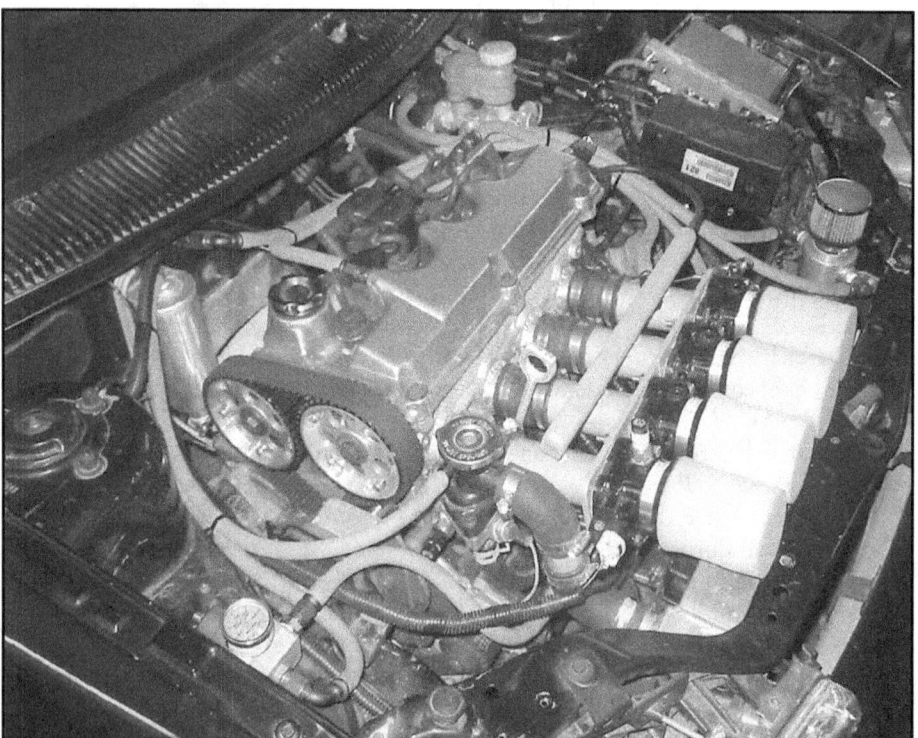

Some engines are out of reach for most of us, but they're still cool to look at. This DOHC 2.0-liter will really deliver the torque you need to break your front axles. Check out the custom intake manifold with individaul throttle bodies.

or even operating your car in an environment where the air contains particles that can get past your air cleaner. So in L.A., you should probably change your oil weekly.

Synthetics do resist foaming, oxidation, and do not contain additives that conventional oils need in order to function properly. These additives tend to break down and contaminate the oil. Synthetics are even more efficient at removing particles from your engine and holding them in suspension until you change your oil. But once the oil contains too many contaminants, synthetic or not, it will no longer be able to suspend them and they'll be redeposited inside your engine. So to change or not to change? The 3,000-mile rule certainly won't hurt your engine, but if you're using synthetics, it could hurt your wallet. Whatever interval you choose, change your oil on a regular schedule to keep your car happy.

If you have an SRT-4, you're probably aware that Chrysler recommends Mobil 1 specifically. We certainly recommend using synthetics with a turbocharged car. The added protection will help extend the life of the turbocharger.

And finally, many enthusiasts feel that in order to help keep a constant supply of oil flowing in and out of your engine, you should consider installing the Moroso aftermarket oil pan. The Moroso pan is a work of art, with its elaborate baffle system with swinging trap doors for maximum oil control. It also has a full windage tray to better strip oil off of the crank. Better yet, its six-quart capacity is two quarts more than stock. Even though we love the Moroso pan installed on the Speednation turbo car, it isn't really necessary. The stock pan is great. We have really challenged the lubrication system of our SSC Neon, racing it at 6,500 rpm for ½ hour at a time. This includes generating over one g of cornering force in several long, sweeping carousels that would challenge any system to keep from getting oil staved, and we haven't had any problems yet.

Chapter 13

Modifications on a Budget

The best way to approach any project is with a budget. This chapter will help you prioritize what you want to do to your Neon or SRT-4. But before you get started, here are a few important points that need to be made.

1. Never buy tires before you buy wheels, but choose your wheel size based on available tires. An example is the guy who buys 18-inch wheels because they were on sale at his local speed shop, but then can't afford the expensive 18-inch tires. Also, if you plan to autocross a Neon that has less than 200 wheel horsepower, then stick with 14-inch rims. You'll be able to take better advantage of the Neon's excellent low-end torque. However, if decent 14-inch autocross tires become phased out (there are rumors), then you should get a 15-inch wheel. There's an excellent selection of 15-inch tires on the market. SRT-4 drivers should also stick with a smaller size rim (no bigger than 17-inch), even though they have enough torque to spin a 20-inch rim. Usually, the smaller the tire, the cheaper the cost, but check out tire selection for your specific racing venue before you buy rims.

2. Don't install cams or cam gears unless you plan on getting (or preferably already have) an intake, header, exhaust, and a performance PCM. Cams and cam gears should be done near the end of your project. The exception to this would be putting a '95 cam into your later-model SOHC, but if you're going through the trouble of swapping, you'd probably want something bigger than that anyway.

3. Ignition systems, wires, and coils are not worth the money unless you have an unlimited budget, or have modified your car past the ability of the stock ignition.

4. If you plan on doing some racing, get a copy of the competition rulebook and read it. Go to a few events and enter your car just the way it is right now, even if it's a rat. Get a feel for that particular racing venue before you spend a

If you're on a budget, you'd better learn how to do things for yourself. Tools can be expensive, but they're usually a one-time expense that can help you save money on future projects. Michael Carpenter is seen here working on his new exhaust.

Chapter 13

Looks like the exhaust modifications worked, as Carpenter's back-up and daily driver Neon is back on the road, and on the autocross course. (Photo courtesy Bob Killmer)

So many people are serious about how shiny their engine compartment is, but you may as well have a little fun with your Neon. A pretty engine won't help you get past a fellow competitor. This JDM (Japanese Domestic Market) power-steering cover is in response to the import guys who buy the expensive dress-up items for their engine – but it probably won't pass a tech inspection at the track. (Photo courtesy Michael Carpenter)

single penny on your car; that way you'll know where it needs help first.

This chapter is all about doing things in an order that will help you get the most out of the modifications you install. So the big question is: Where do you start? This book covers so many different modifications that it's hard to see how they all fit together. The categories that follow will help you determine what set of modifications you should do first. They're organized by what you want to spend on your project, as well as what you want to do with your car. Obviously, I won't suggest that you gut your car to make it lighter if you plan on driving it to work everyday. A straight-through exhaust and race suspension would also make for a long, noisy, and bumpy ride to work. On the other hand, I certainly wouldn't advise someone who is planning to build a full-blown racecar to install a cat-back exhaust, aftermarket ignition, or performance chip. I would skip right over

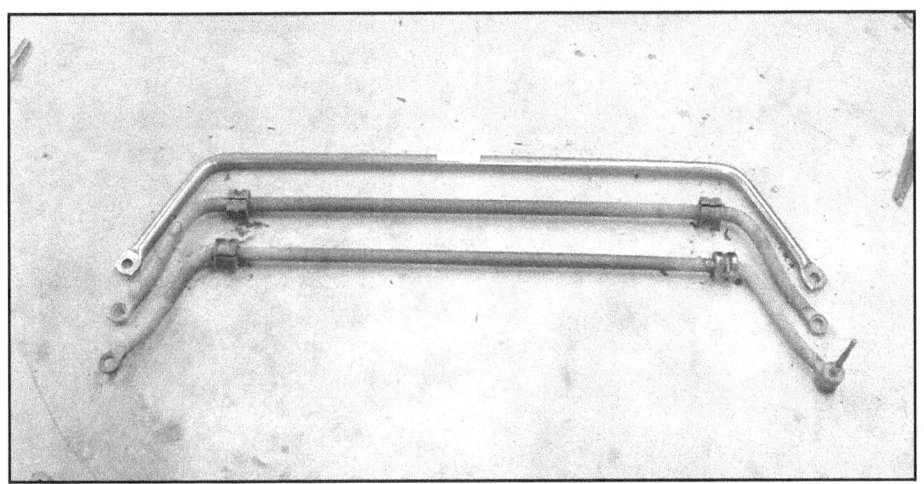

Sway bars are an inexpensive way to get better control of your Neon's handling. Top to bottom, you see a Suspension Techniques bar, an ACR bar, and a standard Neon front sway bar. (Photo courtesy Michael Carpenter)

If you can't afford an expensive air velocity intake system, a $45 K&N stock replacement filter will also give you a few horsepower, and it's washable, so you never need to replace it.

Dual Duty

Do you need your car to get you back and forth to work during the week, but also want to play with it a little on the weekend? Then what you want is a dual-duty project car. Often, serious racing modifications will render your car a pain in the butt to drive on the street (literally). This section is dedicated to providing hop-up alternatives that will work on the track, without compromising comfort on the street. In other words, there needs to be a healthy balance between form and function.

You won't end up with a championship racecar by following these guidelines, but you will be able to preserve your car's street integrity. Only single-purpose racecars have a chance to win championships, unless they have an exceptional driver behind the wheel. Refer to the specific rules for autocross or drag racing to decide which modifications will be in your best interest, as some may prohibit you from competing in the Stock classes. Since there are so many possible scenarios, we have simply outlined modifications that will add to the overall fun in both street driving and weekend amateur racing, even though your car may be ineligible for Stock competition.

Internal engine modifications or rebuilds are not addressed in these sections, as they can completely consume your budget. You can still be competitive without doing anything to your short block. One of our racecars has over 100,000 miles on the odometer. The original bearings were checked and tolerances were measured during a recent ring job, and they were still within factory specs. If you're on a budget, don't fix the engine unless it's broken, or unless you want to add forced induction or Nitrous. If you are starting with an engine that has poor compression, then you'll need to address the problem, which will seriously affect your budget. This shows the importance of starting with the right car. But if you aren't burning too much oil and have decent compression, then just drive it untill it blows. Once it does blow, you can build a killer engine to meet your specific racing needs.

those steps and recommend installing a fully programmable stand-alone aftermarket EFI system and straight-through exhaust. But then I could be giving out the wrong advice if the person doesn't want to spend all that money right away. So you have to define both parameters: 1) how you want to use your car, and 2) how much money you want to spend.

Let's start with the former. There are several levels of race preparation, but we can boil all of them down into these two main categories:

Dual Duty (street during the week – mild autocross, drag, or driver's school on the weekend)

Full Race (Solo I, II, road racing, drag, lapping days)

Under each category, we've listed three budget amounts: *Low Buck* ($1,000); *Moderate Hop-Up* (under $3,000); and *Serious Project* (over $3,000).

Labor costs have not been considered, since they vary greatly. Most of these changes require only a moderate amount of mechanical expertise. For those who plan to go all out, or don't need to consider a financial budget, then you may benefit from reviewing the modifications listed in the Serious Project category to help set your priorities.

Chapter 13

Drag racers aren't the only ones who use different size wheels front and rear. Many autocrossers go with a smaller width in the rear in order to help the car rotate. (Photo courtesy Gil Diaz)

Many FWD cars, such as Hondas and Neons, often go with wider rear wheels for a hillclimb to help the rear stay put. In a hillclimb, you have to compensate for the fact that you'll be negotiating high-speed turns with cold rear tires. By the time this Integra reaches the first turn at the Giants Despair hillclimb, he will be traveling well over 100 mph.

Low Buck ($1,000)

Our goal is to improve both handling and straight-line performance with a budget of $1,000. Without access to used performance parts, this can be a difficult assignment. Assuming you purchase all of the parts new, there are two things that should be given first priority. Low-cost performance struts can usually be found for a few hundred dollars. High-performance Koni adjustables will eat up nearly your entire budget, so you may want to save them for later. You can save money by going with heavier-duty nonadjustable struts. Sway bars are money well spent, but you could also just replace the original factory rubber bushings with polyurethane ones. This can stiffen up the car for only a few dollars. For a low-buck project, we recommend buying a bigger rear bar, unless your class doesn't allow that, in which case you may want to buy a larger front bar. Why some classes won't allow for a rear bar, but do allow for a larger front bar, is beyond me.

Next, spend some money on an alignment. Having ⅛ total toe-out in the front won't eat up your street tires too much on the road, and will really make a difference in "turn in" on the track. Adjust your camber, but don't go more than one degree negative in the front for a street vehicle.

The Mopar High Rate springs are a great budget modification, costing as little as $100 for all four. Check out Neons.org for some leads as to the best places to buy them. These Mopar Performance autocross springs have spring rates of 220 pounds in the front and 180 pounds in the rear. Given the fact that you'll still be driving this car on the street on a regular basis, you should maintain the front/rear balance that was engineered at the factory. In other words, don't make the rear stiffer than the front at this point in your project. Another affordable mod for keeping your Neon flat in the twisties is a strut tower brace (or two).

A cold-air intake system is a cheap and quick way to increase horsepower. A SOHC car can gain three or more extra horsepower, with some extra torque down low. A DOHC will see most of that gain up high. And an SRT-4, well, anything you do to help that turbo breathe better will really pay off. This will only cost you approximately $30 to $40 per horsepower, depending on which intake you choose. Even a replacement K&N filter will add one to two horsepower and costs only about $50.

Weekend drag racers should consider the following, as they emphasize speed over handling. A cold-air intake remains on the top of any list ($150 to $200), and stickier front tires on stock alloy wheels will radically improve your

Money is better spent on your suspension than aftermarket ignition parts. The adjustable coil-over set-up is extremely helpful if you want to get your car balanced. With a set of scales, you can add or subtract weight and raise or lower your suspension to get as close to a 50/50 diagonal weight distribution as possible.

launch. You should also consider stiffer motor mounts to reduce wheel hop at the track. Your quarter-mile times will be faster, and the sticky tires won't cost too much if you are using a smaller diameter rim.

For more engine power on the cheap, you can pick up an auto throttle body for under $50. You can also replace your stock muffler with the high-performance muffler of your choice.

If you have access to used parts (junkyards, Internet), then you can get much more bang for the buck. You may find a cheap intake for less than $100. Find a set of sway bars from an ACR or Sport and grab their sway bars. Some Neon drivers who have rear drum brakes feel cheated, but don't be too quick to do a rear disc swap. We've talked to several people who've done the swap, and most feel it wasn't worth the time or expense. Rear brakes only handle about 20 percent of the braking load. In fact, on our ACR, we converted from the ACR rear disc setup to standard drum brakes to save 16 pounds. Hey, lighter is faster – it all adds up.

A nitrous system is definitely the best bang-for-the-buck modification if you want to go faster in a straight line, but a complete system with all the accessories will practically eat up your entire budget. If you decided to go this route, there'll still be enough money to buy two wider wheels, and then throw on a pair of used slicks for the track.

The cheapest of all modifications you can make is to lighten your Neon wherever you can. If you can live without the A/C, you'll lose 50+ pounds. Don't bother cutting out the door bars on first-generation Neons – it's not worth the weight savings unless you are planning to get involved in serious racing, and it's not safe for the street. Removing the insulation from the floor boards is a long process, but it can save 30 pounds. Follow the recommendations in the Body and Interior Modifications chapter for more suggestions.

After you set up your suspension, get your racecar to an alignment rack to set the toe and camber. This should be the final step of your suspension project, and a great way to spend $75.

Inexpensive, custom offset, lightweight spun-steel Diamond Racing wheels are an excellent choice for racing. Pictured are 14 x 8-inch rims with Kumho V700 tires.

Moderate Hop-Up (Under $3,000)

If you want to get the maximum handling and performance out of your Neon without adding a turbocharger (which wouldn't leave any money to do anything else), then you can build a killer car for under $3,000. The first priority for autocrossers should be to upgrade your struts. You won't believe the difference in handling that a performance strut, like adjustable Konis, can make. That will take a huge, $600+ bite out of your budget, but it's the only way to be competitive. You now can add stiffer springs, going with either the 220/180-pound High-Rate combo, or stepping it up even more to a 310/230-pound X-tra High-Rate set. Serious Solo competitors should also get adjustable camber plates, as well as larger front and rear sway bars.

Depending upon your priorities, and which expert you consult, there could be a great deal of recommendations about what to do next. More power is often the next choice. The problem with more power is that you probably won't be able to take advantage of it on the autocross course. But if your preference is street performance, then more power is the way to go. Since we're working on a bigger budget, you should consider a hotter cam(s) with an adjustable cam gear(s). A reprogrammed PCM like those from Mopar Performance is also an excellent upgrade at this stage. A header can range from $150 to nearly $300 for a very nice unit, such as the one manufactured by Kirk. Remember, you get what you pay for when it comes to headers. Either way, a header can help you save weight and make your car breathe better at the same time. Certainly, replacing the exhaust system would be advised by this point in the project, and would also capture at least five more horsepower. Remember to check the weight of your new system before buying it. Never replace a stock system with one that's heavier – that just doesn't make sense.

However, none of these options should be the next priority for the dual-driver car. In order to take full advantage of all of the suspension modifications performed so far, the best way to spend your money is to buy an extra set of wheels and race tires. Whether you are a weekend autocrosser, do time trials, or hang out at the drag strip, your times will improve substantially with a set of race wheels and tires. Absolutely nothing in racing feels better than getting the traction you need, when you need it. In autocrossing, race tires are worth an average of two seconds per lap on a one-minute course. The time drop is not so dramatic in drag racing, but quarter-mile time will instantly respond to better grip off the line. It's important not to skimp on the wheels, since a good set can last a lifetime of autocrossing. Shortly after buying cheap steel wheels you may begin to wish you had opted for the lighter, higher-quality aluminum rims. The reduction in rotating mass alone is worth the price. If you have a turbo car, the difference won't be as noticeable, since you have so much torque to begin with. Don't buy wheels and tires until you go to the track a few times. Ask questions to see what the best tire for your application is at the moment (it changes so often). Excellent wheel-and-tire combos are often put up for sale by competitors at an event, so keep your eyes open. You can find tons of great

Modifications on a Budget

To help rotate the rear end, Mark Daddio's Turbo Neon was set up with narrower rear tires pumped up to 70 psi. This is not recommended for the average driver unless you like going sideways in every turn.

If your budget can handle it, you can get a lot of horsepower by adding an even larger intercooler to your SRT-4. Colder air is denser air, which makes for better combustion, and more power.

parts for great prices at an event – including complete turnkey racecars.

Serious Project (Over $3,000)

With the right driver and the right combination of parts, $3,000 is often enough money to build yourself a nationally competitive car. At the same time, you may think $3,000 to $5,000 would be plenty to get you where you want to be, but as your car gets more and more competitive, performance seems to come at greater costs. In other words, the first $2,000 could get your car 70 percent of the way, but the next 30 percent will cost you a lot more money.

The trick is to not go crazy. Remember, the goal of this section is to retain the use of your vehicle for the street, and there are many performance parts that would compromise this plan.

$5,000 is enough money to buy a turbo kit, plus do everything else outlined in the under $3K section above. A serious turbo project may also include building up the motor with stronger pistons and rods. There also may be some modifications to the kit to further improve the setup, such as larger injectors or a bigger fuel pump.

This is also a good time to spend some money to save some weight. Lightweight aluminum brackets are available to replace some of the cast-iron parts that came on your Neon. Saving weight this way can be expensive, as these strong but light parts aren't cheap. It all starts to add up, and before you know it, you will have shaved off 100 pounds. You may also want to consider buying a good racing seat. It could weigh as much as 25 pounds less, plus give you more control. Seats can run as high as $800, but there are acceptable options out there for $250.

A monster throttle body combined with a trick intake manifold will complement the cold-air intake you installed earlier. The intake manifold can either be an off-the-shelf item, such as the Indy intake, or you can send your current aluminum intake out for extrude honing.

If you insist on adding an ignition system, now is the time. Make sure it has a rev limiter so that your friends who ask to co-drive your car can't blow up the engine. The two-stage limiter on the MSD DIS-2 is both fun and functional.

No serious project would be complete without a way to keep power going to both front wheels during a race. A limited-slip differential is the only solution, but they are very expensive. Don't be fooled by cheap products that claim to do the same thing. A Quaife will set you back $1,200 plus installation.

Finally, for turbo cars, adding that huge intercooler you had your eye on is a great idea for this phase. We trust Turbonetics (formerly Spearco) when it comes to expertise in the field. Be prepared to spend at least $400 to $800 for

Chapter 13

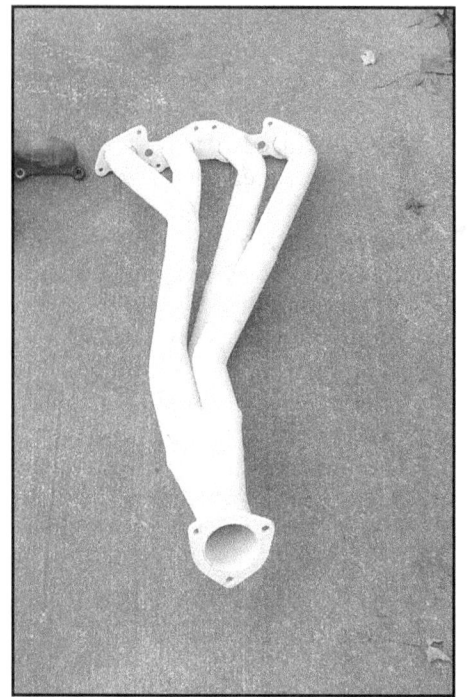

A decent header is a good way to spend your hard-earned cash. You may need to do some modification to your firewall to provide proper clearance for the header. (Photo courtesy Michael Carpenter)

Cam(s) are best suited for cars that have some extra fuel and air to take advantage of the higher lift and longer duration. You can pick up some decent power, but only if you have all the supporting mods.

an upgraded unit. Hahn Racecraft also makes a very nice unit.

Full Race

Building a no-holds-barred racecar need not be more expensive than a dual-duty project. Unlike the parameters described above, there are significant differences in budget allocation depending upon the racing venues: autocross, road racing, and drag. Since you don't need to worry about street worthiness, attention can be focused on all-out performance and handling without concern for comfort. In other words, function takes precedence over form.

Low Buck ($1,000)

Many of the same priorities outlined in the Low Buck Dual Duty section also apply here. Autocrossers need to spend their $1,000 on improving the car's handling before concentrating on speed. Stiffer springs and a rear sway bar will likely eat up a good chunk of this low-buck budget.

Road racers or Solo I competitors, on the other hand, will find a $1,000 budget too restrictive to allow actual track competition. All of the spending will need to concentrate on upgrading safety, as SCCA rules require a full cage, legal harness, a fire bottle, etc. Don't forget the money you will have to spend to protect your body: driver's suit, gloves, nomex socks, shoes, and a Snell SA2000+ helmet. The cost for these items alone is well over $600. To be practical, a minimal budget of at least $1,500 for you and your car pass the initial technical inspection. Conversely, one good thing about building a full road-race project is that you can increase performance simply by taking parts off of the car (check with your class rules before you start cutting). So even if you only have two bucks left in your budget, you can still increase performance by decreasing weight. Just drop your car over at my house for the weekend – I'll take care of it. I've gained a reputation as a hack who can gut a car in just a few hours. One of my friends left me with his CSP autocross car one summer when his job required he leave town for awhile. When he came back, he was shocked as he could barely recognize the gutted carcass. I eventually put everything back after winning my class that season in his car.

On the other hand, building a competent, low-buck drag racer is possible even with a $1,000 spending limit. That's because your focus will be on speed as opposed to handling. As you have read in previous chapters, there are some inexpensive ways to boost power. However, with a $1,000 spending limit, you won't be able to turn 10-second quarter-mile times in any Neon, but you could get well into the 13s with nitrous, some sticky tires, an intake, and some weight reduction. You will also experience a law of decreasing returns as the amount of money you spend increases. In other words, the first $1,000 you put into the car will net you the most bang for the buck, but after that, the cost of speed will increase exponentially.

Finally, gather up whatever cash you have left and get down to the local muffler shop. Cut off the exhaust system right before the cat, and have a pipe welded on so that it exits out the side of the car in front of the rear passenger-side wheel. Low-end torque may suffer, but when you get the RPMs up, there will be a gain in power. You'll also save a ton of weight in the process. If you're not planning on continuing to phase two at some point in the future, then you should get some type of cheap muffler (cherry bomb – about $30) so that some amount of back pressure can be maintained.

Moderate Hop-Up (Under $3,000)

Autocrossers will still primarily be following the formula for dual-duty cars. If you opt for competition in a highly modified class that doesn't require DOT-approved tires, you can save additional funds. A set of lightly used slicks ($200) will make lots of room in the budget for other goodies.

The next priority is to buy the correct super-light alloy wheels for your class. Just see what the national champions are using, and get those same wheels. That could cost between $500 to nearly $1,000. There will still be plenty of cash left in the budget to fabricate a cheap exhaust system (as above) with a nice muffler at the end to provide the back pressure and low-end torque you need for autocrossing. A Supertrapp ($150) can be tuned right at the track to add a little torque where you need it, depending on the course. If money is budgeted properly, $3,000 can get you most of the way to a regionally competitive Solo II car.

Road racers will finally have some money to play with when moving from a low-buck project to this level of modification. Improved handling needs to be the first area of concentration, as the goal is to make the chassis as tight as possible. The parts needed, and their costs, are similar to those used in Solo II (shocks/struts, springs, rear sway bar, bushings). This will consume much of the additional $2,000 that was added to the low-buck modification budget. With any remaining cash, you'll need to buy at least four extra rims (eight would be better). If you're racing in a Stock class, then you can save money by finding a few sets of stock alloys at a boneyard. You'll also need an additional set of race tires, and probably a set of rain tires. If you're racing in a more modified class where wider wheels are necessary to be competitive, then you can likely only afford steel wheels at this time, plus a good set of road-race compound tires. At least with competitive tires, you can get out on the racetrack and try out the new suspension. Power improvements will have to wait for more money to be added to the budget.

Drag racers, on the other hand, will again put power above all other considerations. Once you get going very fast, you'll need to pay more attention to keeping the car pointed in the right direction as it zips down the quarter mile. In the previous section, the goal was to make the car breathe better, so now you should concentrate on giving it some extra fuel. A performance PCM, bigger injectors, and monster throttle body added to the intake purchased in the Low Buck Hop-Up will cost another $1,000.

Now it's decision time. If you plan on going all the way, then stop right here and save the rest of your money for the next section. However, if $3,000 is all

If you start with a cheap car and save money by camping at the track as opposed to staying at a motel, you can afford to spend your money on good racing tires, which can cost $150 to $190 each!

you want to spend, and you want the lowest quarter-mile times possible, then a nitrous system is the answer. A pair of serious drag tires should be your next purchase, which eat up the rest of the money left in your budget.

Serious Project (Over $3,000)

Autocrossers can now go for serious power, but first you should pick a class. There's a lot of money to be saved if you know what you want up front. Don't buy a part that you'll eventually replace with an even better part when you move to a more modified class.

If you choose to go to a Race Prepared or Street Modified class, then it is time for a 2.4-liter engine and/or turbo system. At the very least, you'll need a great ported head. If your goal is Street Prepared or Street Touring, then money should be spent on an aftermarket, stand-alone EFI system. If that is too much for you both financially or in the time needed for installation or tuning, then go for the Mopar PCM and injectors.

Stock class competition can also be expensive, as the price for an extra set of factory alloys plus DOT race tires can cost more than the wheels and tires for other classes. But check out the rules for your class before getting started.

As for the road racer, in addition to what was purchased with the $3,000 budget, the next item to consider is a PCM. Upping the rev limit in a car that has to perform a hundred shifts or more per race can be a major time savings. Adding bigger injectors and some head work to this package will complete your quest to be a competitive regional racer, or even a national competitor as long as you aren't trying for a GT class.

Drag racers with enough money can install a turbo system. This is usually the most rewarding way to go drag racing given a limited budget. The other possibility is to swap on an SRT-4 head/manifolds/turbo along with one of the Mopar Performance Staged kits. Either way, continue with the weight reduction you started in the previous section. Breaking the 10-second barrier is possible with a turbo, nitrous, some good head and engine work, and an extremely lightweight body.

Will 2005 be the final year of Neon production? It looks like the end – unless the popularity of the SRT-4 can save the platform for another year.

Summary

Improving your car's performance while sticking to a budget can often be a difficult thing. There are many decisions to be made based on your priorities. Once you form a plan for your car (street, dual duty or full race), these decisions become easier. Don't give in to pressure from friends who may influence you to buy parts that are either over your budget, or that you simply don't need for your application. They're probably trying to feel better about wasting their money on "cool" new parts that they now know don't work. And don't give in to easy credit. If a particular part is over the budget you set, instead of picking up your MasterCard, pick up your mouse and search the net for used performance parts. eBay is great, but join some forums and message boards as well, such as Neons.org. The accumulated knowledge you find there will make this book seem like it's just scratching the surface when it comes to building a high-performance Neon or SRT-4. You also can't imagine what kinds of deals your fellow users will post on a daily basis.

Where Do We Go From Here?

It really does look like 2005 will be the last year for the Neon, but we hope that the popularity of the SRT-4 can delay its demise for just a little longer. The replacement, with a working title of "PM," will be a true world car, based on the current Neon and Mitsubishi Lancer. It will likely be powered by a modified 2.0-liter Hyundai engine. A turbocharged version will probably be introduced in 2007. Unlike the Neon, which never shared production with any other car manufacturer, Mitsubishi and Hyundai may both have versions of the PM for sale in China and Japan. Hopefully this new car will be as much fun as our beloved Neon. That will be a difficult task to say the least. I can't begin to describe how much fun I have had racing Neons over the years.

We hope this book was able to address your questions and will keep you from wasting valuable resources on parts that either don't work, or that you don't really need. Good luck, and try to save the racing for the track, not the street.

CHAPTER 14

DON'T JUST SIT THERE – GO RACING!

Your Neon wants to go racing. If it could talk, it would tell you straight out, but since it can't, we'll tell you. You're probably driving the best bang-for-the-buck racecar on the planet, but until you get off the couch and stop watching NASCAR and F1 on TV, you won't know what you are missing. (Photo courtesy Gil Diaz)

Solo II Autocross

Autocross is a very popular form of amateur racing in which ordinary people like you and I can participate. Participation has nearly doubled since the SCCA (Sports Car Club of America) introduced several new classes that allowed for common modifications that most import enthusiasts perform. The only special equipment you will need is a vehicle (even pickup trucks qualify), a helmet (usually can be borrowed at the event), a seat belt (no way around this one), a driver's license, and a brain (at times, optional).

Solo II competition usually involves a group of people (usually part of a club) who get together on Sundays (sometimes Saturdays too) to race their cars around parking lots following a course laid out in orange pylons. The cost: about $15 to $20 on the average. For that money you get three to five laps around the course, plus some fun runs (depending on the club). Timing devices keep track of how long it takes you to com-

Chapter 14

Autocross is just one of the great racing opportunities that await you and your Neon. Solo II is inexpensive and low risk, and won't damage your car. It's a great car-control classroom that can help prepare you for high-speed racing. (Photo courtesy Bob Killmer)

plete the course. The quickest times win. Sounds kind of stupid? In a way, it is, but it's also great fun.

The best way to get involved in autocrossing is to get a schedule of events in your area. If you don't know where to turn, go to Speednation and e-mail us and we'll tell you. Most local SCCA regions also have websites, or you can go to SCCA.org. Then just go out and do it! Don't wait until you have your Neon perfectly set up. Chances are, if you've never been autocrossing, but are preparing a Neon to race, you'll likely make some stupid mistakes that you'll regret later. Just go – even with the Neon you're driving to work right now. Even if you don't currently have a Neon and you're reading this book to get some ideas as to which model you should buy, take out your current car, even if it's a

Just do it. Don't wait for your car to be perfect. Don't wait for that new suspension or head. Just take your Neon to an autocross now. A little more prep and experience is needed for track events, but there are entry-level track events put on by both NASA and the SCCA that don't require a roll cage or a driver's suit.

120   High-Performance Dodge Neon Builder's Handbook

Don't Just Sit There – Go Racing!

Hillclimbs are also part of SCCA's Solo I program. Depending on the region and the class, an SCCA legal roll bar may be sufficient, but a driver's suit and Snell helmet are required.

beater. You may find a Neon racer for sale at the event or within the SCCA racing network that's ready to race, for a price less than what you could buy all the go-fast parts for.

Here are a few pointers to make your first event go more smoothly. Take the fuzzy dice down from your rear view mirror, clean out the interior so that there is nothing on the floor or seats that can fly around, leave your hubcaps and floor mats at home, and stop by the gas station along the way to get some extra air in your front tires. Heavier cars like Mustangs, T-birds, or K-cars on DOT-approved street tires should start with at least 45 psi, but lighter cars (like Neons) only need about 35 psi. Rear tire pressures should be around 30 psi. When you get to the event, ask someone at registration to hook you up with someone who's also running a Neon so they can give you further advice on what pressures to use. Don't worry about having to run against a new Corvette Z06 with your little pocket rocket. The SCCA has an excellent grouping of classes that, for the most part, offer a fair and level playing field. But believe it or not, on a local level, much of the time a Neon will be quicker than a Corvette.

There are five main levels of vehicle preparation. The Stock class allows beefier shocks, struts, ignition wires, coil, race tires, and not much else. If you just bought a cool set of rims, a fancy driver's seat, or a slick Momo steering wheel, you'll likely be bumped into Street Prepared. This class allows suspension mods (including lowering), any size wheel, and many of the things outlined in this book. Add a hot cam (even if you do nothing else) and you are instantly in Prepared. This class allows almost everything, except putting a rotary engine in a Spitfire. That'll land you into the Modified class.

In 1997, the SCCA realized that they were making it difficult for those drivers with common, street-legal modifications to compete. Specifically, most Neon owners who want to do some minor hop-up mods for the street have lowered their cars, bought 17-inch or larger wheels, and added a cold-air intake. As long as the car isn't competing on "R" rated race tires (Hoosier, BFG R-1s, etc.), you may fit into the new Street Touring classes, which consist of (in level of modification going from little to lots): Street Touring, Street Touring X, Street Modified, and Street Modified 2 (for 2-seaters). If you have an engine transplant, then you qualify for Street Modified as long as you don't change manufacturers. In other words, you can't put a rotary engine into a Neon, but you can put a Viper engine in an SRT-4 (not that you would want to). Even though it's technically the same company, you couldn't compete in a Neon fitted with a Mercedes powerplant, but you could put in an SRT engine. In fact, adding a turbo or supercharger is fair game. Almost anything goes in the Street Modified classes, but you must retain the car's front interior (you can strip much of the rear). You

Chapter 14

A weekend at the track can be a great way to spend your free time. You take your car off the trailer and go. Once you're hooked, your friends will be shocked when they ask you about the NASCAR or F1 race, and you answer: "I didn't see the race. They don't have televisions at the track." (Photo courtesy Howell Automotive)

also must retain the headlights, glass, etc. These classes are intended for street-legal cars. The good news is that the SCCA has finally put all of the Solo II rules up on their website for all to see. Just go to SCCA.org to review all the classes, and to find the contact numbers of a region near you.

Neons have always done well in the Solo II classes. The SCCA does move the Neon around from time to time, so check the rules, but currently both stock Neons and ACRs are classes in G Stock, where they are very competitive. Neons will commonly turn up in the Street Touring and Modified classes, as well as in D Street Prepared, where Mark Daddio scored a national championship.

Neons and SRT-4s are natural autocrossers. It does take a half-dozen or so races to get a good sense of what class you should run in, and which modifications you should make. That's why you shouldn't do anything until you go to a few events. For example, don't go out and buy new street tires and assume that you will have better traction. Actually, the balder the tire, the better. That's because new tires have full tread – tread that will bend as you go around a sharp turn, causing you to lose traction. We recommend not washing or waxing your car before you go. No one will be impressed. People may actually expect you to drive well if your car looks good.

Most veteran autocrossers are impressed by guys or gals (another good thing about autocrossing) who show up driving beat-up, crappy looking, or tame vehicles (like stock Chevettes or Pintos), then proceed to beat the living hell out of them. You'll become instantly popular if your car looks a little ratty, but you attack the course aggressively.

Over the years, we've seen most every kind of vehicle show up at an autocross, including a 1979 Fury, 1982 Audi station wagon, 1981 Lincoln, etc. We even see rental cars (not that we would ever do such a thing), company cars, and the occasional tow vehicle (as in "my racecar wouldn't start.") Some clubs are affiliated with the SCCA, and some are independent. Plan to get to the event early so that you can have time to walk the course and socialize with some of the more experienced drivers. You shouldn't worry about smashing into your competitors. Autocross is "solo" racing – one car at a time. There are other venues available if you prefer to go door-to-door racing. Most clubs operate a driver's school at the beginning of the season, and there are national schools where you can get instruction from SCCA National Champions. The Evolution school, run by Jean Kinser, is the best. Check out www.autocross.com/ evolution for all the information.

Older Neons are getting booted out of SSC (a national SCCA road racing class), but they're finding their way into ITA (a regional SCCA road racing class).

Former Neon racer and SSC National Champion Joel Lipperini, who defected to Honda in 2004, is nudging his fiancé, Nicole Cooper, at the starting line of the Weatherly Hillclimb. With friends, food, and a great bunch of competitors, what's not to like about racing?

Solo I Hillclimbing, Track Events, and Driver's Schools

If you're looking for a sport that combines some of the best aspects of autocross, rally racing, and road racing, then hillclimbing may be for you. Defined as a category I Solo event, hillclimbing takes you off the track and puts you on the side of a mountain. Actually, it's very much like autocrossing, except that the pylons are made of stone and wood (boulders and trees), and if you go "off course," the consequences are likely to be more serious. You're also going twice as fast. Instead of joking with your autocross friends in the parking lot about the mistake you made on your last run, a similar mistake in hillclimbing may result in discussing your blood type

Chapter 14

Karting is also a great way to get involved in racing. Shifter karts are also welcomed at most autocrosses.

Sport Compact drag racing seems to get more popular every year. Neons are great cars to drag. They're easy and inexpensive to modify, and fun to drive.

and trying to determine how many fingers the paramedic is holding up in front of your face on your way to the hospital. But don't let us scare you out of trying this great sport.

Solo I programs also schedule events on road-race tracks across the country. Passing is sometimes allowed but with strict limitations. You get a great deal more track time when a Solo I is held on a race course. One more word about Solo I: While I was spinning around for the third time after already punting seven heavy wooded guardrail posts, it occurred to me that Neons crash well. My neck didn't even hurt afterwards. Yes, I was lucky, but I would probably have been jerked around a lot more if I was in one of my Hondas going 110 mph around the turn they call "Oh Shit." And if you wreck a Neon, there are used ones around for $500. That way you can transfer over all of your undamaged go-fast parts and your wallet won't hurt as much as if you'd been driving an Aston Martin.

Road Racing – Improved Touring

Improved Touring (IT) racing is a great next step for Solo I or autocrossers. To get involved in IT racing, you'll need to become a member of the SCCA or NASA. They just don't let anyone go out on the track and compete. You have to go to SCCA-approved driver's schools, apply for a novice license, and then you can earn your road-racing license. NASA is way more lax, and regions differ, so check with the program nearest you.

You must have an SCCA-approved roll cage installed in your car, a fire extinguisher with a sold metal mount, and a full SFI approved drivers suit with accompanying Nomex undergarments and socks. Your seat belts and harnesses must be no more than two years old.

Entry fees for IT are also higher (often $150+), but you get a great deal more track time. IT racers tend to feel that the rest of us are wasting our time on racing weekends, because their track time is measured in hours, not in minutes. We, on the other hand, feel that IT racers are wasting their time during the

Don't Just Sit There – Go Racing!

week, as their repair and preparation time is usually measured in days as opposed to hours. IT racing is definitely the best bang for the buck, but it's a major time and money commitment. Parts break and wear out more frequently, and they must be repaired and replaced during the week. Neons were finally approved for IT racing (specifically, ITA) in 2005.

Road racers have something to be proud of. They don't just race around a parking lot; they do real racing in every sense of the word. It requires a great deal of skill, much more than with autocrossing. And although Solo racing is more precise (the clock is unforgiving), most people would rather lose a race to the clock than to the tire wall. Of course, Solo I hillclimbers often lose a race to the trees, but at least they don't have to worry about who's on their tail.

SCCA National Road Racing

The main difference between IT racing and SCCA National Road Racing is that Improved Touring classes are only regional. It's a little confusing. They run on the same tracks, often on the same weekend, and are both part of the SCCA. But IT is where many of the no longer eligible National cars go to race. Newer Neons still qualify for Showroom Stock C, but older ones do not. There's one National Championship for the SCCA (the Runoffs), and it will likely continue at Mid-Ohio. Over the years, however, there have also been several national IT racing championships, including the ARRC (American Road Race of Champions), held at tracks like Road Atlanta.

Showroom Stock classes A, B, and C require the least amount of startup cash as opposed to the GT classes, which consist of tube frame monsters costing as much as $100,000 to build. We have little to say about this aspect of motorsports, since it's far from being an entry-level competition. The Runoffs, however, are a lot of fun to watch.

Basically, you need to decide where you want to build a car for national competition, or whether you are more interested in regional racing. Of course, you can go to any track in the US and run in

After a run, you need to check under your hood to make sure everything is okay. Look for any leaking fluids and check for funny smells. Opening the hood also helps cool down the engine between runs. (Photo courtesy Howell Automotive)

IT. Spec Neon is a newer class that started in 2004, and is run on a regional level. There are limited modifications allowed, more than SSC. It will likely remain a regional class, but Spec Miata was just made a national class, so who knows?

Driver's Schools

A good way to get prepared for high-speed racing is to attend a driver's school. If you want to go road racing, then you will need to make sure the driver's school is certified by the SCCA.

There are also many schools that are manufacturer specific, but they will often let you join in even if you don't have a Porsche or BMW (two of the most popular club schools). You have to bring your own equipment, however. Of course, there are the professional schools, but registration fees can be rather steep. They'll usually provide a vehicle and everything else you need to get some serious track time. Most racetracks conduct driver's schools of their own. In certain parts of the country, there are schools that are run in parking lots! They set up a Solo I type of course and provide you with all of the gear you need (some including the car). These are usually a lot less expensive, so you get a lot of seat time for the money.

Last, but not least, many tracks around the country can be rented for the day. You and a group of your friends (preferably with some racing experience) can ante-up the cash to rent the track for a weekday, and sometimes on a weekend when no formal races are scheduled. Usually passing is restricted to the straight-a-ways, roll cages are not required, and neither are driver's suits, but you can still total your car. The last "lapping day" that I went to before this book was written saw one Porsche 928 roll, one 1990 Civic t-bone an Integra, and another few cars go flying off the course just missing the tire wall.

Drag Racing

The light turns green, and you step on the gas – what could be simpler? Are you tired of this type of attitude, usually coming from the guy wearing a "No Fear" hat who's never competed legally in a racing event before? They should sit in the passenger seat of one of my record-holding hillclimb Neons and I'll show them fear. Another common opinion is that drag rac-

Chapter 14

To further avoid a catastrophic fire, many classes require that your Neon have a fuel cell. They're a bit of a chore to install, but worth the labor if you plan on doing some high-speed, dangerous racing. Also, many fuel cells allow you to run your Neon down to less than one gallon of gas, since the fuel pick-up is better than the stock Neon set-up. Once your racecar (with no fuel cell) gets under a 1/4 tank of gas, the car will starve for fuel in a long, sweeping turn. (Photo courtesy Howell Automotive)

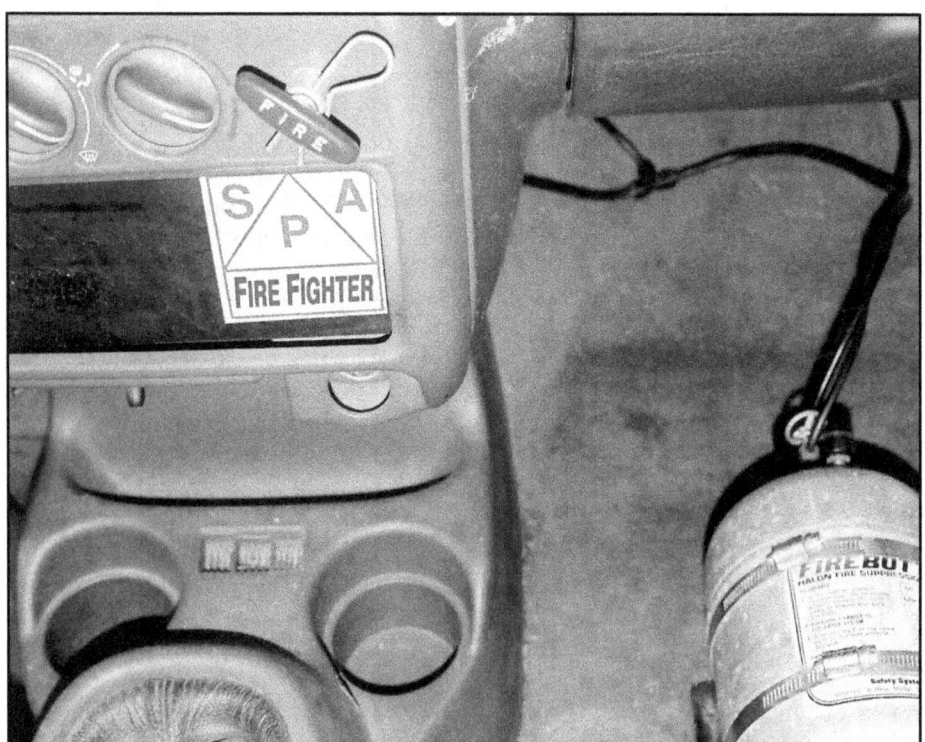

Safety equipment is very important and is mandated by most sanctioning bodies. This onboard fire system is designed to extinguish flames in the engine compartment and cockpit by just pulling the fire switch on the dash.

ing is more about RWD muscle car preparation and engine building than it is about driving. Tell that to the guy in the Neon who's doing the quarter mile in less than 10 seconds. With the recent boom in hopping-up Japanese cars, the drag racing scene has completely changed and is now more popular than ever.

Back in the old days, the only time you would see an import car on a drag strip was at a VW Bug convention. But now, the import and sport-compact drivers outnumber the "Muscle Car Guys" at many strips. In fact, drag racing has become a social event. There are countless local clubs formed for guys and gals who love to work on and modify their FWD sport compacts. These clubs often meet weekly to help a buddy transplant a GSR engine into a Civic, or to just hang out and play video racing games. It's a great way to spend the evening. It's easy to get started with drag racing. Just show up at the local track for a test-and-tune session, or you can hop on to the Internet to get more info. The SRT-4 was made for this venue of racing. Show up with a bone-stock SRT-4 and you'll likely send a lot of those rice-burner Civics home crying. Many of the sport compact car clubs have web pages and can provide details about local drag strips and club meeting times.

Slower cars don't require special equipment (helmets, racing harnesses, fire system, etc.), but if you start turning sub-13-second times, you'll be required to install safety equipment and wear a Snell-rated helmet and/or a driver's suit. You may also need to have roll-up windows and wear long pants. Try organizing a group of your own friends to go drag racing one day, then autocrossing the next. Use combined times to declare bragging rights. Remember, the point is to maximize fun per dollar. As far as fun goes, it's hard to beat this combination. But be warned, drag racing and autocrossing are especially addictive, so caution needs to be taken to insure maintaining stability in your marriage, at work, or at school. Then again, bring along your spouse. Coed racing is more popular now than ever. You also see a lot of father/son and father/daughter racing teams. Use the excuse that it could bring your family closer together. It just might.

Source Guide

AEM and DC Sports
Phone: (310) 484-2322
Fax: (310) 484-0152
www.aempower.com

Diamond Racing Wheels
Phone: (800) 937-4407
Fax: (414) 744-2019
www.diamondracingwheels.com

DynoMax
Phone: (734) 384-7807
www.dynomax.com

Flowmaster
Phone: (800) 544-4761
Fax: (707) 544-4784
www.flowmastermufflers.com

Forward Motion
Phone: (302) 658-2829
Fax: (302) 658-2899
www.forwardmotioninc.com

Howell Automotive
Phone: (800) 531-2184
Fax: (304) 788-3096
www.howellautomotive.com

Iceman Intakes
Phone: (909) 920-5194
Fax: (909) 920-4196
www.icemanmotorsports.com

Modern Performance
Phone: (713) 270-8520
Fax: (713) 270-8890
www.modernperformance.com

Mopar Performance Parts
www.moparperformance.com

Neons.org Forum
www.neons.org
Speednation
Phone: (412) 882-3100
Fax: (724) 926-0215
www.speednation.com

SRTForums
www.srtforums.com

The Tire Rack
(888) 541-1777
www.tirerack.com

Discount Tire Direct
(800) 385-3322
www.tires.com

Notes

More Information for Your Project ...

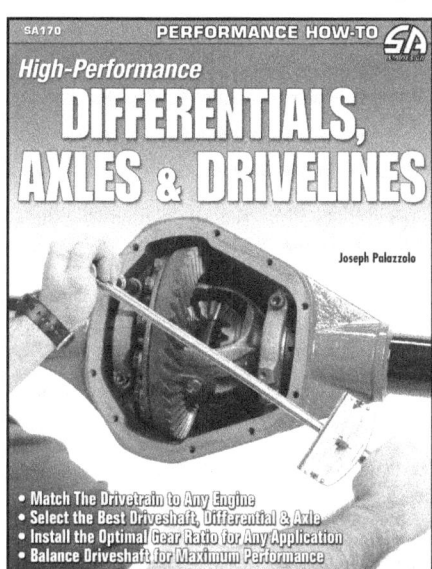

HIGH-PERFORMANCE DIFFERENTIALS, AXELS & DRIVELINES *by Joseph Palazzolo* This book covers everything you need to know about selecting the most desirable gear ratio, rebuilding differentials and other driveline components, and matching driveline components to engine power output. Learn how to set up a limited-slip differential, install high-performance axle shafts, swap out differential gears, and select products for the driveline. This book explains rear differential basics, rear differential housings, rebuilding open rear differentials, limited-slip differentials, and factory differentials. Ring and pinion gears, axle housings, axle shafts, driveshafts, and U-joints are also covered. Softbound, 8-1/2 x 11 inches, 144 pages, approx. 400 color photos. *Item #SA170*

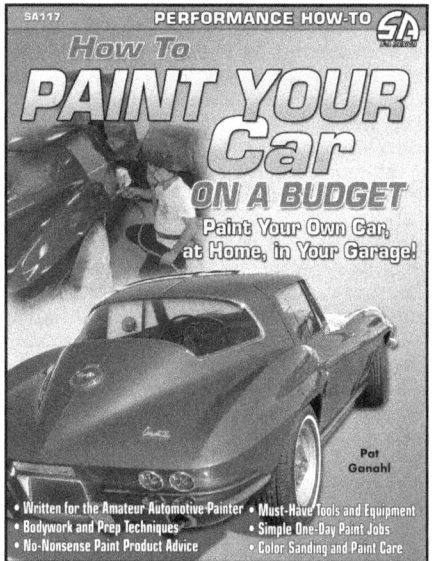

HOW TO PAINT YOUR CAR ON A BUDGET *by Pat Ganahl* If your car needs new paint, or even just a touch-up, the cost involved in getting a professional job can be more than you bargained for. In this book, author Pat Ganahl unveils dozens of secrets that will help anyone paint their own car. From simple scuff-and-squirt jobs to full-on, door-jambs-and-everything paint jobs, Ganahl covers everything you need to know to get a great-looking coat of paint on your car and save lots of money in the process. Covers painting equipment, the ins and outs of prep, masking, painting and sanding products and techniques, and real-world advice on how to budget wisely when painting your own car. Softbound, 8-1/2 x 11 inches, 128 pages, approx. 400 color photos. *Item #SA117*

THE STEP-BY-STEP GUIDE TO ENGINE BLUEPRINTING *by Rick Voegelin* this book is simply the best book available on basic engine preparation for street or racing. Rick Voegelin's writing and wrenching skills put this book in a class by itself. Includes pro's secrets of using tools, selecting and preparing blocks, cranks, rods, pistons, cylinder heads, selecting cams and valvetrain components, balancing and assembly tips, plus worksheets for your engine projects, and much more! Softbound, 8-1/2 x 11 inches, 128 pages, over 400 b/w photos. *Item #SA21*

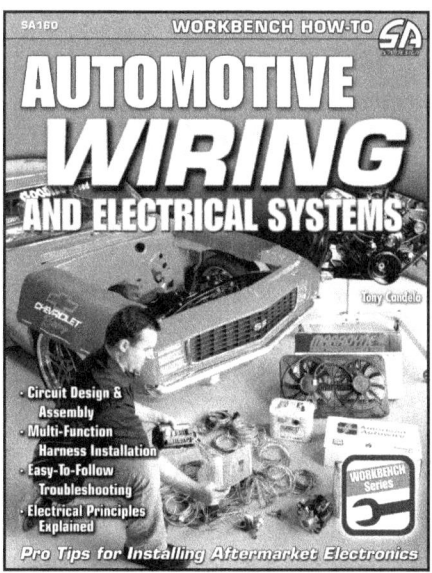

AUTOMOTIVE WIRING AND ELECTRICAL SYSTEMS *by Tony Candela* This book is the perfect book to unshroud the mysteries of automotive electrics and electronic systems. The basics of electrical principles, including voltage, amperage, resistance, and Ohm's law, are revealed in clear and concise detail, so the enthusiast understands what these mean in the construction and repair of automotive electrical circuits. Softbound, 8-1/2 x 11 inches, 144 pages, approx. 350 color photos. *Item #SA160*

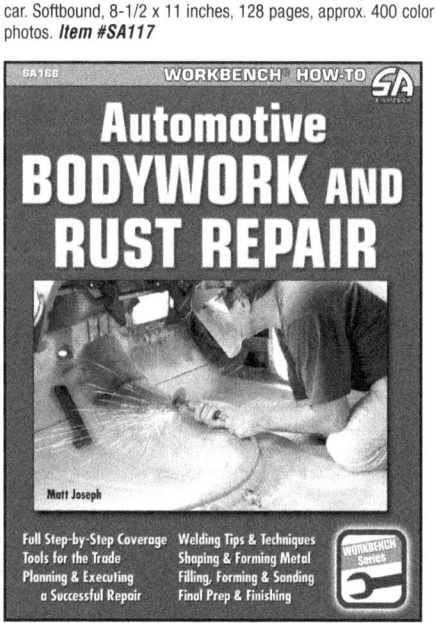

AUTOMOTIVE BODYWORK AND RUST REPAIR *by Matt Joseph* This book shows you the ins and out of tackling both simple and difficult rust and metalwork projects. This book teaches you how to select the proper tools for the job, common-sense approaches to the task ahead of you, preparing and cleaning sheet metal, section fabrications and repair patches, welding options such as gas and electric, forming, fitting and smoothing, cutting metal, final metal finishing including filling and sanding, the secrets of lead filling, making panels fit properly, and more. Softbound, 8-1/2 x 11 inches, 160 pages, 400 color photos. *Item #SA166*

PERFORMANCE AUTOMOTIVE ENGINE MATH *by John Baechtel* When designing or building an automotive engine for improved performance, it's all about the math. From measuring the engine's internal capacities to determine compression ratio to developing the optimal camshaft lift, duration, and overlap specifications, the use of proven math is the only way to design an effective high performance automotive powerplant. This book walks readers through the wide range of dimensions to be measured and formulas used to design and develop powerful engines. Includes reviews the proper tools and measurement techniques, and carefully defines the procedures and equations used in engineering high efficiency and high rpm engines. Softbound, 8.5 x 11 inches, 160 pages, 350 photos. *Item #SA204*

www.cartechbooks.com or 1-800-551-4754

More great titles available from CarTech®...

S-A DESIGN

Super Tuning & Modifying Holley Carburetors — Perf, street and off-road applications. *(SA08)*

Custom Painting — Gives you an overview of the broad spectrum of custom painting types and techniques. *(SA10)*

Street Supercharging, A Complete Guide to — Bolt-on buying, installing and tuning blowers. *(SA17)*

Engine Blueprinting — Using tools, block selection & prep, crank mods, pistons, heads, cams & more! *(SA21)*

David Vizard's How to Build Horsepower — Building horsepower in any engine. *(SA24)*

Chevrolet Small-Block Parts Interchange Manual — Selecting & swapping high-perf. small-block parts. *(SA55)*

High-Performance Ford Engine Parts Interchange — Selecting & swapping big- and small-block Ford parts. *(SA56)*

How To Build Max Perf Chevy Small-Blocks on a Budget — Would you believe 600 hp for $3000? *(SA57)*

How To Build Max Performance Ford V-8s on a Budget — Dyno-tested engine builds for big- & small-blocks. *(SA69)*

How To Build Max-Perf Pontiac V8s — Mild perf apps to all-out performance build-ups. *(SA78)*

How To Build High-Performance Ignition Systems — Guide to understanding auto ignition systems. *(SA79)*

How To Build Max Perf 4.6 Liter Ford Engines — Building & modifying Ford's 2- & 4-valve 4.6/5.4 liter engines. *(SA82)*

How To Build Big-Inch Ford Small-Blocks — Add cubic inches without the hassle of switching to a big-block. *(SA85)*

How To Build High-Perf Chevy LS1/LS6 Engines — Modifying and tuning Gen-III engines for GM cars and trucks. *(SA86)*

How To Build Big-Inch Chevy Small-Blocks — Get the additional torque & horsepower of a big-block. *(SA87)*

Honda Engine Swaps — Step-by-step instructions for all major tasks involved in engine swapping. *(SA93)*

How to Build High-Performance Chevy Small — Block Cams/Valvetrains — Camshaft & valvetrain function, selection, performance, and design. *(SA105)*

High-Performance Jeep Cherokee XJ Builder's Guide 1984-2001 — Build a useful, Cherokee for mountains, the mud, the desert, the street, and more. *(SA109)*

How to Build and Modify Rochester Quadrajet Carburetors — Selecting, rebuilding, and modifying the Quadrajet Carburetors. *(SA113)*

Rebuilding the Small-Block Chevy: Step-by-Step Videobook — 160-pg book plus 2-hour DVD show you how to build a street or racing small-block Chevy. *(SA116)*

How to Paint Your Car on a Budget — Everything you need to know to get a great-looking coat of paint and save money. *(SA117)*

How to Drift: The Art of Oversteer — This comprehensive guide to drifting covers both driving techniques and car setup. *(SA118)*

Turbo: Real World High-Performance Turbocharger Systems — *Turbo* is the most practical book for enthusiasts who want to make more horsepower. Foreword by Gale Banks. *(SA123)*

High-Performance Chevy Small-Block Cylinder Heads — Learn how to make the most power with this popular modification on your small-block Chevy. *(SA125)*

High Performance Brake Systems — Design, selection, and installation of brake systems for Musclecars, Hot Rods, Imports, Modern Era cars and more. *(SA126)*

High Performance C5 Corvette Builder's Guide — Improve the looks, handling and performance of your Corvette C5. *(SA127)*

High Performance Diesel Builder's Guide — The definitive guide to getting maximum performance out of your diesel engine. *(SA129)*

How to Rebuild & Modify Carter/Edelbrock Carbs — The only source for information on rebuilding and tuning these popular carburetors. *(SA130)*

Building Honda K-Series Engine Performance — The first book on the market dedicated exclusively to the Honda K series engine. *(SA134)*

Engine Management-Advanced Tuning — Take your fuel injection and tuning knowledge to the next level. *(SA135)*

How to Drag Race — Car setup, beginning and advanced techniques for bracket racing and pro classes, and racing science and math, and more. *(SA136)*

4x4 Suspension Handbook — Includes suspension basics & theory, advanced/high-performance suspension and lift systems, axles, how-to installations, and more. *(SA137)*

GM Automatic Overdrive Transmission Builder's and Swapper's Guide — Learn to build a bulletproof tranny and how to swap it into an older chassis as well. *(SA140)*

High-Performance Subaru Builder's Guide — Subarus are the hottest compacts on the street. Make yours even hotter. *(SA141)*

How to Build Max-Performance Mitsubishi 4G63t Engines — Covers every system and component of the engine, including a complete history. *(SA148)*

How to Swap GM LS-Series Engines Into Almost Anything — Includes a historical review and detailed information so you can select and fit the best LS engine. *(SA156)*

How to Autocross — Covers basic to more advanced modifications that go beyond the stock classes. *(SA158)*

Designing & Tuning High-Performance Fuel Injection Systems — Complete guide to tuning aftermarket stand-alone systems. *(SA161)*

Design & Install In Car Entertainment Systems — The latest and greatest electronic systems, both audio and video. *(SA163)*

How to Build Max-Performance Hemi Engines — Build the biggest baddest vintage Hemi. *(SA164)*

How to Digitally Photograph Cars — Learn all the modern techniques and post processing too. *(SA168)*

High-Performance Differentials, Axles, & Drivelines — Must have book for anyone thinking about setting up a performance differential. *(SA170)*

How To Build Max-Performance Mopar Big Blocks — Build the baddest wedge Mopar on the block. *(SA171)*

How to Build Max-Performance Oldsmobile V-8s — Make your Oldsmobile keep up with the pack. *(SA172)*

Automotive Diagnostic Systems: Understanding OBD-I & OBD II — Learn how modern diagnostic systems work. *(SA174)*

How to Make Your Muscle Car Handle — Upgrade your musclecar suspension to modern standards. *(SA175)*

Full-Size Fords 1955-1970 — A complete color history of full sized fords. *(SA176)*

Rebuilding Any Automotive Engine: Step-by-Step Videobook — Rebuild any engine with this book DVD combo. DVD is over 3 hours long! *(SA179)*

How to Supercharge & Turbocharge GM LS-Series Engines — Boost the power of todays most popular engine. *(SA180)*

The New MINI Performance Handbook — All the performance tricks for your new MINI. *(SA182)*

How to Build Max-Performance Ford FE Engines — Finally, performance tricks for the FE junkie. *(SA183)*

Builder's Guide to Hot Rod Chassis & Suspension — Ultimate guide to Hot Rod Suspensions. *(SA185)*

How to Build Altered Wheelbase Cars — Build a wild altered car. Complete history too! *(SA189)*

How to Build Period Correct Hot Rods — Build a hot rod true to your favorite period. *(SA192)*

Automotive Sheet Metal Forming & Fabrication — Create and fabricate your own metalwork. *(SA196)*

How to Build Max-Performance Chevy Big Block on a Budget — New Big Block book from the master, David Vizard. *(SA198)*

How to Build Big-Inch GM LS-Series Engines — Get more power through displacement from your LS. *(SA203)*

Performance Automotive Engine Math — All the formulas and facts you will ever need. *(SA204)*

How to Design, Build & Equip Your Automotive Workshop on a Budget — Working man's guide to building a great work space. *(SA207)*

Automotive Electrical Performance Projects — Featuring the most popular electrical mods today. *(SA209)*

How to Port Cylinder Heads — Vizard shares his cylinder head secrets. *(SA215)*

S-A DESIGN RESTORATION SERIES

How to Restore Your Mustang 1964 1/2-1973 — Step by step restoration for your classic Mustang. *(SA165)*

Muscle Car Interior Restoration Guide — Make your interior look and smell new again. Includes dash restoration. *(SA167)*

How to Restore Your Camaro 1967-1969 — Step by step restoration of your 1st gen Camaro. *(SA178)*

S-A DESIGN WORKBENCH® SERIES

Workbench® Series books feature step by step instruction with hundreds of color photos for stock rebuilds and automotive repair.

How To Rebuild the Small-Block Chevrolet — *(SA26)*

How to Rebuild the Small-Block Ford — *(SA102)*

How to Rebuild & Modify High-Performance Manual Transmissions — *(SA103)*

How to Rebuild the Big-Block Chevrolet — *(SA142)*

How to Rebuild the Small-Block Mopar — *(SA143)*

How to Rebuild GM LS-Series Engines — *(SA147)*

How to Rebuild Any Automotive Engine — *(SA151)*

How to Rebuild Honda B-Series Engines — *(SA154)*

How to Rebuild the 4.6/5.4 Liter Ford — *(SA155)*

Automotive Welding: A Practical Guide — *(SA159)*

Automotive Wiring and Electrical Systems — *(SA160)*

How to Rebuild Big-Block Ford Engines — *(SA162)*

Automotive Bodywork & Rust Repair — *(SA166)*

How To Rebuild & Modify GM Turbo 400 Transmissions — *(SA186)*

How to Rebuild Pontiac V-8s — *(SA200)*

HISTORIES AND PERSONALITIES

Quarter-Mile Chaos — Rare & stunning photos of terrifying fires, explosions, and crashes in drag racing's golden age. *(CT425)*

Fuelies: Fuel Injected Corvettes 1957-1965 — The first Corvette book to focus specifically on the fuel injected cars, which are among the most collectible. *(CT452)*

Slingshot Spectacular: Front-Engine Dragster Era — Relive the golden age of front engine dragsters in this photo packed trip down memory lane. *(CT464)*

Chrysler Concept Cars 1940-1970 — Fascinating look at the concept cars created by Chrysler during this golden age of the automotive industry. *(CT470)*

Fuel Altereds Forever — Includes more than 250 photos of the most popular drivers and racecars from the Fuel Altered class. *(CT475)*

Yenko — Complete and thorough of the man, his business and his legendary cars. *(CT485)*

Lost Hot Rods — Great Hot Rods from the past rediscovered. *(CT487)*

Grumpy's Toys — A collection of Grumpy's greats. *(CT489)*

Woodward Avenue: Cruising the Legendary — Revisit the glory days of Woodward! *(CT491)*

Rusted Muscle — A collection of junkyard muscle cars. *(CT492)*

America's Coolest Station Wagons — Wagons are cooler than they ever have been. *(CT493)*

Super Stock — A paperback version of a classic best seller. *(CT495)*

Rusty Pickups: American Workhorses Put to Pasture — Cool collection of old trucks and ads too! *(CT496)*

Jerry Heasley's Rare Finds — Great collection of Heasley's best finds. *(CT497)*

Street Sleepers: The Art of the Deceptively Fast Car — Stealth, horsepower, what's not to love? *(CT498)*

Ed 'Big Daddy' Roth — Paperback reprint of a classic best seller. *(CT500)*

Car Spy: A Look Through the Lens of the Industry's Most Notorious Photographer — Cool behind the scenes stories spanning 40 years. *(CT502)*

CarTech®, Inc. 39966 Grand Ave., North Branch, MN 55056. Ph: 800-551-4754 or 651-277-1200 • Fax: 651-277-1203

Brooklands Books Ltd., PO Box 146 Cobham, Surrey KT11 1LG, England. Ph: 01932 865051 • Fax 01932 868803

Brooklands Books Aus., 3/37-39 Green Street, Banksmeadow, NSW 2019, Australia. Ph: 2 9695 7055 • Fax 2 9695 7355

Visit us online at www.cartechbooks.com for more info!